exile
in the
promised
land

exile
in the
promised
land

a memoir
Marcia Freedman

Firebrand
Books
Ithaca, New York

"Lesbian in the Promised Land" appeared in an earlier version in *Nice Jewish Girls: A Lesbian Anthology* (Persephone/Crossing/Beacon).

Book and cover design by Besty Bayley
Typesetting by Bets Ltd.

Printed on acid-free paper in the United States by McNaughton & Gunn

Library of Congress Cataloging-in-Publication Data

Freedman, Marcia, 1938–
    Exile in the promised land.

    1. Freedman, Marcia, 1938–   2. Israel—Politics
and government. 3. Israel. Knesset—Biography.
4. Jews, American—Israel—Biography. 5. Feminists—
Israel—Biography. I. Title.
DS126.6.F74A3 1990   956.94'004924073   90–3174
ISBN 0-932379-77-X (alk. paper)
ISBN 0-932379-76-1 (pbk. : alk. paper)

This book is dedicated to my father, Phillip Prince,
whose example I have largely followed.

Acknowledgments
◄●►

There are many to whom I owe a great debt, but no one more than E. M. Broner, friend, mentor, and mother to this work. It would not have begun and could not have been finished without her.

My special thanks to Jane Ariel, Sandra Butler, Nan Fink, Jennifer Freedman, Judy Hill, and Liz Prince, who read and criticized the manuscript at various stages; to Amalia Bergman and Judy Mings, who kept me going when the going was difficult; to Sherry Thomas, who got me to pull a yellowing earlier version out of the drawer and begin again; to Natalie Rein, who saved my letters from Israel describing the progress of the women's movement; to Nurit Dagan and Terry Greenblatt, who made a home for me in Jerusalem when I no longer had a home of my own; to Ellie Waxman, who helped me through emotional knots along the way; and to Ilana Berner, Janet Kranzberg, and Jo Oppenheimer for their generous support.

For their support I also thank Myriam Abramowicz, Helene

Aylon, Jewell Belluch, Nahama Broner, Margaret Cecchetti, Phyllis Chesler, Blanche Wiesen Cook, Clare Coss, Roberta Elliot, Eleanor Foa, Louise Gilbert, Carla Javits, Edith Konecky, Beatrice Kreloff, Lucy Lippard, Naomi Newman, Marilyn Pettit, Letty Cottin Pogrebin, Carl Prince, Sue Prince, Rivka Rass, Betty Reiser, Lilly Rivlin, Ruby Rohrlich, Robin Rosenbaum, Sue Saperstein, Susan Schneider, Virginia Snitow, Denise Urdang, Ann Volkes, and Katya Wallin.

Several trips to Israel were made possible by the L. J. Skaggs and Mary C. Skaggs Foundation, and National Community Funds.

I am indebted, too, to Sana Hasan, whose wonderful book, *Enemy In The Promised Land*, provided the insight for the form of my own book. Sana Hasan, an Arab who often passed as a Jew, lived in Israel for three years as a participant-observer. Though she experienced Israel with the consciousness of an outsider exiled from her native land, and I experienced it as my home, we share, remarkably, a common experience of alienation from and compelling attraction to this complex and contradictory land.

Contents

◄●►

Part I: *Aliyah*

Prologue
    Sworn to Allegiance   11

Chapter 1
    Ingathered Exile   27

Chapter 2
    The Women's Movement   41

Chapter 3
    1973   60

◄●►

Part II: The Knesset Years

Chapter 4
    Conspiracies of Silence   79

Chapter 5
    The Natives   106

Chapter 6
    Marcia, *Hamarshah*   120

Chapter 7
Politics   140

Chapter 8
Feminist Politics   169

◄●►

Part II: *Yeridah*

Chapter 9
Women's Aid   189

Chapter 10
Lesbian in the Promised Land   204

Chapter 11
Taking Leave   220

PROLOGUE
Sworn to Allegiance

◄●►

Banging his gavel loudly, the Chairman called the opening session of the Eighth Knesset to order. From my seat at the back of the chamber, I studied the rostrum. It rose from an imposing mahogany dais well above the heads of even the tallest Members. The Chairman's seat was the high point, the rostrum only one step down. It seemed too high, but it was hard to tell.

On one side of the dais hung a grainy enlargement of Theodore Herzl staring trancelike beyond the Knesset, a dream, long dead or yet to be born, frozen in his eyes. On the other side, symbol of the current reality, was the blue-and-white flag of the State of Israel, the Star of David hidden in its folds. Wherever I looked, my eyes returned worriedly to the rostrum. It was definitely too high.

The President of the State of Israel, Ephraim Katzir, made his entrance. "The Knesset will rise," the Sergeant-at-Arms called. Standing, I watched carefully as Katzir made his way to the rostrum and stood behind it. It came to his waist, the bank of microphones to his chest. Katzir was, I knew, about eight inches taller

than I. When the Knesset stood up once again—to sing the national anthem "Hatikva"—I gauged the height of the rostrum on
my body. It was worse than I thought. The rostrum would reach
my nose. Standing behind it, only my forehead would be visible
above the microphones. What does Begin do? I wondered. Or
Golda? Do they stand on a stool?

The President was invited to the Knesset as an honored speaker
only on ceremonial occasions like this one, the opening session
of a new term. It was January 14, 1974. The Yom Kippur War had
officially ended a few days earlier. Not since 1948 had Israel fought
so prolonged a war. Never was it so unprepared. There were days
when the army was in retreat, days when the possibility of being
overrun by Arabs was not just the nightmare of the few but the
reality expected by all. Five thousand soldiers had died, ten times
the number that fell in 1967. The President began by remembering the dead. We stood once more to observe a moment of silence,
a moment to reflect on what the country had been through.

Katzir spoke of what lay ahead. The new Knesset, he warned,
began its term in the shadow of a war that had caught Israel off
guard. The economy was crippled, the country deeply depressed.
The government would have to find a way to revive both the economy and morale. Above all, it would have to provide an explanation for the *mechdal*, as the war was called, the debacle. The near-
miss and the heavy losses had caused an uprecedented crisis of
confidence in the military and political leadership. This was one
of the reasons for my surprise election. It was the reason that, in
another six months, both the Prime Minister and the Minister
of Defense would be forced to resign. It was also the reason the
Labor Party, in another four years, would be out of power for the
first time in Israel's history. Though we didn't know it at the time,
we were experiencing the last gasp of Labor's hegemony on Israeli
politics.

Ephraim Katzir continued to talk about death, listing the names
of former Members of Knesset who had died during the past four
years, especially David Ben Gurion, *zichrono l'bracha*, blessed be
his memory. We stood once more, this time for a moment of si-

lence. When I was a child at my father's side in *shul*, the entire ritual had seemed like a series of inexplicable standings up and sittings down. As then, I kept a sharp eye on my neighbors to know when it was time to sit.

The President finished his *kaddish*, the prayer for the dead, and called upon the doyen of the Knesset to take the oath of office. Golda Meir rose—the oldest, the Prime Minister, one of only ten women in the 120-Member Knesset, and the only woman ever to hold a position in the cabinet. It was said of the Prime Minister and her Cabinet that she was the only man among them.

I held my breath as Golda walked from her seat to the rostrum. Nobody brought a stool. Perhaps there was one already there, conveniently at hand for those who needed it. As I watched, the thick mahogany column supporting the rostrum began to sink slowly, almost imperceptibly, into the bowels of the dais. By the time Golda mounted the few steps to take her place behind the rostrum, it was just the right height for her. For years I tried to catch the invisible hand that controlled the rostrum, but I never did discover whose it was. Each time I mounted those steps to the speaker's platform, however, I said a silent prayer of thanks to the great leveler who made us all the same height.

The Prime Minister took the oath of office. "I swear," she said, "to be loyal to the State of Israel and to faithfully carry out my mission to the Knesset." Free-floating anxiety found a new home. I wouldn't be able to remember the words of the oath. I'd never sworn allegiance in Hebrew before. It was only a single sentence, but I'd never heard most of the words. One of my most agonizing campaign experiences had been urging a crowd to attend a peace demonstration in *Emek Hamatzlaiva*, the Valley of the Cross. I called it *Emek Hamatzlaima*, the valley of the camera. I was the only one who didn't get the joke. What was I doing here anyway? I was about to take an oath that would bind me irrevocably to the state of Israel and I didn't even know all the words.

Golda called the first name in the alphabet, Aharon Abuchatzira, to take the oath after her. I waited for him to stand and make his way to the rostrum. Instead, he turned the switch on the small

microphone in front of him and said, "*Mitchayev ani,*" I so swear.
Two words. There were just two words to remember. I rehearsed
them silently as I waited my turn. In Hebrew, F is a variant of P
and comes near the end of the alphabet. There was plenty of time.
I even remembered to add the feminine ending. My voice didn't
crack, I didn't stumble, I didn't knock my chair over when I stood
up, the microphone worked. "*Mitchayevet ani,*" I said. I so swear.

◄●►

Trying to decide what to wear that morning, I thought about
something Esther Broner once said about Bella Abzug. "When Bella
was sworn in as a Congresswoman, do you know what everyone
talked about? Her hat. That's all, just the hat!"
It was hard to find anything in my closet no one would talk about.
Jeans, long Oriental dresses from the *shuk* in the Old City, India-
print wraparound skirts. Even a few leftover miniskirts. It hadn't
occurred to me to buy a new outfit for the swearing in. Once it
would have been second nature. Too late, I heard my mother's voice,
only a faint echo now. "What are you going to wear? Here, go buy
a new outfit," she'd say, handing me a credit card. "Maybe a tailored suit. Look like a *mensch.*"
I settled, finally, on a long tweed skirt that reached my ankles
and a turtleneck sweater that was all right for academe but a little
too tight for politics. I pinned my hair up, trying to make it neat,
but several long strands came loose within minutes. Taking a last
look at myself in the mirror, I counted the white hairs beginning
to sprout at my temples—there were ten. I remembered my mother
at my age, two white wings spreading elegantly from her temples.
I had to run to catch the Tel Aviv bus, and though it was winter,
I was sweating by the time I gave the driver the fare. Handing me
my change, he held it a moment just beyond my reach. "Don't
I know you from somewhere?" he said, staring at me. My picture
had been in all the papers for the past month, ever since the election. Of course he knew me from somewhere. It only took him
a few seconds to remember. "*Betach,*" he shouted, "Sure, you're
Marcia Freedman." Heads turned as I walked toward an empty seat

in the back. *"Ha'amerikanit,"* I heard someone say. *"Hafeministit hameshuga'at."* The American. The crazy feminist.

The bus headed south along the coast road, the highway hugging the beaches. Both sea and sky were the color of lapis, the horizon a line of haze dividing one solid patch of blue from the other. On the other side of the road were fields of bananas and grapes. Here and there in smaller patches sunflowers, alfalfa, and cucumbers were growing. The fields spread from the road on one side to the base of the Carmel on the other, filling every available bit of arable land.

The Carmel, a low coastal range, is only a protrusion of rock that stretches for miles along the shore of the Mediterranean, its bare copper and sand-colored rock dotted with caves and rutted by wadis. The caves were used by Neanderthals according to archeologists. Their bones and artifacts, found in these caves, fill display cases at the Rockefeller Museum in Jerusalem. In one, an entire skeleton, as if in situ, lies in the fetal position surrounded by bowls and rough-hewn tools.

In the distance I could see the ruins of Atlit, modern by comparison. The outer walls of a Crusader fortress stand at the furthest reach of a small peninsula. Inside, I knew by rumor only, the Israeli navy maintained an observation post. The Crusader ruins were visible in the distance; the navy was not.

Eyes closed, I visualized what I knew of the Knesset. I'd been there only once, to see the Chagall tapestries that hang in the Foyer. I recalled a square glass-and-marble building that was cold and, except for the rugs, unadorned. It seemed deliberately designed to intimidate. The massive five-story square was a beehive of passageways, doors, and staircases, most of them roped off from the public. Today I would undo those ropes. See what was on the other side. Me, the crazy American feminist.

The beaches gave way to low-lying dunes covered with cactus and scrub. We passed a large kibbutz built on the sand, its fields on the other side of the highway. A few miles down the road we passed a small Arab village, also built on the dunes, the same crops growing in smaller fields. But these fields, I knew, no longer belonged to the villagers. They had been declared abandoned property in 1949, taken over by the state and given to the neighboring kibbutz for cultivation. The Arab villagers were no longer farmers, but traveled twenty miles in either direction to work as poorly paid day laborers, only one rung up the economic ladder from the Palestinians from the occupied territories. The houses of the village ramble along the dunes, preserving the outlines of the land, facing modestly away from one another. As the years passed, this little village became more and more crowded. Locked in by state lands, the road, and the sea, it had no room for expansion.

Nearing Hadera, we passed a Bedouin encampment along a foul-smelling creek that drained water and waste from the wadis into the sea. The settlement was a well-known pocket of resistance to the government's plan to move all the nomadic tent-dwelling Bedouin into permanent homes within clearly defined boundaries. These few Bedouin were the last families to remain on the beach, driven back to this sewage ditch. Many said they held out only to get more money. Some defended the Bedouin, saying that this beach land had been their tribal property for generations. They were fighting for their territory and a way of life, practicing a tactic that would later become policy among the Palestinians of the West Bank—samud, steadfastly holding to the land, no matter how oppressive the conditions or tempting the offer to leave it.

There were few Arabs on the Tel Aviv express. At mid-morning, the bus was filled with young married Ashkenazi women going to buy clothes in the big city. There were a few Sephardic women surrounded by empty plastic baskets and net bags they would fill with bargains from the open-air market of Tel Aviv near the central bus station. The woman sitting across the aisle from me looked, from the lines on her face, to be about sixty. There was no grey in the jet black hair that showed around her flowered cotton headscarf. We looked at one another and smiled. She revealed a gold tooth. She wore gold earrings and bracelets. Her personal wealth, hers to keep if her husband ever divorced her, perhaps all she would be able to keep. She is smarter than I am, I thought, thinking about so many Ashkenazi women I knew who were pauperized by divorce, getting to keep only the thin gold band on their finger.

I wondered if this woman, or anyone on this bus or in the settlements we'd passed had voted for me. I'd been third on the list. Shulamit Aloni, who founded the Citizens Rights Movement and headed the list, claimed that she'd carried us all in. Perhaps she had. But just as likely, with two feminists on the list, there had been an underground women's vote. Still, even I hadn't taken my candidacy seriously. Giving my name to her list had been a gesture of feminist support for Aloni. Getting elected had been a political accident. So was Boaz Moav's election, number two on Aloni's list. Neither of us had expected to win when we agreed to be candidates.

Shulamit Aloni and Boaz Moav were waiting for me at party headquarters in Tel Aviv. We greeted one another uncomfortably. I hadn't seen Aloni since before the election. We had spoken on the phone only to make these arrangements. I'd seen Boaz, though. He'd been part of the delegation Aloni sent to Haifa just after the election to persuade me to resign. I was too much of an amateur, too much a new immigrant, and too much of a feminist for Israeli politics, they argued. "I bet you weren't even planning to wear a bra to the Knesset," one had said. I refused to resign but promised to wear a bra. Aloni and I never discussed that meeting. It was one of many things we never mentioned.

Aloni was in high spirits. This was her big day. Golda Meir's refusal to give her a second term in the Knesset had cost Labor three seats. Meir and Aloni were bitter enemies. Aloni had been elected the first time under the wing of Pinchas Sapir, until his death Israel's Finance Minister and one of Labor's most powerful politicians. Shulamit Aloni and Golda Meir had been notoriously hostile to one another from the very beginning. Aloni, young, attractive, often witty and sometimes stinging in her attacks, had won the media battles easily. But Golda had power. She could and did veto a second term for Aloni, and even Pinchas Sapir couldn't change her mind. Aloni declared herself an independent candidate in a daring last-minute gamble that had paid off handsomely.

We met in Tel Aviv in order to travel together to Jerusalem.

Shulamit drove and did most of the talking. Boaz sat in the back, silent. The tension in the small car was triangulated. Boaz shared the amateur category with me and was almost as nervous as I. But he was Aloni's faithful man Friday. He and I might empathize with one another, but he always sided with Shulamit.

I would have been happy to stare out the window silently and listen to Shulamit's cheerful talk. I had a charge to fulfill, however. A winning party has wealth, government funding determined by the number of seats held by each party. The women's movement in Tel Aviv had instructed me to demand its fair share of the spoils. In Haifa, I'd been told to ask for an office and staff. Now it was time to carry out my charge. Aloni's answer was brief and left no room for discussion: she'd won the election, not me. There would be no budget for me, or for the movement.

In silence, the tension more palpable each mile traveled, we reached Sha'ar Hagai, Bab el Wad in Arabic, the gateway to the wadi through which the road to Jerusalem makes its ascent. We passed pine groves planted by the Jewish National Fund. A guide had once explained that water had to be brought by the bucketful to the newly planted saplings. We passed overturned armored vehicles left at the side of the road to commemorate breaking the siege of Jerusalem during the War of Independence.

Boaz Moav, who had been quiet until then, said slowly, "We had discussions with the Labor Party last week and agreed to support their candidate for Chairman." The election of the Chairman was on the day's agenda, immediately following the swearing-in. Every party could propose a candidate, but since the Labor coalition had a majority of the votes, with or without our help its candidate would win. We had campaigned against Labor as much or more than against the Likud. The votes that we got, Labor lost. We'd been elected as an opposition party. Was Aloni hoping to be invited to join the coalition? Did she want her options open because she sought to rejoin the Labor Party some day? But Boaz wasn't asking for my opinion. He merely instructed me how to vote. I'd been committed without being consulted. First disinherited, then disenfranchised. The line had to be drawn somewhere. I claimed my rights. "Since I wasn't at the meeting," I said, "my vote remains unpledged."

Shulamit's hands tightened around the steering wheel. I don't represent myself, she told me. I had been elected on her coattails and was honor-bound to vote as she, the party's leader, told me to. Honor-bound, perhaps, but not legally bound, I reminded her. Once sworn in, the seat belonged to me, not to the party. Always uncomfortable with confrontation, I was more scared than angry. As Shulamit drove on in punishing silence, I began to feel childishly guilty for spoiling her day. She'd been in such a good mood when we started out.

◄●►

We reached Jerusalem and passed through the black iron gates guarding the President's House and were greeted at the door by Ephraim Katzir, a well-known scientist from the Weitzman Institute with no background in politics or public life. He seemed shy and ill at ease. A large man who bobbled amoeba-like as he walked, Katzir led us to a capacious room with nothing in it but four formal high-backed chairs around an inlaid mosaic table. On the table was a large ornate ashtray and a cigarette lighter. The President lit up and so did we. Off to one corner a small crowd of photographers gossiped, paying no attention to us.'

The President turned first to Shulamit Aloni, the party's leader, and asked her if the Citizens Rights Movement would accept a coalition led by Labor. This was his one official political function—to ascertain which party had the greatest potential Knesset support and to ask that party's leader to put a government together. The outcome was foreknown in 1974, as it had been since the very first Knesset session twenty-five years earlier. Traditionally, Labor won a majority, but not large enough to establish a government without the support of the National Religious Party. Together they had dominated Israeli politics since before the establishment of the state.

Aloni told Katzir that the CRM would support a Labor government, looking at me pointedly as she did so. I nodded. With that, the scripted portion of the meeting ended. As we improvised political small talk to fill the remaining minutes allotted to the meeting, the photographers gathered round, flashbulbs popping, but they soon lost interest. They'd been taking the same picture all day. The President stood up and showed us out.

The drive from the President's House to the Knesset took only a few minutes. Again we passed through guarded steel gates which secured the Members parking lot and private entrance. Aloni led the way into the inner sanctum, the Members Dining Room, where a reception for new Members was in progress. The long, narrow room had two glass walls looking out on the green expanse of Knesset lawn and the bare Judean hills in the distance.

Shulamit took Boaz by the arm and led him away, leaving me to follow behind or to make my own way. The latter seemed preferable. A waiter passing with a tray of drinks gave me something to do. I hated large parties, especially formal ones. Normally, I would have finished my drink and left. This time I was trapped, one of the honored guests. The room was crowded, mostly with faces I didn't know. But there was Golda, unmistakable even from the back. And Dayan, Begin, Peres, Rabin, Sharon, and others who were familiar images. Surprised, I noticed that Begin was as short as I, that Sharon was disgustingly obese.

But Dayan was the biggest surprise. Every man in Israel would have given his right eye to be Moshe Dayan. He was the archetypal New Jew—a military and political leader, powerful but understated, a warrior and a womanizer. The sinister black eye-patch lodged comfortably in the hollow of his high cheekbone. His tight-lipped smile was rare. His face suggested an equally lean, tight body, not the Humpty-Dumpty shape I saw for the first time that day. The archetype of sabra masculinity was seriously bottom-heavy.

Looking around, I saw a courtly gentleman with a fringe of grey hair and a Charlie Chaplin moustache coming toward me. He shook my hand, almost clicking his heels together. "Welcome," he said, "and good luck. I'll support you whenever I can."

I was astonished, but even more, I was embarrassed. I didn't know who he was. "Thank you," I said, "and what is your name?"

Victor Shem-Tov, leader of Mapam, Israel's socialist Zionist party, was clearly startled. His back stiffened as he told me his name, adding, "I'm the Minister of Health." He was as embarrassed as I. Like the bus driver and the Minister of Health, people generally recognized me. One after another politicians and journalists came over to shake my hand. "Brucha haba'ah," blessed be your arrival, they said. Most stayed to chat cordially.

Some of the women of the Knesset surprised me with their expressions of solidarity. Chaika Grossman, another Mapam leader and chair of the Health and Social Services Committee, let me know that she expected me to be her ally. She was a short woman who delighted in the fact that I was shorter still. Her lined round face had a determined look that became impish when she smiled. Her blue eyes were sharp and attentive, her short blonde hair curled naturally. She looked like and was a kibbutz woman, used to hard work and no pretentions. But Chaika Grossman had also been a member of the Warsaw Ghetto resistance; she had demonstrated her courage early and exercised leadership ever since.

Geula Cohen, another early heroine and Menachem Begin's protégée, had operated a clandestine radio for the Irgun, a breakaway commando group that espoused and practiced terrorism against the British. Geula was an exciting woman. Unlike all the others, save for Shulamit and me, the Knesset women dressed conservatively, from tailored to matronly. Geula's clothes were like a frumpy schoolgirl's—mostly I remember a black skirt, white blouse, and a black cardigan, always a little disheveled. Her body, ungirdled beneath the incongruous clothing, was unself-consciously sensual. But it was her face that earned her the name of La Passionara. The dark rings under her eyes and the thick dark brows that drooped above outlined deep black eyes that seemed to burn even in repose. All her features were large, all her expressions intense.

Menachem Begin, then leader of an opposition that had not yet come to power, kissed my hand gallantly. A Polish gentleman, it was his way with the ladies. I was speechless. Begin patted me on the head, as though he were six-feet tall. "Maideleh," he said, "you're too young to be in the Knesset." "Look Mr. Begin," I said, holding my hand level between my forehead and his, "we're exactly the same height."

Later that day there was a second meeting between us, this time a confrontation over who was to get out of a crowded elevator first—he, who was standing right in front of the door as it opened, or I, in the back and the only woman. Begin stood aside, waiting for me to work my way through from the back. The crowd in front of me parted. I could feel the eyes on me, waiting to see what I would do. As *hafeministit*, I was expected to reject meaningless gallantry that bespoke condescension. I could be gracious about it and publicly compromise what were supposed to be my principles, or I could stand my ground and refuse to get out of the elevator first. Personally, elevator etiquette is of no interest, but this was a challenge. How militant are you? I stood still and waited. So did Begin and everyone else. Finally, the absurdity of it, or perhaps waning interest in the contest, moved Begin to take the first step. I hurried to catch up. Wordlessly, we exited side by side.

In the lobby of the Knesset Chamber just before the swearing-in, I stood only a few feet from Golda Meir, the closest I'd been all day. If she looked my way, I planned to introduce myself. But she never did. Her formidable presence, the back she turned toward me, didn't encourage me to introduce myself to the Prime Minister. During the six months I was part of her orbit, we never exchanged a word or even a glance. In an interview with Oriana Fallaci in *Ms.* magazine, Golda was asked what she thought of the feminist movement. "They're nuts," she said. I knew that if I tried to speak to her, she would cut me short. Like Aloni, Golda Meir did not like other women, especially political women.

I entered the Knesset chamber for the first time and was shown to my seat by a deferential usher. I followed him up the three carpeted steps to the raised floor that held the horseshoe rows of seats. On the small desk in front of me was a leather stationery case bearing my name on a small brass plate. The seats were the kind you see in corporate offices and airports, naugahyde variations on a theme, degrees of comfort marking degrees of privilege. The Chairman's chair had the highest back, the widest arms, and the deepest seat. It rocked and it swiveled. The Ministers' chairs, too, had high backs but were somewhat narrower, not quite as padded, and the frames were chrome, not wood. The Members' seats had arms and were well-padded, but they had low backs and swiveled on a fixed base. And so on. The amount of naugahyde one sat on also distinguished the honored guests from the press and the press from those in the glassed-in visitors' gallery.

One by one, Cabinet Ministers made their way through the back rows shaking hands with the freshmen they hadn't greeted in the Dining Room. Yoseph Burg, Minister of the Interior and leader of the National Religious Party, reached me as he came down the line. Burg was an Orthodox Jew who considered himself an enlightened traditionalist. For decades, he was one of the most powerful politicians in Israel. Here comes the enemy, I thought, as I watched Burg approach. The photographers in the gallery overhead turned their cameras on us as we shook hands and talked. "We have something in common," he said in English. "I, too, studied philosophy, in Germany before the war. What are you doing your dissertation on?"

"Wittgenstein and Kant," I answered, to Burg's delight, as I wondered how he knew that I was even doing a dissertation. We were still talking about Wittgenstein when the Chairman's gavel called the first session of the Eighth Knesset to order.

◄●►

I watched the sunrise from the balcony of Shoshana's apartment where I'd spent my first night as a Member of Knesset, a sleepless night. Fear and anger toward Shulamit, Burg's surprising camaraderie, Golda's rejection, my embarrassment about not recognizing the Minister of Health, the ridiculous confrontations with Begin—all claimed their hour. The power and privilege of mounting those three steps to the floor of the Knesset competed for attention with helpless anxiety that I wouldn't be able to reach the microphones.

I looked out over the bare, steeply rolling Judean Hills. The rising sun cast rose-beige shadows on the dusty brown hills. Off to the right, alone on a low hill, I could see the Knesset. Its square heaviness stood out against the gently curved hills and the golden stone of the rest of the city. On an opposite hill was the graceful white dome of the Shrine of the Book. They seemed appropriate symbols for the day's passage from academe to agora.

Falling asleep finally, a scene from my childhood drifted in among the static and clutter of the day's events. Once, coming into my grandmother's kitchen for one of the strawberry sodas she made by squirting seltzer over a spoonful of jam, I found my mother sitting on a chair, crying. I'd never seen my mother cry before. I don't know why she was crying. What I remember most is the image of my grandmother standing in front of her, her arms folded across her chest, her back straight, her head held high. "Annie, *zul zein a mensch*," I heard her say just before they noticed me. Be a *mensch*.

What exactly is a *mensch*, Grandma? It was her most singular compliment, reserved for the few, though literally it only means "person." What was it you had to do to be a person in my grandmother's eyes? When these four years were over, would my grandmother think I was a *mensch*?

PART I:
Aliyah

Chapter 1
Ingathered Exile
◄●►

The plane landed at Lod Airport on a hot July night and tax-
ied to the sliding-glass doors of the main terminal, a two-story concrete building. Deplaning, the moist, breezeless air seemed to wrap
itself around me in welcome. The blue-black night sky was dense
with stars. I stopped for a moment to look at it, suddenly overwhelmed by memories of an earlier romance with Israel, a summer affair that was hot but short-lived. Now I was back, eager to
take it up again.

"What's she stopping for?" I heard someone ask behind me.
"Is something wrong?" It was 1967, just three weeks since the Six-
Day War began and ended. The passengers were tense. I picked
up my daughter and started down the stairs.

We were a small group, but passport control was slow and the
line at customs long. Each suitcase, every bundle was inspected
carefully. The customs men pulled radios, toasters, watches, tape
recorders from passengers' suitcases, motioning their owners to the
cashier's window to pay customs duties. Bill and I were waved

through. As new immigrants, we could bring in whatever we wished tax-free. There was a murmur of resentment from the citizens behind us in the line. We were guided toward a sign that said Ministry of the Interior and entered a long, narrow room filled with small cubicles. In each there was a table and two wooden chairs facing a tired clerk. It was midnight. Here, too, the line was long. We'd been traveling twenty-four hours and were all cranky. "Why do they have to do this now?" I muttered. Bill, looking glum, didn't answer. Jenny began to cry.

Finally we heard "*Freedmann!*" and took our turn in one of the cubicles. The weary bald-headed man opposite us had a thick pile of papers that he began to fill out by hand. We saw our names being written in Hebrew as the clerk struggled to render Marcia, William, and Jennifer in a language that didn't accommodate them. He asked for my father's first name. On impulse, I gave his Yiddish name, instinctively covering my political tracks—my father was a Communist, and I was a child of the McCarthy era. Or did I redefine my identity for some other reason? To be more Jewish, perhaps? The clerk wrote it down. I became Marcia *bat* Feivel Shrage, Feivel Shrage's daughter. So I would be buried.

"My mother's name is Anne," I offered, but he didn't write it down. He asked my nationality. "I'm an American," I said.

"That's your citizenship," he answered. "Is your mother a Jew? Then you're a Jew. That's your nationality."

How strange that my mother determines whether I can be a citizen, but my father's name is my official identity. But these were prefeminist times, and I found the customs of the land merely curious.

We traveled from the airport in a Mercedes taxicab on the only road that connected Tel Aviv and Haifa. We passed an occasional billboard with large Hebrew letters I couldn't read. Road signs in Hebrew and English told us how many miles to Netanya, Caesaria, Hadera, and Haifa. After Hadera, the two-lane highway wound around the base of the Carmel coastal range. At one stretch, the space between mountain and shoreline was so narrow that only a small beach separated us from the sea, smooth and silvery in the moonlight. We could see the lights of Haifa approaching, lighting up an expanse of the Carmel slope. The driver turned onto a road that wound serpentine up the mountainside. The sign said Sea Road. Each curve in the road revealed a different view of the coastline, the deserted highway, and the city sprawling down the side of the mountain encircling the bay. For most of the distance there was nothing but the view on one side and dark pine woods on the other. We turned a steep curve and suddenly a statue of the Virgin Mary loomed in front of us. "Stella Maris," the driver said, as the road turned at a ninety-degree angle away from the statue. "It means 'Star of the Sea.' There is a monastery here," he said, pointing to the pine woods on the left. "Carmelites."

The road continued to wind gently toward the crest of the Carmel, with a few stores and houses on both sides. Nearly at the top, the Mercedes stopped and let us out in front of a three-story concrete building with two broad balconies on each floor. The concrete was painted cream, the balconies maroon. The house was surrounded by flowerbeds, trees, and shrubs. Cyclamen grew wild in the grass. Near the entrance was a large poinsettia. The poinsettia was a surprise. I had never seen one that wasn't potted and on display for Christmas. A Jewish highway, a Jewish taxi driver, even a Jewish poinsettia, I thought, as Bill looked for the key that would let us into our new home.

In the morning, Bill went out to shop for food, and I looked around the apartment. Flecked beige tile floors and whitewashed walls. Square sinks and high faucets that were extended by a bit of rubber hose to keep them from splashing. Rectangular rooms filled with rectangular foam-rubber furniture. There was a sofa and two matching chairs facing it across a coffee table. Here and there was an odd antique. Most of the walls were covered with bookshelves, a whole wall full of books in Yiddish.

Jenny slept on in the white metal crib as I toured the sublet apartment. "How can there be a crib in this apartment and no washing machine?" I wondered, worrying about the diapers. There was a knock at the door. "I'm Shelly," said the grey-haired woman on the other side, "your upstairs neighbor." She held out a bouquet of flowers. Shelly looked to be my mother's age, about sixty. She was small and bosomy. She wore no make-up, and her steel-grey hair was pulled back into a bun. "Welcome to the *aretz*, the Land," she said, and handed me the flowers.

Over coffee, Shelly taught me how to be a *ba'alat bayit*, an Israeli housewife. "You clean the floors by tossing a pail of water over them," she said. "Then you push all the dirty water out the front door with this," showing me what looked like a squeegee on a long stick. "We call it a *sponjeh*." She warned me that the city shut down between one and four. "The husbands and children come home for lunch," she said. "It is our meat meal, so we all cook in the morning."

"How do the women who work manage to make the meal?" I asked.

"None of the neighbors work," she said, "except Bracha. She's a teacher. She comes home with the children and cooks."

"From two to four, everyone takes a nap," Shelly told me before she left. If the children don't sleep, they have to be quiet. The *schlaffshtunde*, she called it. No, there are no laundromats, there's no diaper service, and she had never heard of disposables.

When Bill returned he brought food and a story. At the bus stop across the street, he had asked directions in English. A woman standing nearby overheard. "You must be Mr. Freedman," she had said. "I heard you were coming. I live a few blocks from here, but my son is your next-door neighbor." She invited us to spend Rosh Hashana with her family, just in case we had no family of our own nearby.

As the day went on, each of the five neighboring families stopped by with flowers and chocolates to welcome the Freedmans to the Land. We had just come from a New York apartment building where we exchanged greetings only with the couple whose door directly faced ours. I could go for days in the neighborhood without once seeing anyone I knew except for the man who sold me newspapers and cigarettes each day. In Israel, we became members of a community within twenty-four hours.

These neighbors became our family for the next ten years. Jenny grew up calling Shelly and her husband, Alec, *Bubba* and *Zeide*, grandmother and grandfather. Other friendships were quickly made and often ran deep. We left New York voluntary exiles to a land of strangers and found instead, unexpectedly, that we had come home.

◄●►

It is too hot in the Middle East to conceal the tattooed numbers under long sleeves. The arms of the couple who owned the neighborhood grocery store as they handed me my change; the electrician as he hung a fixture for us in the hallway; the waiter at the cafe as he set coffee down on the table.

I fought to keep myself from staring at the numbered wrists that moved the Holocaust from the realm of metaphor for my worst fears to the reality of everyday life. The threat of unimaginable, inexplicable disaster had haunted me since childhood, ever since I had met my two cousins, the only survivors of my father's family in Europe, gaunt, the horror still in their eyes when they arrived in Brooklyn. I fit easily into the culture of survival that surrounded me. I had been a child during the Holocaust, safely in America. But it could have been me instead of Anne Frank. I understood that early. It could have been me, but it wasn't. While she was being gassed to death, I was worrying about saving my bubble gum in a glass of water to be chewed again the next day, the major deprivation of the war years for American children. Why had she died and not I? Why had it happened at all? Unanswered, unanswerable questions were tattooed on my brain as surely as the numbers on wrists.

The sense of imminent danger that pervades daily life in Israel fed my fear of extinction in a way that was so familiar it was almost comforting. Pay Attention to Suspicious Objects, the signs in public places said. As we walked into movies or the supermarket, members of the Civil Guard, older men no longer fit for combat duty, checked purses and packages for bombs. When we made trips to the Galilee, or Acco, or the newly conquered territories, our friends and guides placed loaded weapons in their glove compartments. On city streets, young soldiers flirted with their girlfriends while their automatic rifles dangled casually from one shoulder. "Me against them" is a way of life in Israel. *Them* may be the Arabs, the bureaucracy, the car trying to cut in front of you, or people shoving and pushing to get on the bus. At some level, for all of us it seemed, everyone else was *them*.

During our first year of sightseeing, Bill and I visited *Lochmei Haghetto'ot*, a museum of the Warsaw Ghetto fighters. The Warsaw Ghetto was the epitome of Jewish resistance, the ghetto fighters' museum its national monument. We went to *Yad Vashem*, a memorial to Holocaust victims where their names are recorded, their pictures and artifacts of the camps displayed. We climbed the snake path to Masada, a desert fortress built by Herod where the Jewish rebellion against the Romans was finally crushed. The surviving Jews had committed mass suicide rather than be conquered by the Romans. School children learn about Yoseph Trumpeldor, a hero of the Jewish settlement in Palestine, whose words, *Tov lamut b'ad artzenu*, it is good to die for our Land, are carved in stone at the site where he was killed. These are points of reference on the map of Israeli consciousness. They say Never Again, not as an article of faith but as a warning to the world. We will destroy ourselves if necessary, but will never again be destroyed.

◄●►

Bill and I arrived in Israel during a moment of optimism that was fleeting and never to return. We stepped off the plane just three weeks after the end of the Six-Day War, a war that thrilled Israelis and Jews all over the world. The enemy had seemed formidable, and Israelis were told by their government to expect the worst. Instead, the enemy planes never got off the ground, and much of its land was quickly conquered.

The Six-Day War vindicated the heroes of the ghetto resistance. It proved that Jews could be legendary warriors once again. It suggested that we had become invincible. There was relief and joy in Israel at the time we arrived. The sense of closeness and community—the greater *we* who stands against the greater *them*—

was heightened by wartime and by the easy victory.

There was also a rare feeling of hope. "Eshkol is just waiting for a phone call from the Arabs," said Alec Bassin, during our first Friday night visit with our neighbors. He said it with a big grin, but he seemed to say everything with a big grin. Alec loved to talk, and most of all he loved to talk politics.

Mixed nuts and raisins, a bowl of fruit, and artfully sliced melon were on the coffee table between us. By the time Shelly served her homemade cake, I learned the prevailing political wisdom from Alec. With Israeli troops in control of the West Bank and Gaza, the Golan Heights, and the Sinai Desert, the Arab states would be anxious to negotiate a permanent peace. For the first time, Israel had a winning hand in the negotiations that would surely start within the next few months. No one thought, then, of holding on to the territories for long.

"This was our last war," Alec said. I was naive; I wanted to believe him. But just that week, the Israeli government announced the permanent annexation of Arab Jerusalem. The newspapers called it reunification.

"What happens if Eshkol's phone rings and the Arabs want to negotiate about Jerusalem?" I asked.

"Jerusalem is our Holy City," said Alec, a passionately secular Jew. "We left her once and wandered in exile for almost two thousand years. We must never leave Jerusalem again."

By November, Moshe Dayan, the Defense Minister who determined Israeli policy on peace and war, called the occupied territories security zones. While all Israel believed that peace was around the corner, Dayan was digging in for an indefinitely prolonged occupation. The policy that Dayan established and Prime Minister Golda Meir espoused was to maintain the status quo, in those very words, until conditions were propitious for peace negotiations on Israel's terms. Even Alec Bassin no longer talked of peace negotiations. "The most important thing," he said, "is *bitachon*, security. Nothing else really matters."

It wasn't a statement one could argue with. It had been historically determined. The primary concern of a society of survivors is *bitachon*—an interesting word whose meanings are several. The Defense Ministry is *Misrad Ha'bitachon*, and a child who is insecure is said to lack *bitachon*. You can have or not have *bitachon* in someone, confidence; you can buy *bituach*, insurance; and you can express something *b'bitachon*, with certainty. Security, defense, insurance, confidence, certainty. It's all the same thing in Hebrew.

◄●►

The land, not its politics, preoccupied us most of that first year. We bought a secondhand car from a UNIFIL officer in Jerusalem and toured the *aretz*. There were excavations everywhere revealing the layers of Biblical prehistory when the Hebrew tribes had dominated. I'd read the Bible only once, for an undergraduate course in mythology. The first semester fairy tales, second semester the Bible. I never questioned the rightness of the conjunction until I stood on the ground where Solomon stabled his horses and where the people, defying their priests and kings, worshipped the Canaanite goddess. In the museums I saw their pottery and the earliest texts of the history they had recorded. I reread the Bible in 1967. No longer a fairy tale, but history. My history. A history I had known only as a religious precept, an arcane fact that could never be more than an abstraction. I, who could not trace my genealogy back more than three generations, and even those incompletely, acquired ancient ancestors. This earth was mine.

The sun, too, was mine. I lay beneath it on the shores of the Mediterranean, in the Negev and the Sinai, by the Sea of Galilee, and in the rarefied air of Jerusalem. A loaf in the oven. I lay beneath the sun for hours, not moving, not even thinking. The white light, the heat that baked me, were consuming. I sought out the sun as an addict her drug of choice. I wore no hat and did not drink enough water, against everyone's constant advice. And I fared well. I fared well in the desert. I fared well in the mountains. My skin grew darker. When winter came, the outlines of my bikini did not fade. I thought my skin color was going to alter permanently and wondered what to do about these white reminders of non-Semitic blood.

I hungered for the sun when the winter rains began. But the dramatic winter weather was as intense as the sun's heat. The power failed easily. We sat for hours in candlelight, our shadows dancing eerily on the walls. The wind whistled and howled, the rain beat down in torrents and sudden cracks of thunder seemed to come from no distance at all. These storms never abated, they just ended. And when they did, the sun's rays broke through from behind the clouds, reminding me always of Christian depictions of the second coming. I thought a great deal about religion that first winter.

L'alot artzah, to ascend to the land, is a bureaucratic act of immigration. It is a physical act of emigration from one country to another. It is a socioeconomic state of being for a few years. It is an existential act of identity as a Jew. It is a moral commitment to the Jewish liberation movement. It is also a spiritual act of rebirth and renewal.

Aliyah is a ubiquitous word in the Hebrew language. You do *aliyah* when you get on a bus, ascend to the throne, climb stairs, read from the Torah in synagogue, ride in an elevator, or make a pilgrimage to the Temple in Jerusalem. Jews taking up residency in Israel make *aliyah*. The state has replaced the Temple.

I heard the word before I actually did it and never took its literal meaning seriously. A whimsical archaism, I thought. But ascent is what it was, physically and spiritually. I sensed it in the air that first night just off the plane and in the welcome of our first day in Haifa. In the immediacy of my connection and identification with complete strangers. In the depth of new friendships and a shared history of survival that I was just beginning to make mine. In the way my senses welcomed what to many would seem a harsh climate and desolate scenery.

◄●►

Shelly Bassin's lessons on Israeli housekeeping were not overdrawn. I stood barefoot in an inch of dirty water, wielding my squeegee in a losing struggle to keep the water from washing over the legs of the furniture. The water washed to its own rhythms, prodded by my squeegee toward the front door, down the stairs, and into the garden. Most of the neighbors called the antique furniture I brought from America *alteh zachen*, old things, junk. They offered no advice to solve my *sponjeh* problem. Much as I worried about the cracks appearing in claw legs, I loved the fresh smell of wet tile that filled the house afterward and the feel of the clean, cold floor under my feet.

Most of what I learned about keeping house in Israel was by anamnesis. The laundry dried in the heat of the sun. Like my mother, I hung it on the line with wooden clothespins. Like her, I had a neighbor to gossip with while hanging clothes. I remember my mother and Mrs. Melnick leaning dangerously over their second-story windowsills to reach the clothesline, shouting to one another from house to house, sometimes a recipe, sometimes neighborhood gossip.

Since Barbara Prager's family and mine occupied the two first-floor apartments, our shared clothesline was strung at the back of the house. We did not have to shout. The Pragers were also American immigrants, Barbara a convert to Judaism and Leonard a Yiddishist. We sublet their apartment during our first year in Israel, while they were on sabbatical in New York, and then moved into the apartment next door. Barbara and I were both part-time professionals. She played viola with the Haifa Symphony, and I taught philosophy at Haifa University. Leonard, like Bill, taught in the English Department. We were Siamese twinned along our kitchen wall. Intensifying the affinities, our children grew up together. It was a sign of their near-sibling status that they could step into one another's homes through our adjoining kitchen windows. During the nine years we shared the ground floor of 66 Derech Hayam, the Road to the Sea, we often talked about tearing down the wall that separated us and living communally. In truth, we never really had to tear it down. In all the important respects, it didn't exist.

Shopping with Shelly Bassin, watching her cook to become familiar with the spices, the cuts of meat, the narrow range of vegetables, I remembered my grandmother and the sanctuary that was her kitchen when I was a child. I sat on a high stool as she worked,

listening as she sang in Yiddish. Sometimes she let me wrap the
blintzes or pinch the edges of the kreplach. But I was never allowed to touch the babka. Nor even to go near the corner where
it sat under its cloth, rising.

Preparing for Shabbat had been the heart of my grandmother's
domestic ritual, and it became the heart of mine. The preparation
began early Friday morning. With three or four large plastic baskets
in hand, the women headed for the Mercaz, the Center, to shop.
Some drove, most took the bus. Between eight in the morning
and noon, we converged on the only supermarket in the city, the
Supersol, the superbasket. Irritable women pushed loaded carts
through crowded narrow aisles. Driving them as their husbands
drove their cars, they cut one another off, held up traffic to select
the very best tomatoes in the pile. Impatient women shouted, "Nu?
Gveret!, Hey, lady," the phrase echoing back upon itself from one
jammed aisle to another.

My grandmother walked the aisles with me, pointing to cel-
ery roots, onions, turnips, carrots, and fresh dill for the chicken
soup. The potatoes and onions still had the dirt of the field on
them. The smell of oranges, cucumbers, and tomatoes mingled with
the human smell of sweat. Hundreds of kosher chickens were stuffed
into glass showcases, their heads and feet still attached. The feet,
I remembered, went into the soup. My grandma knew I loved to
suck the skin and bits of flesh off the soft-jointed bones of the
fiselach. Doing so is my earliest memory of sensuality. She always
saved the feet for me. She also never made gribbenehs and schmaltz
without letting me know. I ate the gribbenehs, the fried pieces of
fat left after the rendering of the schmaltz, as they came out of the
frying pan. Then I spread the thick, warm chicken fat over a slab
of rye bread and sprinkled it with salt.

My grandmother was with me in the kitchen later in the afternoon as I cleaned the chicken the way she had, plucking out
the remaining feathers with a knife, scraping off yellow underskin
that still clung here and there, and, finally, holding the chicken
over an open flame to singe the fuzz from the legs and wings.

The meal on Friday night was the queen of meals. Chicken

soup and matzoh balls, roasted chicken and vegetables so fresh their
tastes were unfamiliar, and finishing up with homemade cake. It
was at least nine before we finished, time for the babysitter to come
so that Bill and I could go to the neighbors or to friends for a
glass of wine and someone else's homemade cake.

We were six families in identical three-bedroom flats in a three-
story building. We cooperatively owned the land and the building. Because of our common rhythms and the common space we
shared, there were strong bonds between the neighbors, particularly the women whose lives so resembled one another's. We
shopped and cooked in the morning and did our housework in
the afternoon. The children were in school in the mornings and
played outside in the afternoons. There were many children on
the block, nine in our building alone. It was safe for them to play
outside, even the littlest ones. Everyone, including strangers, kept
an eye on the children. And they watched one another. They all
knew the rules: stay on the sidewalk and away from "suspicious
objects." There were pictures of suspicious objects in all the schools
and post offices—button bombs that could be left in an empty pack
of cigarettes or a box of candy, time bombs in a plastic shopping
bag or briefcase. There was no way for the children to learn these
lessons without learning, too, that it was Arabs who put these le-
thal toys in their paths.

From the age of two, most of the children were in school for
half the day, six days a week. These were the hours considered
suitable for women to be away from home. For the minority with
jobs (less than one in three), the schoolday determined our working hours. Barbara rehearsed in the mornings and performed in
the evenings. I always scheduled my classes in the morning. An
occasional afternoon faculty meeting threw me into a frenzied spin
arranging childcare. Bracha, our other working neighbor, was a
teacher. She came home on the same bus as her children.

We rushed home from work, changed our clothes, and put
on our aprons. We still had to make up for the missed morning
hours of housework by hiring other women, usually Moroccan,
to help us. But even with the help, Bracha, Barbara, and I usually

felt harassed. We received no sympathy from our nonworking neighbors. They were harassed, too, and couldn't imagine why we wanted to make more work for ourselves.

Only Barbara and I, the two American immigrants in the building, got any assistance from our husbands. Bill and Leonard did some childcare and a little cooking, but hardly any housework. What they did was noticed, however, and remarked upon by the rest of the neighbors. None approved, but there was an edge of envy to it as they complained to one another about how much work there was to do. They complained most often to Barbara and me.

Shlomit, dark-haired and dark-skinned, was the most volatile. We could hear dishes crash against the walls, her tirades screamed full throat out the windows. She was angry because her husband was once again out of the country on business, and one of her three children had once again dirtied the newly washed floor. Bracha's outbursts were verbal only, but no less public. Shelly complained incessantly about aches and pains and an impossible amount of work still to be done, but she always finished up with a joke and a good laugh. Stella did the same, without the joke. Each time she stopped at my landing, resting for a moment, Stella sighed, *Ain li co'ach*. I have no strength. Though she was twenty years younger than Shelly, none of us thought to wonder at Stella's constant ailments. We treated them as metaphors for her life and thought we understood until, a few years later, she died of breast cancer. Then, two years after that, her husband Ytzchak suddenly dropped dead. Of a broken heart, we agreed, sharing the rewards of martyrdom for a moment. They left two young daughters who, with a housekeeper, remained in the third-floor apartment.

I knew these neighbors, and they me, most intimately. We met over the clotheslines, or at the *macolet*, the grocery store across the street. Sometimes our squeegees touched on the landing. We shared some Friday evenings together. We borrowed staples from one another. Together we wove a fabric of domesticity and security that sheltered 66 Derech Hayam.

I was part of *kibbutz galuyot*, a term I first learned because it is the name of a street in Haifa. "The ingathering of the exiles" is a messianic concept, the final stage before the coming of the Messiah. The Jewish state, the new secular messiah of the Jewish people, adopted the term to describe the heroic dream of the early pioneers, that with the establishment of the state all Jews would leave exile behind and regather in Israel. For contemporary Israelis, *kibbutz galuyot* is more modest. It describes the diversity of Jewish racial and ethnic identity. I was one of many different sorts, not so much a Jew in Israel where almost all non-Arabs are Jews, but an *Anglo-Saxit*, from an English-speaking country and therefore a distinct minority not quite trusted by most others. Still, I belonged. I felt totally at home and could not imagine ever living anywhere but in Haifa for the rest of my life.

Chapter 2
The Women's Movement
◄●►

Back in New York for a visit in 1968, I was browsing in a Greenwich Village bookstore and passed a table of books and tabloids by women's liberationists who called themselves Redstockings, Furies, Witches. The book titles talked about sex, politics, and power. A tabloid was called *Notes from the Third Year*. Third year of what? I picked from the newspapers, magazines, and books on the table at random, reading first and last paragraphs, making a little stack that grew quite large. I carried them to the counter where Bill was already on line. "Let's see what you bought," he said. It was an innocent, even expected question, an expression of one of the strongest bonds between us, the books we shared. This time it felt intrusive. I wanted to hide the books but could not. Nervously, I handed them over. "What do you want to read this stuff for?" For a brief moment Bill's usually impassive eyes were angry. I cringed. My heart began to beat wildly. The hint of anger did its work. I had to resist the impulse to lose the books while carrying them home. They remained unread on the shelf. Soon I forgot I ever bought them.

Two years later, my father died by suicide. Depression opened inside me like an endless chasm that seemed to suck me deeper and deeper as the days, the weeks, and the months dragged on. It was as if I had taken in the depression that must have caused my father's death, a depression born of dissatisfaction and frustration with the turn in his life from labor leader to small businessman. My own depression focused on what was wrong with my life— so ordinary, so uneventful, so mired in the details of housework and childcare.

At the point where coping with the daily routine began to feel impossible, I thought about seeing a psychiatrist, but hesitated. Wouldn't I be told that I hadn't adjusted sufficiently to my destiny as wife and mother? I identified with my father. I always expected my life to be like his early life had been, revolutionary and passionate. Would I be accused of penis envy? I thought about seeing a psychiatrist and fleetingly remembered the books.

One day, sitting at the edge of a pool watching Jenny take a swimming lesson, and wanting more than anything to join my father in his death, the incident in the Greenwich Village bookstore came to mind in full detail. I understood what a coward I had been in the face of Bill's disapproval. It took me several days to find the books—I had hidden them so well—and I began to read. As I did, the heavy depression that had lasted more than a year dissolved into anger.

I read Simone de Beauvoir, Betty Friedan, Shulamit Firestone, Ellen Willis, Charlotte Bunch, Kate Millet. These were intelligent works by intelligent women. Their minds, like mine, were fine-tuned by higher education and, for some, the study of Marx to the patterns of oppression and exploitation. Philosophy was my field, political theory my favorite corner. I recognized well-formed formulas and well-reasoned arguments when I saw them, and I could add my own personal experience to the weight of evidence. Though passionate and often personal, the arguments were convincing. I was a quick study.

I learned from these writings that I'd been taken in by the

mythology of romantic love that lives happily ever after; that house-work and childcare are exploitative when unshared; that anatomy need not be destiny; that anger is a rational response to oppression; that an imbalance of power determined my relationship to my husband, to my child, to my colleagues at the university. I learned that like all oppressed peoples, women would have to resist and fight back, not individually but together. I learned that like Blacks, like Jews, women needed a liberation movement.

This was not theoretical learning about a new social cause. It was about me, and my entire life was in question. Why do I do all the housework? Did I really ever choose to become pregnant? Why are men excused and women punished for sexual transgressions? Why did I take on Bill's name when we married when my own, Prince, was so much nicer? Why am I the only woman in the philosophy department? Why, if we were both in graduate school when we met, was Bill now the chairman of his department and I unable to finish my doctorate?

Daily incidents provided the materials of transformation, real life as allegory. Bill, standing in front of the refrigerator preparing to make his usual grilled cheese sandwiches for lunch, complains that we're out of cheese. I, apologetic, run out to buy some. My department chairman tells me he needs help ordering books and journals for the library. Would I mind doing the paperwork? My friend's Phi Beta Kappa key hangs on her kitchen wall, above the sink, where she can look at it each evening while she does the dishes. Such moments are historical markers of developing feminist consciousness. They are the stuff of personal legend. They flag the moments after which whatever was before is never to be again.

So began a struggle with myself, with Bill, with Jenny, with my academic colleagues, against the impulse to serve that was the habit of a lifetime. As far as I knew, I was the only feminist in Israel. I felt unbearably alone. As never before, I needed women friends, women who could share the agony of change I was experiencing. From that need came the behavior that organizers call recruiting, though it didn't seem that way at the time.

Judy Hill was the first. We were both part-time junior faculty.

We and our professor husbands were friends. Our daughters took the same ballet class. As we waited for the class to end, I asked Judy if she had ever heard of the women's liberation movement. Yes, she said. She'd been in a consciousness-raising group in Chapel Hill during a sabbatical year, but Moshe was upset about it. "He said he didn't think it was possible to be a feminist and remain married. I didn't leave the group," she said, "but I'd be scared to join one now." The next week I arrived early to wait for Jenny and so did Judy. I brought her a book which she took hesitantly. For a moment I thought she would give it back. The following week we talked about the book, collapsing long hours of conversation into fifteen minutes before the class and after it. I brought Judy another book and wondered if she kept them hidden from Moshe. We began to meet at a nearby cafe during the ballet class, discussing our reading, then our lives. During one of these meetings, we were so engrossed that I was fifteen minutes late when I came to pick up Jenny. She was traumatized with fear. I had never been late before. She never took another ballet lesson. Even now, my adult daughter looks at me accusingly whenever ballet comes up in our conversation.

Judy and I met at the Cafe Carmel, a sidewalk cafe with round white tables and bright umbrellas. Over the years, the cafe became a meeting place for Haifa's feminists and women wanting to get to know us. But at first it was just Judy and me and our little joke about how revolutions are spawned in cafes just like this one. Perhaps, we said, one day there will be a plaque that reads, "The Israel feminist movement began here."

At first there was only Judy, but soon there was Shoshana Eilings as well. I met her through our mutual connection to the philosophy department, she, a reentry student, and I, a junior faculty member. Shoshana grew up in the Jewish Quarter of Jerusalem in the 1930s and '40s, one of six children of Orthodox working-class parents whose family lived in the Jewish Quarter for six generations. She was fifteen in 1948 when the War of Independence broke out, lied about her age, and joined the Palmach, the elite commandos of the Jewish underground. At eighteen she married, had

two daughters, divorced, married again, divorced again, and, finally, in her forties, passed high-school equivalency exams and entered the university to study psychology and philosophy.

Through Shoshana, Judy and I met Marilyn Safer, another
American immigrant and a feminist, who taught in the psychology department. Marilyn brought a graduate student with her,
Malka Ma'on, like Shoshana a reentry woman and Israeli-born.
Malka's younger sister, Nomi Nimrod, was also a student at the
university and joined the table in the cafeteria that became our
regular meeting place. Nomi brought in another student, Malka
Perkal, a slight young woman, only eighteen, whose tightly curled
golden brown hair matched the color of her eyes. Malka, an American, was really Marcia. To avoid confusion we called her Malka-
Marcia. Natalie was the last of the original organizers to join the
group that met at the Cafe Carmel. Another *Anglo-Saxiot*, a new
immigrant from England, she read an interview I gave to the *Jerusalem Post* about women's liberation. The next day she knocked on
the door at 66 Derech Hayam. "My name is Natalie Rein," she
said. "I've come to help. My goodness! I didn't realize you were
so short."

We became Israel's first consciousness-raising group and the innocent founders of a movement that for most Israelis was anathema.

◄●►

Later that same year, the campus Hillel organization asked me
to give an extracurricular seminar on a topic of my choice. "We'll
provide a budget for coffee and cookies," said Bernie Och, the young
Reform rabbi who ran Haifa's Hillel. "Choose any subject you like,
preferably controversial."

"Women's liberation," I said. "But I'll only do it if the course
is open just to women."

Bernie was a liberal and spent a good deal of his American
budget trying to promote Arab-Jewish relations at Haifa University, a school with a large number of Arab students. He was usually
agreeable to new ideas, listened carefully, let himself be persuaded.
But at that moment his large brown eyes, magnified by the round

glasses he wore, registered shock. His upraised eyebrows knit his brow, making him look worried as well. "Why?" he asked, "What's the point? What if someone else wants to exclude women?"

I explained to Bernie that there weren't any texts, the issues were not a common subject of public discourse. I explained that we had to use our own lives as raw material and create our own analysis. I explained that we needed space and privacy to do that, that the material would be threatening to men, and they would only be disruptive. I explained that the habits of being dominated by men were too strong and that the women would be silenced.

He agreed. Reluctantly. He was so nervous about what I planned to do, I was sure he would promote the class discreetly. Instead he posted flyers all over the university. I couldn't go anywhere without seeing them—large black-and-white signs that were low-budget stark. In three-inch letters they said:

WOMEN'S LIBERATION
MARCIA FREEDMAN
WOMEN ONLY

The campus buzzed. The press sought me out.

Eight students came the first evening. All had dark hair and olive complexions, were single and in their early twenties. I proposed what I had in mind for process. We would choose an autobiographical subject and go round the room saying whatever we wished about our own experience. Afterward, we would see if we could discern patterns, analyze common threads, and draw conclusions.

The women looked at one another in bewilderment. "You mean we're going to talk about our private lives?" one of them asked. "I thought you would lecture." Israelis hardly ever speak of their private lives, even in private, and still less about their feelings. I knew they were scared. But so was I. My risk was no less than theirs. Greater, perhaps, since gossip about me would travel fastest and widest.

There was complete silence in the room. Occasionally one student looked at another, then back down at her lap. I thought we would sit like that forever. Hannah, a student in one of my classes and the only one there I knew, broke the silence. "I'll do it," she said, "if I can be sure that everyone will protect my privacy. Haifa is a small town." Others nodded. The pact lent solemnity to our proceedings.

Childhood was the obvious place to start. Safer than the present. I began, since it had been my idea. I expected to be an anomaly among these women, not only older, married, and a mother, I was the only American. But as I spoke about my tomboy childhood, I could see the young Israeli women around me nodding in recognition. They, too, had rejected the constraints of femininity early and then had to come to terms with them in adolescence. Some were still coming to terms. Those with older brothers chimed in "Me, too," when I spoke of endless parental conversations about my brother's future. Lofty possibilities were raised—a doctor, a lawyer, a professor even. Why not? Didn't my brother always get A's in history? My future career possibilities were never mentioned, though I got A's in everything.

We went around the circle, speaking out of turn only to offer support or ask a question. After a while, the stories, so similar, began to blur into one another. As the circle moved on it picked up the basic patterns and embellished them with the fine detail of things remembered perhaps for the first time.

Then it was Aida's turn. "I grew up in Um-al-Facham, a village in the Galilee," she said, as we all stared at her. She spoke Hebrew with perfect *sabra* accents. Her name, pronounced *I-da*, could well have been Eastern European. We all assumed she was Jewish until she said where she was from. Aida knew that. "I'm an Arab," she said. "Most Jews don't know until I tell them." Her father was one of a small but growing number of Arab professionals who believed in education for their daughters. Aida's father, an educator too familiar with the deficits of underfunded education in the Arab sector, encouraged Aida to attend a Jewish high school.

Aida and two of her brothers all attended the university and shared an apartment in Haifa. They colluded in not telling her parents that in Haifa, Aida sometimes wore pants and went freely about the city by herself. "I came here alone tonight and I'll go home alone. But it's not customary for an Arab woman to be out on the streets like that at night. My parents would be very upset if they knew. When I'm at home, I wear long skirts and keep house with my mother. Even here I'm expected to keep house for my brothers. I can't object. If my parents knew my brothers weren't chaperoning me, they might insist I come home."

Penina was last. She had a bad case of acne, was very near-sighted, and talked in the staccato rhythm of a pneumatic drill. Her sentences were an assault on the ears and the brain. She was impervious to our pleas to slow down. She simply couldn't. "All through high school," she said, "we were prepared for army service. We thought we were going to be soldiers. In paramilitary training, we did everything the boys did and we did them together. They took us on twenty-mile hikes carrying packs, had us set up our tents, and then ordered us to get up in the middle of the night and take them down again. They wanted to teach us to be tough, the boys and the girls. I thought the army would be like that, too. I thought I would be a soldier. But I was never a soldier, except for the uniform. I was a typist. I took orders from men. We all took orders from men, even the women officers. It was humiliating. I never thought of myself as inferior to anyone before, certainly not because of my sex. By the time I got out of the army, I knew what the score was."

The women murmured and nodded. "I was a typist too," Hannah said. So were four of the others. One had been a behind-the-lines radio operator, and the other was sent to a hospital to work as a nurse's aide. She distributed and collected bedpans.

"You know what they say about the army," Etti said, looking around for confirmation, "the best of the men to the air force, the best of the women to the pilots."

Eight women came to the first meeting, twelve to the second, and twenty-five to the third. We split into two groups. "I don't think we should call ourselves study groups any more," Hannah said. "What we really need is a movement." Aida put up signs in Arabic for the third group. In order not to identify herself as an organizer, she took out a post office box. The groups reproduced like amoebae. Soon there were fifty women, then a hundred.

Feminism isn't just a political movement; it's also a personal transformation, fearful but heady. Our friends and our neighbors noticed the changes. They saw dozens of women coming into and going out of our apartments for meetings, parties, just to visit. They saw us at the cafe. They were curious. Recruiting was easy.

◄●►

Malka, Nomi, Malka-Marcia, and I stood in front of the Supersol on Saturday mornings selling the movement's first newspaper. Friday, when women did their shopping, would have been better, but like all the rest, we, too, were busy on Friday mornings. It was an understood imperative among us—no demonstrations, no meetings on Friday.

Saturday was a day when families strolled in the Mercaz, window-shopping, resting a while in *Gan Ha'em*, the Mother's Park, having a drink at a sidewalk cafe. Standing on the edge of the sidewalk, close to one another for protection, we hawked the newspaper. We disturbed the peace. Crowds of the curious and the hostile gathered around, mostly in couples. The men challenged us loudly. They made lewd jokes. They wagged their fingers in our faces. They jostled and pushed, as though by accident. Young men, walking together in groups, shouted obscenities. The women watched silently. Husbands steered their wives away. Occasionally, someone bought a paper. By the end of the day we'd sold ten, maybe fifteen papers. Shaken, but triumphant that we'd held our ground, we had coffee at the Cafe Carmel and agreed to come out again the following Saturday.

During those earliest years, we supported a wildcat strike of women factory workers demanding equal pay. We collected signatures on a petition for abortion reform. We protested at the Rabbinical Court. We demanded and won a day-care center at the university. Wherever we demonstrated, rallied, petitioned, sat-in, or marched, there were only a few of us, and angry crowds gathered. Tranquil Haifa, and the rest of the country, was shocked.

Friday-evening gatherings with the neighbors or with friends, those amiable get-togethers over cake and coffee, turned into an angry battleground between husbands and wives whenever one of us was present. Good-humored teasing about feminism grew with repetition to baiting. Finally, it became a matter of honor to take the bait and defend the movement. Most often, the men, except our own husbands, joined ranks against us. The women were apologetic. The evening invariably came to a head when it was time to serve coffee and cake. Who would get up and do it? The host was hostile. He wasn't about to move. The hostess hesitated, ashamed to play the servant after all. Still the guests had to be served. She'd baked the cake and would clean up afterward. That was the reality of our lives, no matter how much we claimed otherwise. Over coffee and cake, couples argued with one another. At the end, everyone went home confused and angry. Surely no one slept well that night. I dreaded these evenings that once I'd found so pleasant. Later, I refused to go. Bill, who by then was comfortable helping serve guests in our home, complained that I was ruining his social life and separating him from his friends.

The fear and hostility that feminism aroused in widening circles lasted throughout the seventies and into the eighties, fed by an unflagging negative press. We were described routinely as aggressive, shrill, emotional, unkempt, ugly, and, of course, utterly wrong. "Feminism sometimes borders on the absurd," wrote Heda Boshes, one of the few influential women of the press. Feminists, she wrote, think "that in order to demonstrate their liberation and their rights, they have to be ugly, hairy. . . perhaps they would do away with bathing." Under the headline, "The Battle Front Has Shifted to the Home Front," Ruth Schreiber wrote that "Israeli men will soon have to defend a third front. It's not enough that they have to sit in the trenches and on the tanks at the borders defending our cities and towns from terrorists. In the future they will also have to defend themselves at home, against their wives. At least these are the hopes of the women of the feminist movement in

Israel." Others wrote that they wanted nothing to do with feminism. They liked being feminine. A few, like Yael Dayan, embraced feminism as a way of life but attacked the movement. She was already liberated, she wrote in a mass-circulation women's magazine, and she hadn't needed the help of a movement.

The media attention, distorted as it was, ignited small sparks all over the country. I received letters from women in Tel Aviv, Jerusalem, Eilat, various kibbutzim. I replied, by mail or by phone, with the same message: Try to organize a group. "Oh, I couldn't do that," they said. But in Tel Aviv and in Herzliyah, a suburb of Tel Aviv, there were two women willing to organize—Esther Eilam and Ruth Resnik. Through their efforts, the movement spread to Tel Aviv.

In Jerusalem, the movement came into being without connection to what we were doing in Haifa and Tel Aviv. It grew out of the left, first as a kind of ladies' auxiliary to Matzpen, the Israeli Socialist Worker's Party. We learned about its existence through the media, and in the early years we coexisted uneasily. Matzpen was anti-Zionist and, in Israeli terms as well as our own at the time, it was beyond the pale. The Matzpen literature, written by men, saw the women's movement as a new avenue for anti-Zionist organizing. Its women were encouraged to become feminists in order to bring the entire movement into Matzpen. In Haifa, we'd found the men of the left to be less cooperative, less sympathetic, and more threatened than moderate liberals like Bill or Bernie Och. We did not trust Matzpen and, in those days, we did not trust the Jerusalem movement.

The Jerusalem women, in turn, did not trust our careful disassociation of women's oppression from the oppression of Arabs and the poor. There was little collaboration between us and a great deal of tension.

All together, we were no more than fifty active feminists in the whole country. We knew that we needed one another and we tried to bridge the differences. On a hot summer's day in 1972, we all met in Tel Aviv to try to find common ground. It was the first time we had had a national meeting. For twelve hours, we sat in a circle on the floor and argued about feminist theory.

—"Women's liberation is a struggle against male domination and patriarchal institutions."

—"The women's movement has to be part of the struggle against all oppressions. We must join with the Palestinians, with the poor. Women's oppression is part of the class struggle, not separate from it."

—"Arab women and poor women are just as oppressed by their men as we are, even more. Our struggle cuts through race, class, and nationality."

—"It's the economic system that oppresses women, not men."

—"We want to be a mass movement of women. If we identify with the anti-Zionist left, we will alienate most Israelis. You are crippling the women's movement."

We shouted at one another, we sweated profusely, and we never resolved our differences. When the Jerusalem women were shown on television marching in the May Day parade carrying signs for women's liberation and for a binational state, the rest of us could only grit our teeth. The other choices, to denounce the Jerusalem women or to loudly proclaim our Zionism, would only feed the media the message that this tiny new movement was already in disarray. I remembered my father's warnings about the abuse of united fronts, but also his anger about red-baiting. I remembered the McCarthy era of the 1950s and responded with confusion and ambivalence. For many, it was an early warning that we needed to keep the politics of the Middle East out of the women's movement. But try as we would, the Arab-Jewish conflict always played a decisive role in the development of Israeli feminism.

◄●►

Irgun Emahot Ovdot, The Working Mothers Organization, originally a feminist organization aligned with the labor movement, ran a network of childcare centers throughout the country during the 1970s. But once, in the prestate days of the pioneers, they had been militant socialist feminists organized around the demand for wages for housework. The Working Mothers no longer recalled the specifics of their past, but they remembered enough of their history to invite me to Tel Aviv in 1972 to speak to them about women's rights.

I wrote the speech in English and rehearsed reading it aloud in Hebrew from the English text. Shoshana provided much of the translation and wrote the words I might forget in the margins. I added phonetic markers.

I would have been safe had I talked about discrimination in the rabbinical courts. I would have been on familiar ground if I had complained of underrepresentation in politics. In the Israeli catechism, that was the unfinished business of the pioneers. But mine was a different message and a harsher one.

"There are myths about Israeli women," I began, "that are part of our Zionist orthodoxy." Not a safe beginning. "We have our images of pioneer women driving tractors and believe that we are equal in the workplace. We see pictures of women in uniform bearing arms and believe that we have an equal role in Israel's defense. We see Golda Meir, our Prime Minister, a role model for women all over the world, and tell ourselves that each of us could be Golda if we wished. But none of this is true any more. It probably never was."

I drew a picture of systematic discrimination relentlessly full of facts and figures. I spoke of the deepest levels of oppression—in our personal relationships, sexuality, marriage, and the family. The women in the audience stirred in their seats, whispering to one another. The whispers turned to shouts.

—"Golda proves that if a woman deserves it, she can be the equal of men. Maybe the rest of us just don't deserve it."

—"If there's inequality, it's our own fault."

—"I'm as free as I want to be. Look at the price Golda's had to pay. Divorced, estranged from her children. No, thank you."

—"You want to put men in aprons! What man would want a woman like that?"

—"What's wrong," a very red-faced and carefully groomed woman in the front row shouted, "if I prefer to spend the evening ironing while my husband reads the newspaper? We just have different ways of relaxing."

—"Relaxing! You call that relaxing?"

In a far corner a woman in her seventies stood talking to a growing group around her. I couldn't hear at first, but slowly, everyone turned to listen. "I fought for women's rights forty years ago," she was saying, "and I'm glad that women are organizing again. You should listen to this young woman and you should be helping, not arguing with her."

Afterward, only two of the two hundred women in the hall took her advice. I felt battered driving home to Haifa, taking solace where I could—two women who asked for the address of the movement in Tel Aviv and the support of a *chalutza*, one of the pioneers.

◄●►

The family is central in Jewish thought, going back to the Biblical period when the Hebrews were tribes subdivided into patriarchal clans. It is a commonplace among Jews, scholars and laypersons agree, that the centrality of family plays a key role in the survival of the Jews. Throughout two thousand years of exile, the study house, the synagogue, and the home replaced the Temple as the place of worship. Religiously, home life was ritualized and sanctified.

Be fruitful and multiply, the Biblical injunction to Jews, takes on special importance within the framework of survival. Two thousand years of persecution culminating in the Holocaust and the halving of the Jewish population of the world created enormous pressure on survivors to bear children. The history of the Zionist enterprise only served to reinforce the injunction. With constant wars and endless casualties, procreation became a national ideology. As early as 1948, Ben Gurion told women they could best serve the homeland by bearing at least four children for the state. He called it *aliya p'nimit*, internal immigration.

Twenty-five years later, *aliya p'nimit* determined public policy. Access to information about birth control was strictly controlled. Social workers were not allowed to mention it to their clients, even when asked. Abortion was legal only if pregnancy and childbirth threatened the life of the mother. Economic incentives encouraged large families, and marriage exempted women from service in the army. C'vod bat melech p'nima, the rabbis said. Honorable women remain indoors.

The women's movement questioned all the accepted norms about women's role within the family. It challenged the sacred—and nationalist—duty of women to bear children; the absence of women in the public sphere; the role of women in the army; and the segregation of women in the workforce into poorly paid ghettos of "women's work." But most especially, in taking our case to the streets we violated religious and cultural norms of femininity.

The Israeli response was to label feminism an American import. No matter that American brands of tobacco, cars, appliances, and liquor were in demand. When applied to the women's movement, American import was decidedly and uniquely pejorative.

For the sabra, Israeli-born, women in the movement, American import was doubly insulting. Many began to research the pioneer period seeking their own Israeli feminist roots. What they found challenged the deeply held mythology about the role of women in Israel's golden age.

The pioneer women's history, their struggle, the nature of their demands, their successes and failures were not recorded in the official history books. Instead, the chalutzot were shown at work in the fields, milking cows and riding tractors. The pictures are of liberated women working alongside men to build the homeland. The official mythology was widespread, not just in Israel but throughout the world. In 1961, Betty Friedan had cited Israel as the only place in the world where women were equal to men.

Through a painstaking search for documents—diaries, letters, an occasional out-of-print book—Israeli feminists began to reconstruct the truth about women in prestate Israel. The reality is that the chalutzot worked the land, built roads, or constructed houses only when, as part of their rebellion, they separated from the men and set up their own communal farms and businesses. The truth is that these women fought long and bitterly to win the right to vote and the right to inherit and own property. They fought against bigamy and the traffic in child brides. They won only those rights that feminists in the west had won a generation earlier.

Early Zionist theorists advocated a "renaissance of the Jewish people," one that would produce a New Jew. But they wrote as if only men inhabited the Jewish world. The New Jew would place the highest value on manual labor and self-sufficiency. He would be prepared to defend himself. The *Shomrim*, the Jewish Guardians of the early Zionist period, were the heroes of the *chalutzim*. A self-appointed organization of guardsmen, the *Shomrim*, dressed in Bedouin clothes and carrying long rifles, rode from settlement to settlement defending against thieves and raiders.

This resurgence of Jewish machismo was at the heart of early Zionist ideology. And though lip service was paid to feminism and the "liberation of women from their biological tragedy," the *chalutzim* were either dismissive of or hostile to the feminist struggle of the *chalutzot*. They decreed that women's proper role in the new agricultural settlements was in the kitchen or the laundry. In the days when all the pioneers, men and women, were sustained on payments from a central fund operated by *Misrad Eretz Ysraeli*, the Land of Israel Office, women were paid less then men. Women—who perform services—were employed by men—who do productive labor—it was said, and thus deserved less. The *chalutzim* were tyrannical and arrogant in their personal relationships as well.

In the early seventies, Israel still revered the founding fathers, but the founding mothers were disparaged as dowdy old women in orthopedic shoes who had sacrificed their femininity in a futile attempt to be like men.

Kibbutz women were even more resistant to the revival of feminism in Israel than city women. They, the daughters and granddaughters of the *chalutzot*, understood the anger and disappointment of the founding mothers as the result, not the cause, of their feminism. They originated the official ideology of the kibbutz, extended to the larger society, that Israeli women had long ago been liberated but had since discovered that true happiness was to be found in family life.

Speaking about women's liberation at kibbutzim was a very different experience from speaking in the city. Instead of the usual hostile uproar, I encountered a silent audience, on the surface, at least, unresponsive. "The kibbutz," I reminded them, "was founded at least in part to liberate women from traditional roles as wives and mothers. But look around you. All the women on this kibbutz do housework. What does it matter if women are housekeeping for an entire community or only for their own families? It's still housework. Who runs the kibbutz? Who speaks up at community meetings? Who do you send to the Knesset to represent you?" Invariably the older women would say quietly, "She's right," and the younger people, men and women, stared down at their shoes, ashamed, or so it seemed to me, of betraying the foremothers' struggle.

◄●►

Purim is a carnival holiday lasting three days. It is a time for adults to shed the serious, sober demeanor of everyday life for costume parties and sanctioned drunkenness. But mostly it is a holiday for children. Mothers devote long hours to creating the costumes their children will wear for three days, in school and on the streets. One time I dressed Jenny as a rabbit, once as a rose. It was only during my third Purim in Israel—Jenny was dressed as a witch—that I realized I was seriously out of step with the culture.

Walking the streets of the Mercaz, a newly enlightened feminist, I saw the pattern for the first time. The boys were dressed as Haman the Wicked, or soldiers, pirates, policemen, cowboys, even Indian chiefs—all armed. Some of the girls were ballerinas and nurses, but most of them wore long white dresses with flowing trains and crowns, and carried jeweled scepters. They were dressed as Queen Esther. They learned about Esther as the savior of the Jewish people, but they dressed as brides. According to the story they were taught in school, Esther was a heroine because she was chosen to replace Vashti, King Achoshveros' disobedient wife. Afterward, "He sent letters into all the king's provinces...that every man shall govern his own home...." Esther was chosen to marry the king because of her extreme modesty, her chastity, and her submissiveness.

Esther, the obedient bride, was the ideal of womanhood expressed year after year at Purim. Where, I wondered, walking with Jenny the witch through the Mercaz, is Deborah, the judge, the leader, the warrior woman? Certainly, looking at the other mothers, I saw Deborah in the strong, determined faces around me. Surely Deborah, not Esther, was the heroine of the *chalutzot*. Why did they dress their daughters as Esther?

There is a yearly competition in Israel for *Eshet Cha'il*, a woman of valor. It is awarded to a woman who combines volunteer service to the community with exemplary service to a large family. Having at least six children seems to be one of the criteria for being Israel's woman of the year. The Biblical psalm about *Eshet Cha'il* tells of a woman who "girdeth her loins with power, and strengthens her arms." She wheels and deals, buying and selling real estate and shiploads of merchandise. She is in the world and of it. But at home "her husband doth safely trust in her," and she "looketh well to the ways of her household."

This is the double message given Israeli women, Jewish women everywhere. "Be strong, be assertive, but do it in the service of the family and under your husband's dominance." *C'vod bat melech p'nima*, the princess is honored at home.

◄●►

Israeli feminists exposed the contradictions inherent in the Jewish/Zionist idealizations of women, the fierce warrior and the obedient wife. We challenged the resurgence of machismo among Jewish men that was the ultimate message of Zionism. We stirred the waters of guilt and ambivalence for men and women who both embraced and rejected their mothers' struggle. We aroused the deep-seated fears of Israeli women that they weren't feminine enough. We threatened the stability of the family and, by extension, the security of the state. We rejected the call to become pregnant in order to repopulate the Jewish people or keep up with the Arab reproduction.

We were called an extremist movement. But we were not extremists, and the angry, shamed, but always threatened response we evoked was painful and confusing. We felt rejected and embattled, even as we understood the profound nature of our challenge to Israeli society.

It was hard to remain committed, and some dropped out, overwhelmed by the burden we'd taken upon ourselves. But for most, myself included, the women's movement was a journey of personal liberation. We could turn back only at the price of self-respect and growth. We had to go forward, and because of that the movement, even in the face of intense hostility, could not be stopped.

Chapter 3
1973

◄●►

It became more and more difficult to talk with Alec Bassin, as much because of his politics as his unreconstructed sexism. He beamed whenever he caught me barefoot on the landing, squee-gee in hand. "You see," he boomed, "even feminists do the *sponjeh*."

"We've never been so secure," Alec said, as he held forth one Friday evening. It was summer. We sat on the Bassin's balcony over-looking Derech Hayam. There were no buses or trucks on the road, and only an occasional car passed by. We looked out over the empty field of wildflowers across the street. On the other side of the wadi, the lights that dotted the hillside came from Chalissah, an Arab village that had once been on the outskirts of Haifa and was now surrounded by it.

"Why should we give them back the Golan Heights and let them start firing down on our kibbutzim again?" Alec went on. "Peace? First the Arabs have to want peace. For us, security is more important. When they're convinced they can't get rid of us, then there can be peace." Alec's demeanor, though commanding, was amiable. He assumed our agreement and beamed his delight as he refilled our glasses with wine. Alec, as usual, planned to vote for Labor in the upcoming elections.

I listened carefully to Alec and to everyone else, thinking about how I would vote in October, the first time I voted as an Israeli citizen. Locating myself on the political spectrum was an existential quest: it would mark the way I defined myself as an Israeli.

I followed the news closely. The headlines bespoke a society at peace with itself, an era of prosperity and growth, of military self-confidence, perhaps even arrogance. All seemed quiet on the West Bank. In 1970, King Hussein brutally suppressed a Palestinian uprising and drove PLO leaders and thousands of refugees out of Jordan. Since then there had been relatively little terrorist activity on the West Bank and even less indigenous protest. The military had an easy time with the occupation. Nor did it strain Israel's economy. The cost of the occupation was more than offset by the benefit of an almost 50 percent increase in the domestic market, cheap labor, and an expanded tax base.

But there were small items, only a few paragraphs long, stuffed into corners or used as fillers. Stories about curfews imposed on the West Bank, for hours or days. Stories about expulsions, demolition of homes, administrative detentions. These were the predictors of things to come.

Discussion of the future of the occupied territories or even the possibilities of peace in the Middle East engaged neither the media nor the politicians prior to the 1977 elections scheduled for the end of October. The Labor Party, when asked, referred as briefly as possible to the Jordanian option and the Allon plan, whereby Israel and Jordan would agree to redraw the border between them. The leader of the opposition, Menachem Begin, had a clearer agenda. Begin called for a "Unified Land of Israel," *Eretz Ysrael Hashlema*. There was a semantic map of territorial politics. In the 1970s, one could not use the word *occupation* without being accused of anti-Zionism, a term, in Israel, akin to traitor. The annexationists talked about the liberated territories. Labor, trying to hold the middle between annexation and withdrawal, called them the administered territories.

Neither major party recognized that the people living on these lands had a legitimate claim to them. They were called only refugees. The term *Palestinian* was rarely used. Golda Meir reiterated publicly that there was no such thing as a Palestinian people. Together the two major coalitions, the Labor Alignment and Begin's Likud, represented the great majority of the people, including some of my friends and many of my neighbors. Like the politicians, most people did not talk about the present or future of the territories, and when they did, the talk was peculiarly abstracted. It was as if there were plenty of time, the issues still academic.

◄●►

I saw Shulamit Aloni for the first time in 1970 when she lectured in Haifa on the need for a women's movement. She had just returned from the United States where she'd been inspired by American feminism. To my knowledge, this was the original call for action by anyone remotely connected to the political mainstream. At the time I had only just begun my reading. I was excited to see the title of her talk advertised: Does Israel Need a Women's Liberation Movement?

Aloni spoke passionately and brilliantly about the oppression of women under the system of religious law governing marriage and divorce. When she finished, I rushed out of the auditorium, hoping to talk to her before she left. I caught up with her in the parking lot. "If you're starting a movement, I want to help," I called to her.

Aloni turned to me scornfully, I thought, though it was dark and I couldn't be sure. I was sure about her voice, however. It was full of contempt. "Start it yourself," she called as she got into her car.

The memory of that encounter was still fresh when Ruth Resnik called in August to ask me to be a candidate for the Knesset on Aloni's list. Ruth was one of the founding mothers in Tel Aviv. "Shulamit has decided to run independently," she told me. "Golda won't give her a safe place on Labor's list. There's a small group of people supporting her for an independent run. She wants our help." And then Ruth said the most astonishing thing. "She's offered us third place on her list, and she wants you to be the candidate."

Ruth paused, giving me a chance to respond. When I didn't, she mercifully went on with the details. The party would be called the Citizens Rights Movement (CRM), Shulamit would be first on the list, then a microbiologist from Tel Aviv University named Boaz Moav. There was another man involved in the founding group, Shulamit's brother-in-law, whose office would be campaign headquarters. "He'll probably be fourth," Ruth said. "But the important thing right now is to get enough signatures to file. The deadline is in three days."

So that was it. Aloni didn't have any organization in place, nothing but a small group of supporters. She needed drones, and we were the closest thing at hand. Why not do it? She had spoken eloquently that night, at least from the stage. If we succeeded in helping her get elected, she would owe a debt to feminism. "Why don't you be the candidate?" I asked Ruth. "After all, you're Shulamit's friend."

"She asked me," Ruth said, "but I won't be able to be active in the campaign. I'm scheduled for surgery next month."

And so our pact was struck. I knew little about Shulamit Aloni, except that she was a liberal maverick, articulate and witty, perhaps one of the best orators in politics. Her ad hominum quips often made headlines. Aloni was also one of the few politicians who understood the institutions, attitudes, and processes of western-style democracy. She was a woman, and with uneven enthusiasm, a feminist. I knew, too, what I'd experienced in the parking lot. She would have been my candidate, but did I want to work for her?

Ruth mobilized the movement in Tel Aviv and I in Haifa. With only a few days to gather fifteen hundred signatures, we canvassed the Mercaz day and night—during the day at the entrance to the Supersol, at night working the cafes. There were about fifteen feminists on the street, and between us we knew enough of the people who frequented the Mercaz to collect more than the required number of signatures.

Three days after Ruth's call, I traveled to Tel Aviv for my first meeting with the new party's leadership—Aloni, Boaz Moav, and Ram Ron, her brother-in-law. Aloni wore jeans and a plaid shirt. She was exuberant. "Wait and see," she said, "I'll get us all into the Knesset."

Until that moment, the possibility of election never dawned on me. When it did, I couldn't take it seriously. Still, the images conjured up were slow to fade, and, as usual, my first reaction was fear. "You're going to have to take me there by the hand," I said. "I won't even know how to find the ladies room." It was supposed to be amusing, but Aloni's mood shifted. She looked at me scornfully. I was sure of it this time. Her intense blue eyes cut through to my vulnerability, and it was clear that she didn't like what she saw. Nevertheless, when her brother-in-law tried to challenge my right to third place, Aloni made an impassioned little speech about her commitment to feminism. "The women's liberation movement is my movement, too," she said. "Marcia stays."

That was the honeymoon, and it was a brief one. Aloni and I had our first blow-up with Shulamit in absentia. The party platform was written hastily during the first months of the campaign and, eventually, the drafters got to women's issues. This was the only platform meeting that Aloni did not attend. In her stead, Dina Goren chaired the meeting. Goren, a professor of communications at Hebrew University, a large woman with fiery red hair, was recruited largely because the list needed another woman. She was unknown in feminist circles.

I came to the meeting with a draft plank prepared by the Haifa movement. It was deliberately moderate, we thought. In the space of a brief paragraph, it called for an end to job discrimination, equal opportunities in education, and reproductive freedom—issues, we thought, that would arouse no opposition. "It's too radical," Goren said immediately, as though she'd planned to say that about whatever I suggested. An angry red flush crept from her throat to her forehead where it clashed with her hair. There was a virtual Greek chorus of agreement. I looked at Moshe Hill, who had not yet spoken. Moshe was Judy's husband, a CRM candidate because he was an environmentalist and a respected expert in urban planning. The feminists of the CRM had recruited him because he was Judy's husband, and we thought we could trust him. I assumed that he, at least, would be loyal.

"All we need is one sentence promising to work for equal rights for women," Moshe said. I waited quietly as the anger flooded through me. If I'd learned anything during the past few weeks, it was that you get your way by being angry. When I spoke, I heard an unfamiliar sound. I was shouting. "Why that's even less than what the Labor Party has. I'm sure even the Likud will have more than one sentence on women. It's ridiculous. There are two feminists heading the list. For God's sake, Moshe!"

"That's why one sentence is enough," he said.

I was the lone hand against a sentence that read that the CRM would work toward equal rights for women. Embarrassed and defeated, I left the meeting.

Ruth Resnik called the next morning. She had just heard from Shulamit that I'd been extremist and hysterical, she said. Ruth begged me to behave. "Shulamit wasn't at the meeting, Ruth," I told her.

"She knows what she's been told," Ruth said. "You acted like a hothead, Marcia. The platform's not that important."

"What is important, Ruth?"

"Winning, Marcia, winning."

◄●►

According to the Jewish calendar, the ten days between Rosh Hashanah and Yom Kippur are the Days of Awe. It is the time set to prepare to meet the Maker. Taken literally, the Days of Awe are a matter of life or death. On Yom Kippur, the names of those who shall live and those who shall die are inscribed in the Book of Life. On the morning of Yom Kippur, the neighbors stopped by to say "*Gmar chatimah tovah*," may it end with a favorable inscription.

Yom Kippur 1973 was a sunny October day. Except for the foot traffic to and from the synagogue down the street, Derech Hayam was deserted. I sat on the balcony doing *cheshbon nefesh*, moral stock-taking, thinking mostly of the year gone by, a year that had changed so much. The air was still and mild. The muffled sounds of prayer from the synagogue carried up the Sea Road. For once, there was neither the sound nor smell of traffic. The shabby synagogue occupied an abandoned British army barracks that had once guarded both forks of Derech Hayam. Today, the synagogue guarded them. No one would drive past a synagogue on Yom Kippur.

I sat alone on the balcony enjoying the silence as the first army truck roared by. It was filled with soldiers. Comically I expected it to screech to a halt as soon as it spotted the synagogue. But no, it drove right on by. I stared after it in amazement. Then I heard the rumble of more heavy traffic coming down Derech Hayam. A line of jeeps went by followed by more trucks filled with soldiers. The synagogue emptied onto the street, householders ran out to their balconies to witness the spectacle of military convoys traveling down Derech Hayam.

As I watched, Alec Bassin came in without knocking, a transistor radio held close to his ear. "The Egyptians have attacked the Bar Lev line in the Sinai. The Syrians are attempting to retake the Golan Heights," he shouted, for once not smiling. Then the sirens went off. "Down to the shelter," Alec barked, leading us to the storage room under the house. It was filled with the flotsom of six families, but now I noticed for the first time that the walls and ceiling were made of foot-thick concrete. Except for about twelve inches of air space, the structure was entirely underground. Our common storage bin had been built to double as an air-raid shelter.

We spent the day emptying and cleaning out the shelter, fitting it with chairs, camp beds, food, water, first-aid kits. Every once in a while the sirens sounded again. We stopped working and sat still until the all-clear. The eeriest thing of all was that the children, even the smallest, were utterly silent during the air raids. On orders from our radios, we crisscrossed our windows with masking tape and got our first-aid kits in order. We couldn't replenish food supplies because it was Yom Kippur and everything was closed. A blackout was imposed.

No news came over our transistor radios about the progress of the battle. Only a terse announcement, repeated for several days, that there had been a surprise attack. Since most of the army had been on leave, it would take a few days to mobilize and gain the offensive, the radio assured us. "Don't worry," Alec said, and everyone agreed. "They never say anything while the battle is going on. It was the same in '67. It will be all over in a few days."

All the next day, the transistor called up reserve units, using code names that were mostly the names of flowers, animals, trees, precious stones—the machinery of death hidden in the guise of life. That night at midnight, booted footsteps descended Derech Hayam on the run. "Freedmann. Vilyam Freedmann!" shouted the phantom runner. We opened the shutters, a light in the dark to the runner his signal to stop. Bill's reserve unit was called up. They were too new to have a code name. The truck was on its way, rounding them up. "Hurry up," the runner said. "You have about ten minutes." Bill got out of his pajamas and into the brand-new uniform which had seen three weeks of basic training and no more. The rest of the unit was made up of other overaged new immigrants, mostly Russians. More than the silence of the radio, this unit's call-up made me anxious.

By morning there wasn't a man between eighteen and fifty-five left in Haifa. The men simply disappeared from the city. Of the neighbors, only Alec was left.

On the third day, *erev Shabbat*, David Elazar, the Chief of Staff, appeared on the evening news to assure us that everything was under control and that the war would soon be over. It was true that the Syrians and Egyptians had mounted a successful surprise attack. They had recaptured part of the Golan Heights and the Sinai. But Israeli troops were now regrouped behind new lines of defense. The attack had been halted. Soon the enemy would be driven back. Daddo, Elazar's popular nickname, tried to sound reassuring. But there was something, perhaps the worry lines crossing his forehead, that undermined his credibility. Even Alec wasn't convinced.

That night, closed in behind tightly drawn shutters, I heard canon fire echoing up through the wadis of the Carmel. I blew out the candles and opened the shutters, expecting to see Syrian troups fighting their way up Derech Hayam. There were short bursts of gunfire followed by long pauses. I imagined the Syrians banging open doors and firing in at random, stopping during the silences to rape. Just as I thought it was over it would start again. I was panicky, not sure whether Jenny would be safer awake or asleep, or where I could take her for protection. My mind ransacked the small apartment for a hiding place.

"The gunfire is from the harbor," I heard Nomi say behind me. "The navy is test-firing." I hadn't heard her come in. Nomi was a member of my consciousness-raising group, the one I loved most. "I didn't want to frighten you," she said, putting her arms around me. "You look scared enough already. In wartime, so much fear is dangerous. Would you like company? Would you like me to live here until Bill gets home?" Nomi moved in, and so did Malka-Marcia, who also didn't want to be alone during the war.

One of the worst things about the home front was that there was nothing at all to do. Factories, offices, and schools were closed. There were few buses on the streets. Without men, the country's economy ground to a halt. Only the military machine functioned. Civil life was totally disrupted.

During the first days of the war, teen-age boys and older men were mobilized to provide essential services. When women volunteered, they were turned away. We were asked to knit woolen hats and bake cakes for the men at the front. This finally was an insult so brazen it provoked a response. Women, not just feminists, complained that they weren't being taken seriously in Israel's hour of need. A feminist voice could be heard in the land, in private conversations during the active weeks of the war and in organized forums during the months that followed. It was noticed that there were no women bus drivers, for instance. Why was that so? Because, it appeared, the charter of the bus cooperative, an early paradigm of socialist Zionist urban ideology, barred women.

It seemed during those long, inactive days that women didn't exist. I felt humiliated and enraged. I needed to do something to redeem my existence. One morning I packed Jenny and some home-made cakes into the back of the car and drove north to find Bill. I didn't know where he was stationed, only that it was somewhere along the border.

Lebanon under the Maronites had not entered the war, and the military capacity of the PLO forces in Southern Lebanon was limited to infrequent, rarely successful commando attacks and oc-casional rounds of Russian-*Katyusha* rockets. I hadn't felt particu-larly worried about Bill's safety, and I didn't worry about Jenny's or mine. The Northern Road, I thought, was hardly a war zone.

The road along the border was dotted with checkpoints. At each one, the soldiers on duty looked us over and asked where we were going. Women did not often drive along this road alone, even in peacetime. For that reason, perhaps, no one bothered to issue orders barring civilian travel. "I'm just taking these cakes to my husband," I said, trying to make it sound like a nice Israeli thing to do. "I also knit him a hat." I had the advantage of surprise on my side. Before they could tell me to turn back, I put the car in gear, waved good-bye, and drove on. No one tried to stop us.

Military camps lined both sides of the road. Those on the right, on the Israeli side, had a look of permanence. Those on the left were field camps set up inside the chain-link fence that marked the no man's land between Israel and Lebanon. I drove into one after another looking for Bill. Each time, the guards were surprised, shaking their heads when I asked for a unit of Russian *olim*. "You should go back," they all said, but no one stopped us from going on.

Poor Bill was astonished and probably embarrassed when I found him and delivered the cake. It was not exactly my sort of gesture, the cake at least. I was sure he understood my need for bravado to break the boredom. I cut the cake, someone made Turk-ish coffee, and we had a little party. Bill had apparently told them that I was a candidate for the Knesset, and they treated me like someone on the campaign trail. Bill finally ended it. "Come on," he said, "I'll show you what I do here."

I followed him deep into the no man's land until he stopped at a spot marked by a small tripod. He told me how he sat there alone, during the night, manning a submachine gun. It was set up in the middle of what would otherwise be grazing ground for goats. He spent the nights here, easy game for terrorists attempting to infiltrate. Somehow this outpost was supposed to deter them. "Do you know how to use the gun?" I asked. "They taught us when we got here," he said. "I think I know how to use it. I know how to take it apart and put it back together."

It was already getting dark when we left. The sun sets quickly in the Middle East. Within minutes the sky and the road were black, so dark that I couldn't even make out Jenny's shape asleep on the back seat. Only two dim beams of light lit the road in front of me. This time I welcomed the checkpoints. The soldiers were different ones. They looked at me oddly, suspiciously it seemed. What was I doing here? Where was I coming from? My identity card please. What's that in the back seat? They shined their lights around the car thoroughly, lifting up the blanket I'd thrown over Jenny, who slept through it all. When they let us go it was with a warning. "Don't stop for anything or anyone. Get home as fast as you can."

It was midnight when we got home. The phone was ringing. "Oh my God," Bill's voice screamed in agonized relief. "I thought you were all dead." Terrorists had gotten through the fence that night, he told me. "I thought...." I could see the pictures in his mind—taken hostage, raped, killed. He had been living with them for hours. "It's all right," I said, "we're home. Everything's all right." That night I dreamed that Bill's position was surrounded by terrorists. His machine gun lay in pieces around him. As he frantically tried to put it together, the enemy moved in closer, spraying bullets, not quite sure where their target was. I wanted to help but couldn't. Though I could see it all clearly, I was far away, an impotent bystander.

◄●►

At last there was a job for women. The country's small hotels were turned into rest homes for the mentally and emotionally wounded. We were asked to be "hostesses"—to serve coffee, try to talk with patients, play *sheshbesh*, backgammon. We were to raise morale, to be a reminder of normalcy. All that was required of us was our womanhood. We were not expected to have any therapeutic skills.

The lobby of the Pension Wohlman was a parody of Israeli gender. The men, suffering from shell shock, were taciturn. The women, ever smiling and cheerful, tried to draw them out of the silence into which most of them had withdrawn.

I was, at first, as speechless as the men around me, afraid to talk with anyone for fear of what I might hear and too shy to strike up conversations with perfect strangers. Finally, I gathered up my courage. "*Boker tov*," good morning, I said to a small, swarthy man sitting silently in a corner, still in the striped army-issue pajamas that made the patients at the Wohlman look like prisoners. He didn't even look at me. "How are you this morning?" No answer. "Would you like some coffee?" He shook his head. It was all I could do not to walk away from the dark shell of silence he created around him. "How about a game of *sheshbesh*," I said, not asking but reaching for the board and beginning to set it up. Still without a word, he turned his chair around and reached for the dice.

We played, silently, for hours. Still silently, a small group gathered around, some the grandsons of the New Jew and some the sons of Moroccan immigrants. Shell shock cut across class lines. I lost every game, hardly able to keep up with the speed of my opponent. Some of the men smiled with what seemed like satisfaction as I lost. Most stared at the board, refusing to look at one another or at me. Their faces were entirely expressionless except for the eyes. Dark eyes mostly, that burned deeply with fear and pain, that looked about wildly at even the slightest unexpected sound. I played the game, futilely seeking eye contact, accepting the rule of silence they established, and struggling with myself not to take it personally. They made me feel ashamed of the fear I'd experienced in the early days of the war, guilty that I was sitting there unscathed and ready to chatter about the weather with these men who couldn't talk at all. What had those eyes seen?

When I arrived the next morning, the board was set up, the

dark, silent man waiting. I brought us both some coffee, nodded wordlessly and sat down to play. The group of men gathered around. It was the same each day for a week. Then, one morning, an hour into the game, the silence broke. "You shouldn't have done that. You should have played this way," my opponent said, rearranging the pieces on the board. He spoke with a strong Yemenite accent. "What's your name?" I asked, overjoyed to hear a sound, any sound. "Yosef," he answered.

It was like a signal. From that moment, our corner became noisy, the onlookers kibbitzing, teaching me how to play. I began to win a few games now and then. Only Yosef, who had made speech possible for the others, remained silent.

One morning, Yosef was waiting for me as usual, the board open and ready to play. But instead of reaching for the dice, he reached into a pocket and brought out some pictures—his wife and children. We didn't play *sheshbesh* that morning; we sat and talked. Not about the war, never about the war. Yosef talked about his job as an automobile mechanic, his family, the life that existed before the war. As he did so, I recognized him, an Israeli man like most that I knew, slightly arrogant, a little boastful, but nervously and obviously wanting to impress me with his manhood. He told me how many girlfriends he had before he was married, that he had many sons because he never used birth control, what a good wife he had, how attentive she was to him, how well she cooked and never complained when he spent long evenings away from home with his friends.

After a few weeks, Yosef began to flirt with me. Once again, the group around the *sheshbesh* board followed his lead. The dark silence was replaced with the bravado of sexual innuendo. The men took turns beating me at *sheshbesh*, and now my occasional wins were greeted with general disapproval, the man who lost teased by the others.

One morning, an officer in crisp khakis took me aside. "You're doing wonders with my group," he said.

"Your group?" I responded.

"Yes," he said, "that whole bunch are in a therapy group together. You've really made a difference for them. Maybe it's because you play *sheshbesh* so badly," he laughed.

A month later Yosef went home, and soon they all left. Bragging, flirting, and acting cocksure, they were once again normal as far as the army was concerned. Except that Yosef and the others still jumped nervously if a car backfired or a dish dropped and broke, and their eyes, when they thought no one was watching, still looked inward with terror. We women saw our clients "recover" and knew what they carried home with them. We knew, too, that it would be waiting for us when our men came home.

When the active part of the war ended, our husbands, relatives, and friends were given leave—a few days, some a week at home. As they told their war stories, the truth about the first weeks of the war began to emerge. The Syrians had broken through on the Golan and were poised to advance on Tiberius, only forty-five minutes from Haifa. The famous Bar Lev line in the Sinai, believed by most Israelis to be impregnable, had been easily overrun. The Egyptians had poured over our initial line of defense. The homecoming soldiers, the first of those who served on the front lines, told tales of a barefoot retreat. It was a particularly humiliating circumstance for Israelis who liked to describe Arab cowardice with reference to the 1956 Sinai campaign and barefoot Egyptian soldiers running for their lives across the desert.

The unthinkable had happened. The army had not failed us, but it was taken by surprise and for several days forced to retreat. When finally the army was able to hold a line, it was unable, for weeks, to gain back lost ground. No territory was lost to the enemy during the 1973 war. But for a certain while, it seemed that the whole war might be lost. Israelis could not forgive the army for that sort of failure.

The death toll mounted daily. I knew some of the dead. Everyone did. It was a gruesome chore to pick up the newspaper each morning and read through the pages of funeral announcements, looking for and finding familiar names. Once the ceasefire was in place, there were rumblings and whisperings about incompetence. Soon the media began to call the first stages of the war the *mech-*

dal, the debacle. The finger pointed to the Minister of Defense, Moshe Dayan, the hero's hero. It is axiomatic in Israel that if the army is not invincible, it isn't strong enough. Only certainty guarantees security. A vulnerability uncovered, the collective wound oozed. We blamed our leaders. Very soon they would be forced to resign, first Dayan and then Golda. Israel's Mother and Her Glorious Son fell from Grace.

First they tried to stonewall. The consideration seems to have been electoral more than anything else. The Meir government set December 31 as the new election date and appointed a commission of inquiry to investigate the *mechdal*. A respected jurist, Moshe Agronat, was placed at the commission's head. With the *mechdal* effectively sub judicia, Labor felt it safe to go ahead with the elections.

The campaign went on almost as it had before, except that the opposition now blamed Labor for the *mechdal*. Neither side saw anything about the war that prompted them to think about peace. The CRM participated in the general silence, and the small parties of the left continued saying what they had always said: that security without peace was impossible, that peace without withdrawal from the conquered territories was impossible. Few could listen. The campaign took place as Israel mourned its dead and nursed its wounded, as the government negotiated a truce with the Egyptians and Syrians, and as the economy struggled to revive.

The polls predicted a reduced but sufficiently large victory for Labor and one seat for Shulamit Aloni. Voter response eluded the pollsters that year. Most voters, like Alec Bassin, remained steadfast for Labor. But even Alec lost the cocky certainty he'd had before the war. Once again, Israel was on the defensive and no one felt secure. It was both a political and emotional reality. Invincibility gave way to vulnerability, grandiosity to depression, arrogance to uncertainty. Politically it was a volatile situation.

People intent on survival do not easily rock their own boat. Instead they often give it a gentle but clear nudge. Some Labor support appeared to be going to the Likud. Some voters looked toward the CRM for an alternative. There had been an earlier, prewar poll that suggested I could get elected. If anything, the war had made that more likely. There was undeniable evidence not only of discrimination against, but disdain for, women; we had had our noses rubbed in it. Women might be angry enough to vote feminist.

◄●►

Midnight, New Year's Eve 1973, in Kiryat Shprintzak, a neighborhood of cheaply built high-rise apartments standing one next to the other and exactly alike. The neighborhood begins at sea level and rises along the western slope of the Carmel. There, in an enormous auditorium, the final returns from all Haifa precincts were counted.

I was there on party assignment. The room was filled with smoke. The officials were mostly men. Every few minutes another precinct reported—two men carried in a padlocked wooden ballot box that was filled with small squares of cheap white paper printed with the identifying initials of each party. Selecting the piece of paper of choice and putting it through the slot of the ballot box constituted the entire act of voting.

As the precincts checked in, a tally was kept on a huge chalkboard that dominated one wall. Returns from other cities were updated on a second chalkboard. The CRM was doing better in Haifa than anywhere else in the country, even Shulamit's own city of Tel Aviv. Almost 5 percent of the vote, enough for five seats. Elsewhere we did less well, but well enough, with almost three percent, enough for three seats. By midnight it was clear. Happy New Year, Marcia. You've just been elected to the Knesset.

"You see that?" I said to the Likud functionary sitting next to me, pointing to the CRM's count. "That's me. I've been elected."

"You?" he said. "Who are you?"

PART II:
The Knesset Years
◄●►

Chapter 4
Conspiracies of Silence

◄●►

My maiden speech was deliberately noncontroversial. Like everyone else I read the speech from a prepared text, intent on getting it over with. The chamber filled to hear the young feminist with the American accent. As I walked the long walk back to my seat, relieved and grateful to my colleagues for listening politely, I barely heard the Chair announce the next speaker, Akiva Nof, a young member of the Likud, and I didn't realize he was speaking about me until I heard my name. Nof, following the custom of the Knesset, said words of welcome for the no-longer virgin Member, ritualistically nice things. But then he went too far. "I hope that in the course of your struggle to liberate women," he said, "Israeli men can be liberated as well."

The Knesset was scandalized. "Which men do you mean?" someone shouted angrily. "We don't need any liberated men here." Those who attacked Nof were not backbenchers. One was the Minister of Transportation. Another was a wealthy industrialist who would become Minister of Commerce and Industry under Begin.

"I meant that nation of men who are dominated by women," Nof said, lamely trying to extricate himself. "What you should have wished for is that this country be liberated from women," shouted someone else who remains anonymous in the Knesset Record.

For several minutes, as the Chair futilely tried to bring the Knesset to order, there was pandemonium. Women's liberation and I had only one guarded defender, Meir Pa'il, a reserve general and leader of a leftist peace movement called Moked. He responded angrily to the antifeminist outburst. "This movement may have something important to say to us," he said. "Maybe we don't understand and cover it over with typical *sabra* cynicism. Marcia Freedman is a unique phenomenon in this Knesset."

Unique I was. My opinions, my frames of reference, my age, my accent, my size, and my sex conspired to differentiate me from everyone else. Above all, I was identified with a movement that seemed to terrify my colleagues. I would never have to worry about being co-opted.

◄●►

In the early 1940s, the attendants at Greystone, a state asylum for the mentally ill in New Jersey, went out on strike. My father, then regional director of a new union—the State, County, and Municipal Workers of the CIO—had organized them. The strike dragged on. The State of New Jersey cared as little about those who worked at Greystone as it did about those locked up inside.

The turning point in the strike, as my father told the story, was a visit to Greystone by a commissioner negotiating for the state. On the invitation of the union, he came to learn about working conditions firsthand. My father took the commissioner on a tour of the facility, bringing him finally to the rows of padded cells. "Knock on that door and open the peephole," my father suggested. As the commissioner did so, the inmate did what he did every day. "He shoved a load of shit right in the commissioner's face," my father told us, laughing until the tears came to his eyes.

I grew up on such stories, a child of the left. I cannot remember a time when I was not political. In grade school I argued with the teachers who taught us capitalism as though it were history. I was six years old when I watched my father burn an entire library of books and papers because he feared investigation by the Dies Committee, an early precursor of HUAC, the House Un-American Activities Committee. I was ten when American labor unions were purged of Communists, my father among them. I was in high school during the McCarthy era when some of my favorite teachers lost their jobs for refusing to name names. My brother and I both feared we would be denied college scholarships because our father was a "red."

I sat close to the radio in 1948, listening and cheering with my family as the United Nations voted to establish a homeland for the Jews, and I understood that this was the ultimate act of resistance. I was taught at home that the new Jewish state was socialist, democratic, and committed to equality, and social justice. I learned at home that these were Jewish values, that being Jewish placed a special burden on me. Not the burden of fear, but the burden of resistance.

I entered the Knesset, in January 1974, just three months after the Yom Kippur War, with my contradictions intact—distrust of authority and a belief that the social-democratic Jewish state embodied the values I'd been taught at home. I was soon disabused.

The war had strained the already fragile economy to the breaking point. The government had to raise money to pay for it. The budget was the first important item on the Knesset agenda. The government warned that we all had to tighten our belts. The fat budget on my desk revealed that only some of us would have to do so—those who could least afford it. The Religious Ministry, through which government funds were channeled to religious institutions, was uncut. Subsidies to state-owned corporations were uncut. Corporate and individual taxes remained the same. Instead, the subsidies on food staples were cut. The price of milk, eggs, bread, oil, and rice would rise. The budgets for education, health, and welfare were slashed. I studied the numbers on my desk, the first governmental budget I'd ever seen. And then I talked to Rivka, who cleaned my house twice a week. She and her husband supported four children.

"Rivka, how much do you and Chaim take home every month?"

"I make about 450 pounds," she said, "and he makes about 750. We get another 300 pounds from the National Insurance."

"If you have to spend 150 pounds more a month on food," I asked, "what would it mean?"

"What would it mean?" she said. "It means we'll eat less."

Rivka and I sat down together to work out her family's monthly budget. The next day I was scheduled to speak on the national budget. Instead I spoke of Rivka's budget. I wondered aloud how Labor, who sent its delegates every year to the Socialist International, carried the red flag on May Day, and sang the "Internationale" at the start of every party meeting, could place the burden of the war on Rivka and Chaim.

The budget speech aligned me with the few socialists in the Knesset, who welcomed me with their congratulations, surprised that the CRM had produced one of their own. Among the elected representatives of the state of Israel, only about 15 percent were socialists, and they saw themselves as an embattled minority. Nothing I'd been taught at home about Israel had prepared me for this.

During the first year I learned that Israel was not only not socialist, but was questionably democratic. Though nominally a parliamentary democracy, Israel's parliament is relatively powerless. Even the first day was instructive. "Where is my office?" I asked one of the administrative staff. I was directed to the third floor where I found Shulamit Aloni and Boaz Moav in a small room crowded by two desks. I learned that this was the only work space allotted the three of us. Each party is allocated one or two rooms, depending on its size. Only Ministers have offices of their own. Shulamit, Boaz, and I shared our one room with a staff of two: a Secretary, who is a legislative aide, and a secretary. Most Secretaries are men, and most secretaries are women. There were no speech writers, no researchers, and no one to handle the media. Even the large parties had no more than a staff of two. Rank-and-file Members were expected to do the work of legislating by themselves.

Israel's parliamentary system is based on the English Parliament, but in many respects it is a toothless copy. In the British system, parliamentary questions put by MPs to government ministers are used effectively as a parliamentary check on ministerial power. Often they are used to expose abuses or to challenge policy.

In the Israeli system, parliamentary questions are mostly a waste of time, as I found out with one of my first. I had been informed by someone in a position to know that the government had military advisors in South Africa. I asked the Minister of Defense if this was true. But unlike England, where the question is presented from the floor, giving the Minister no time to prepare an answer, I had to present the question in writing. According to the rules, the Minister of Defense had to answer within three weeks. In reality, it was several months before my question was answered, and only one additional spontaneous question from the floor was permitted. The Minister of Defense flatly denied the accusation implicit in my question. Though I suspected he was not telling the truth, there was no way to uncover it. The situation was too carefully controlled, and the Minister was under no obligation to tell the truth to the parliament. There was, I learned, no reason to ask a parliamentary question except for the possibility that it might get a paragraph of coverage in the press, the small headlines that only news junkies read. In this case, the Israeli press never reported on the question and the Minister's answer, although the *New York Times* did. Even so, it made no difference. Israel's relations with South Africa continued as before.

I was assigned to two Knesset committees—Education, and Health and Social Services. We met once a week, for two hours, on subjects that were sent to the committees by a vote of the plenary. Committee Chairs and Members had no power to initiate subjects on their own. It took only a few weeks before I understood that Knesset committees have no power to subpoena, neither witnesses nor documents. No testimony before them is under oath. Their recommendations, though forwarded to the appropriate government ministry, can be and often are ignored. Most important, Knesset Members' votes are controlled in committee as tightly as in the plenary. Strict party discipline is an inviolable rule.

Because of party discipline, the outcome of every debate, every vote on the Knesset floor was predictable. The consequences for not voting as instructed by one's party leaders were well known—undisciplined Members would not be renominated by their party's leaders who controlled the process of slate selection absolutely. Since the government is formed by the party with the majority of votes in the Knesset, and Members must vote as instructed, the government—a handful of party leaders—completely controlled the legislative process. As a consequence, there was no good reason to be present during Knesset debates other than to give a speech, and usually the chamber was empty except for the twenty or so Members who were scheduled to speak. We rarely listened to one another while waiting our turn. Instead, we wrote our speeches or took care of correspondence. It was a desultory chore to make up the quorum as one dull speech followed another, the legislative outcome completely predetermined.

In contrast, the Members Dining Room was always crowded and noisy. Members and staff ate and drank, especially drank, and courted the media. If I wanted to reward supporters, I invited them to lunch in the Members Dining Room. If I sought a private place for a conversation, it was in the Members Dining Room. If I tried to get journalists interested in my issues, I sought them out in the Members Dining Room. I spent three days a week at the Knesset, the days it was in session, most of the time in the Members Dining Room, where the work felt most useful.

B. Michael, a witty and liberal columnist for one of the major dailies, asked me during those early days what I thought of being in the Knesset. When I shrugged and said it didn't seem that one could accomplish much, he grinned. "It's like having a soapbox in Hyde Park," he said, "except that your soapbox is higher than most."

Knesset Members also had direct access to Ministers and their appointees and could try to intervene on behalf of individual citizens with *ta'anot*, complaints. Over the years, the constituencies that turned to me with *ta'anot* were those who were marginal, those without enough status to command the attention of more powerful Members—women seeking divorces and frustrated by the rabbinical courts, Israeli Arabs denied jobs for reasons of security that were never made specific, the families of political prisoners who claimed to be mistreated by prison authorities, non-Jews who wished to settle in Israel but were denied permanent residence for reasons unknown and potentially unknowable. Occasionally, but not ordinarily, it was possible to redress an injustice by asking a Minister to intervene personally in a particular case. These interventions did not constitute precedent; they benefited a single individual but were of no political consequence.

With neither staff, nor office, nor real power within a system of highly centralized political and economic control, most of us didn't take our legislative roles nearly as seriously as our speaking engagements or our positions within our parties.

◄●►

In the spring of 1974, three terrorists crossed the border from Lebanon and took over a building in which a hundred children and two adults were camping overnight. The terrorists demanded the release of all the Palestinian terrorists being held in Israeli jails in exchange for the hostages. Moshe Dayan, Minister of Defense, was at the scene with the troops he had sent to surround the building, poised to storm it. The cabinet, meeting in emergency session, decided to negotiate. What happened next was then, and still is, a mystery. The government's decision to negotiate was never carried out. Instead, Dayan gave the order to storm the building. The three terrorists died. So did thirty children.

A commission of inquiry was appointed to investigate what had happened at Ma'alot. The Horev Commission report held no one accountable for what occurred there. If it explained how it was that the Minister of Defense failed to carry out the orders of the Prime Minister, only the then-current members of the cabinet were privy to the information for only they saw the complete report.

The report distributed to Members of the Knesset barely a few hours before it was scheduled for debate was heavily blue-penciled. It was rumored that the Prime Minister had censored it to protect Dayan.

During the debate on Ma'alot, a sullen-looking Moshe Dayan sat alone in the back row of the Knesset. The Jewish Prince was temporarily in disgrace. Dayan's resentment was palpable. This was the second commission report in just a few months that had found the hero lacking.

Dayan took notes, only rarely looking up at the speakers who, one after another, rose to blame him for what most considered a military failure. Even as I registered for the debate, I knew I would be out of step. I spoke of excessive secrecy in government and its relation to the abuse of power, about the rule of law, and about the public's right to know. My knees trembled, my stomach ached, my head throbbed. Though he could do nothing to me, I feared Moshe Dayan, as did everyone else in the room.

With very few exceptions, Members of Knesset found my speech irrelevant. That the Minister of Defense could do as he wished regardless of an explicit government decision to the contrary, that the report the Members read was censored—this aroused no opposition. My speech about accepted western democratic process flew over the heads of my fellow Members.

◄●►

One morning, the seven o'clock news led off with the story of a drug bust at a high school in one of Jerusalem's best neighborhoods. Three students were arrested for selling small quantities of hashish. That day my colleagues made speeches about hallucinations, immediate and hopeless addiction, depravity, bad trips, psychotic episodes. They warned of the dangers of becoming "levantine," i.e., lazy, slothful, and stoned. The Members, even the most liberal among them, called the three teen-agers pushers and *narkomanim*, narcotics addicts. They demanded full prosecution and maximum penalties. They wanted to make an example of the three, who could have been their own sons.

The menace is at our very doorstep, they said. It must be destroyed. The hash of today is the heroin of tomorrow, they said. No one said anything about the heroin of today. There was an increasingly serious problem of criminal traffic in drugs and growing numbers of addicts. When the government finally released official figures, the estimate was a hundred thousand. No one spoke of it, and few knew anything about it. But for the fact that one of these addicts was the son of friends, I wouldn't have known anything about it either. There were hints, however, that Israel was becoming an important crossroads in the international drug trade, especially the arrests abroad of drug lords with Hebrew names.

I entered the debate with enormous misgivings. A young American, part of a generation in which smoking marijuana and hashish was socially accepted behavior, I was the in-house expert. I spoke to a full house and, for the first time, almost extemporaneously. I tried to calm their fears about hashish. I compared its effects to the buzz after a few glasses of cognac, a habit regularly indulged by many of the Members. The real problem, that neither we nor the police are paying attention to, is the traffic in heroin and opium and the growing number of those addicted to hard drugs, not the use of marijuana and hashish. I called for the legalization of drugs as a first step in dealing with a problem that Israeli society had yet to recognize. A weekend editorial item appeared that called me "Marcia, *hamarshah*," Marcia, the permissive one.

◄●►

Nomi Nimrod, who worked as a social worker with *na'arot b'm'tzukah*," teen-age girls in distress, came home one day shouting her frustration. Zahava, one of her clients, had been beaten by her father and thrown out of the house once again. She was only fourteen years old, and there was nowhere to send her, Nomi said, nowhere at all. "I can't take them all in to live with me!" she said. "What am I supposed to do?"

All Nomi's clients were like Zahava, young teen-age girls from poor families. They were encouraged to stay at home and help their mothers, to marry early, to maintain a virtuous reputation until then, and, like them, to bear large numbers of children. Some were the victims of incest, but that was never talked about. Some, like Zahava, rebelled. They dropped out of school and ran away from home. Often they fell into the arms of pimps who waited around the neighborhood knowing there would always be a fresh supply of youngsters to enliven their business.

Nomi and a handful of others worked with these girls, trying to keep them out of prostitution or pregnancy and in school, trying to get them to stop hating themselves. And most often they failed. From Nomi, I learned what it means to be poor and female in Israel, and I began to investigate the government's programs and policies for dealing with the problem.

I discovered that the Welfare Ministry's entire budget for these girls was only about a million pounds out of the two billion allocated to the Ministry's Youth Division. All the rest went to *no'ar b'm'tzukah*, boys in distress. I learned that there were only seven social workers in the field assigned to teen-age girls and a staff of one in the Ministry to supervise them. The Welfare Ministry's study of the target population predicted that there were as many as twenty thousand *na'arot b'm tuzkah*. But the Defense Ministry told an even worse story. Twenty-five percent of all teen-age Israeli women were annually rejected from army service for not having finished eight grades of school. Their male counterparts were taken into the army and put into remedial rehabilitation programs. Twenty-five percent of the country's prostitutes were between fourteen and eighteen.

I asked that the subject be debated in the Knesset. It was sent instead to committee for discussion, which effectively kept it behind closed doors and away from the media. Eventually, and as a result of committee recommendations, the budget for "distressed girls" was increased from one million to seven million pounds. A new facility was opened in Haifa that could handle fifteen girls at a time, a few more social workers and administrative staff were added, but Nomi still came home each day as frustrated as before.

◄●►

Abortion is an explosive issue in a country where everyone is obsessed with the Arab birthrate. The figures are updated as fast as the Bureau of Statistics can gather the data. When survival is the question, it seems, having babies is one of the answers. And since it's in most men's power and not within most women's choice, having a large family remains a masculine form of heroism and a feminine form of service to the state. The requirements of survival find a powerful echo in the Biblical commandment, *proo urvo*, be fruitful and multiply. Each pogrom, each expulsion, and finally the Holocaust itself has carved this lesson into the hearts of a nation.

Abortion is a divisive issue everywhere, but perhaps nowhere more so than in Israel. The "Woman Question" cuts through Israeli society with a finely sharpened blade. The wound bleeds for those who have died and those yet to die. With constant reminders of the Holocaust, the losses of three wars, and countless acts of terrorism, life in Israel is a continuous ceremony of mourning.

Official Israeli policy declared most abortions illegal, but unofficially the authorities sanctioned abortion for those who could afford it. The law in force in 1974 conformed with *Halacha*, Jewish religious law. It prohibited doctors from performing abortions except to save the life of the mother. In practice, the law was not enforced. Almost all Israeli gynecologists ran abortion clinics in their private offices. Of the sixty thousand abortions carried out in Israel each year, three-quarters were illegal. Legal abortions done in hospitals were, on paper, performed to save the mother's life. In fact, they took place for all sorts of other reasons. In extreme cases, poor women who could not afford the cost of a private abortion were served publicly. No one ever questioned the high number of ostensibly life-threatening pregnancies terminated in hospitals around the country, just as no one ever questioned the illegal black market in abortion.

The situation was embarrassing for the government and difficult for gynecologists. The women's movement had demanded abortion reform since 1971. Abortion was on the national agendas of most western countries during the early 1970s. The Labor government responded by appointing a commission, the Baki Commission, charged with recommending new legislation.

The commission recommendations, issued in 1974, proposed

to restrict access to abortion to those for whom pregnancy is a misfortune: rape and incest victims, mothers out-of-wedlock, menopausal women, teen-agers, the medically and mentally ill. The commission recommendations embodied an overlapping of the moderate wings of medical and religious opinion. Religious law permits abortions for *pikuach nefesh*, saving lives. Though two living beings are recognized, moderate orthodoxy recognizes the precedence of the mother. The gynecologists were interested in preserving their market. The legislation that the Baki Commission drafted respected both the wishes of the dominant religious party, as well as the gynecological establishment, by legalizing current practice without altering it.

Anticipating publication of the Baki recommendations, I introduced a bill drafted by Nitza Libai-Shapira, then professor of law at Tel Aviv University. The bill was modeled on the *Roe* v. *Wade* decision as well as the new French and Italian laws. It ended all restrictions on free choice during the first trimester of pregnancy. Our strategy was to try and get the jump on public opinion as well as to win Knesset support before the Baki Commission could set the standard for what was acceptable.

Labor adopted a strategy that was the first of many parliamentary anomalies that marked the history of the Knesset's response to women's issues. The government adopted a rarely used tactic that was surely a sign of extremity. The Labor Alignment released its Members from party discipline, allowing each a vote of conscience. Likud, equally divided, did the same. Even the National Religious Party was divided, with some of its Members unopposed to reform. It seemed for a while that the field was clear for a rare expression of majority opinion.

Formally, all Labor Members were free to vote their conscience. There was a small group, in fact, all the Labor Alignment women, who were not. Informally, but in a way that bound them all, they were asked to unite around the Baki Commission recommendations. For any one of them to have refused the request would have meant courting disfavor in the party leaders' eyes and the possible end of their political careers. Through these seven women, the

government managed to control the legislation of abortion reform
without ever having to take an official position. The women introduced and carried legislation based on the Baki recommendations. Some of them were prochoice and even publicly supported
my bill. Some were prolife, and there were varying shades between.
But they were all equally committed to one proposition: the survival of the coalition—and their own political survival—took precedence over the interests of women, whatever they believed them
to be.

I watched, at first with dismay but ultimately with a growing
sense of betrayal, as the Labor women met secretly to hammer out
an initial amorphous version of the Baki recommendations that
more or less satisfied them all as a starting position. Then they
convinced fifteen of the twenty-two Members who had agreed to
cosponsor prochoice legislation to change their minds. The women
refused to meet with Nitza and me, and they refused any offers
of compromise or cooperation. My advocacy of free choice was
part of their strategy. If they could isolate me and define choice
as too radical, they could legislate conservatively but appear to be
moderate on the one issue about which most Israeli women were
in agreement.

The abortion issue, the first piece of legislation I introduced
into the Knesset and the issue on which I gave my last speech in
1977, was my introduction to the devious ugliness of parliamentary intrigue. I was an innocent, at first outraged and then discouraged by the hypocrisy of the process and furiously at odds with
the Labor Alignment women. Their commitment to women had
always been tenuous, subordinate to their commitment to their
careers in politics. I was their sacrifice, offered up on the altar of
political fortune.

But if I was an innocent within the Knesset, I was an experienced organizer outside. By then there were a few hundred active feminists around the country and three centers of organized
support—Haifa, Tel Aviv, and Jerusalem. All mobilized behind
prochoice reform of the abortion law. There were demonstrations,
street theater, rallies, petitions, and letters of support from Jewish

feminists in the United States and Europe. I was able to keep the movement informed about the legislative timetable and I was able to draw the media. Most journalists were liberal and sympathetic to the abortion issue. The television crews assigned to cover our demonstrations took pains to make our small numbers look good. Women journalists rushed to get on the story, one of the few that might move them off the women's pages. The women's movement took the lead on an issue that had broad public support. Though the Labor women ultimately won the battle in the Knesset, their public opinion strategy backfired. By isolating me as the sole proponent of prochoice legislation, a position that was overwhelmingly popular, I became the heroine of abortion reform.

◄●►

I dressed slowly the morning of the first vote on the two abortion bills. My eye caught a red silk blouse and a floor-length denim skirt. Good, I thought, I'll dress for a party, a victory party. I brushed my long dark hair and decided to leave it loose. I dabbed patchouli oil behind my ears and drew lines of kohl around my eyes. "You've never dressed like this for work before," I accused myself in the mirror. "Use whatever weapons you have," the painted image replied. I undid another button of my blouse. I entered the Knesset that morning entirely focused on winning the vote.

It was the last session of the week, and the abortion bill was the final item on the agenda. I had to secure the fence-sitters, capture some of the indifferent, and make sure my supporters remained on the floor for the vote. Long Bedouin earrings chimed gently as I made the rounds of tables in the Members Dining Room, persuading and cajoling, charming and, where necessary, flirting. I watched the clock, counting and recounting the numbers. When the bell rang signaling the vote, I was ready. The Labor women's bill passed by forty-three to thirteen. Prochoice passed too, twenty-six to thirteen.

The debate was raucous throughout but became fevered when I ascended to the rostrum. There was hardly a sentence in my speech that didn't arouse the opponents of abortion, most particularly the ultra-Orthodox Members:

—"Sixty thousand abortions a year are performed in this country, most of them illegal."

—"Tens of millions of Arabs, who are fruitful and multiply, surround our borders."

—"Countless children are born against their mothers' wills."

—"There are no unwanted Jewish children."

—"Illegal abortions are performed routinely in private clinics."

—"They destroy fetuses, souls, spirits of Israel's children while they are still in their mother's womb."

—"It is women's right to choose."

—"I want to ask you something. Has Arafat given his consent to this law?"

—"These private abortions cost two thousand shekels each, the price of maintaining a family of four for a month."

—"The Jewish people are being annihilated."

—"Ninety million shekels a year go into the pockets of six hundred gynecologists, tax free."

—"Murderers! To lose a single soul for Israel is to lose the whole world."

—"Abortion is the right of the rich, unwanted pregnancies the fate of the poor."

—"There are no unwanted Jewish children."

—"There are government documents instructing law enforcement authorities to turn a blind eye on abortions performed by licensed gynecologists."

—"In this generation, when Hitler, may his name be blotted out, murdered a third of our people, threw a million of our children into the ovens, how is it possible to permit the murder of Jewish fetuses still inside their mothers' wombs?"

—"The freedom to plan a family is an elementary civil right."

—"We've already heard your proposals to legalize prostitution and drugs, but this is the worst yet. Why not permit bigamy as well? Women could have ten husbands, twenty husbands."

—"Unwanted children are abused, psychologically and even physically."

—"There are no unwanted Jewish children!"

◄●►

On an intensely sunny June day in 1976, the Israel Association of Obstetricians and Gynecologists held its annual convention at the Hilton Hotel in Tel Aviv. A few weeks earlier, the Association warned in published advertisements that Israel's gynecologists would refuse to cooperate with prochoice abortion legislation on the grounds that it is unsafe.

The doctors were listening to a paper on the latest advances in obstetric surgery when a small group of women carrying placards and shouting slogans entered through a side door of the Hilton that led directly into the main ballroom of the hotel. The demonstrators marched noisily across the room and onto the dais. They stood facing the audience, shouting slogans that demanded legal and free abortion. They accused the doctors of getting rich from black-market abortion. The astonished doctors, trying to drown out the slogans, began clapping their hands rhythmically, as Israelis do both when demanding an encore and when expressing displeasure with a performance. Like cheerleaders before a willing crowd, the women chanted in time to the doctors' beat. The chair called for order, but there was no order.

I could see the four security guards coming toward us out of the corner of my eye. They closed in on our signs and when they were able, tore them to shreds. The largest, six-feet tall and two-hundred pounds, grabbed the sign I held in my right hand. With the instincts of a childhood spent fighting neighborhood bullies, I reached up for his open shirt collar and held on tight. We glared at one another. He was afraid to touch me, I knew, but his fury and frustration would eventually win out over the restraint he was struggling to maintain. I watched, trying to gauge the moment, as his face turned from pink to rose to purple. The guard intensified his attempt to take the sign from me. That was the moment. I let go of both the sign and the shirt collar at once and with my free hands pushed him. Off balance, the giant fell. That must have been what caused the first of the doctors to throw a cast-iron water pitcher at my head. A picture in the next day's paper shows the doctor throwing and me blocking. A torrent of water pitchers, flower vases, and ashtrays rained down on us. We ducked some, caught some, and piled the ammunition up behind us. Disarmed finally, the doctors backed off, stopping only when they reached the far walls. They were afraid, I suppose, that we would throw the stuff back at them. It was a curious sight, eleven women holding six hundred gynecologists at bay.

Left standing in the middle of the room, taking pictures rapidly, were the photographers—one woman and several men. The security guards bore down on them, grabbing cameras and confiscating the film. The female photographer stuffed rolls of film inside her bra, signaling us with the other hand to help her. One of the guards closed in, grabbed her flashgun and hit her over the head with it. A few of us diverted the guard while others surrounded Carol Gutter, the photographer, and led her to the side door she'd opened for us earlier that day.

Later, the press described the action as "unseemly," "scandalous," "shameless," and "hysterical." "Eleven wild-haired, sloppily dressed women" caused a "wild riot." They used "unprintable" language. They violently attacked the doctors and the hotel security guards.

Israel had never seen anything like it before. Disrespect for Jewish doctors, disruption of a professional meeting, disheveled women carried off in paddy wagons with raised fists, brazen women confronting enraged gynecologists, eleven against six hundred. The Hilton Affair made the headlines, as we knew it would. The black market in abortion was exposed. The country, in living rooms and at work, talked about abortion and reproductive rights. Opinion polls showed that 75 percent were prochoice.

Spilled blood spread beneath the surface of my skin. I was black and blue, green and yellow. A symbolic sacrifice only, the stigmata disappeared in a few weeks. But their effects lingered. Our action, though successful in our terms, was deemed inexcusably rude. The country was prochoice but once again antifeminist.

"Why did you do it, Marcia?" asked Lova Eliav, a former Secretary-General of the Labor Party who had bolted and eventu-

ally became my political mentor and father figure. Lova, who had
spent months trying to clean up my act, looked exasperated. I began what promised to be a long speech on the history of feminist
civil disobedience when he interrupted impatiently. "Yes, but why
did *you* do it?" Lova clearly didn't expect a response, and indeed
there was none.

Grassroots activism and electoral politics may share the same
causes, but they obey entirely different rules. Politicians, by definition, have to be popular to survive. A politician never willingly
creates a scandal. Grassroots organizers do little else.

◄●►

Both abortion bills were voted to committee, but three months
later prochoice was defeated by a carefully engineered vote of seven
to six. The committee chair, Chaika Grossman, was a member of
Mapam, the Labor Alignment's left wing. With patience and enormous skill, she moved the committee from a majority in favor of
choice to a majority in support of the Baki Commission recommendations with the addition of a *sa'if sotziali*, a poverty clause.
Poor mothers of large families would be exempt from the general
prohibition of abortion recommended by the Baki Commission,
along with the infirm and the victimized.

Preparing for the hearings as though for a doctoral thesis, I
gathered information, kept notes scrupulously, and checked the
accuracy of my sources. I came to the abortion hearings more expert than most of the expert witnesses. But the facts were hardly
central to the committee's deliberations. Sex was on everyone's mind
throughout the months and years of committee hearings on abortion. The committee room often filled with jokes and lewd remarks,
guffaws, and snickers. Sexual matters were the focus of most of
our discussions—incest, rape, teen-age pregnancy, menopause. It
made everyone nervous. The Member who sat to my right, a dandy
of a man with long white hair and flashy clothes, leaned toward
me tittering, "Before a woman needs an abortion, there's something else she has to do first." He thought it was so funny he could
hardly stop laughing.

These meetings, always loud and excited, so dismissive of women, and punctuated with suggestive jokes—these meetings enraged me. I could hardly recognize the abrasive, loud, disruptive person I became, for once no different than those around me.

Two years later, with the Likud in power and the ultra-Orthodox parties included in the coalition, the *sa'if sotziali* was repealed. The official statistics on abortion reported in 1979 were identical to those reported in 1974, before the reform. Fifteen thousand legal abortions and at least forty-five thousand illegal ones were performed yearly. The Knesset labored mightily for four years, some Members in genuine struggle with their conscience, to change nothing. Those who could afford it planned their families. Those who could not continued to contribute more than their share to the country's demographic war with the Arabs.

◄●►

My role in politics was to place feminist issues on the agenda and try to keep them there. It was a mission that, in political terms, was doomed. Unless I turned my back on the cause that had put me in office, I was bound to fail as a politician. To succeed, I would have to fail as a feminist. It took the Hilton Affair for me to understand that although I could and should have known it on the day of my maiden speech. In fact, I could have known it much earlier.

When I first heard Rachel Kagan's stories about her time in the Knesset, I had no idea that the information would be so pertinent. Years before I was elected, Kagan taught me what it would be like to be a woman and a feminist in politics. I met her in 1972 when she was eighty-five. Kagan had been a Member of the First Knesset (1949–52), elected by an independent Women's List. The Women's List represented two prestate feminist organizations, the Union of Hebrew Women for Equal Rights in Eretz Ysrael and WIZO/Hadassah, the latter created by Henrietta Szold. Kagan was Szold's protégée and heir to the leadership of Israeli WIZO (Women's Independent Zionist Organization). Kagan, one of two women who signed Israel's Declaration of Independence in 1948, headed the

Women's List in 1949 and was the only one elected.

Kagan was a small, delicate woman who looked like an eagle. Her eyes were jet black and beady. Her nose, though small, curved like a beak. She wore her long white hair pinned back in a loose bun. She walked at least ten miles a day, she told me years later at ninety-three. I'd just followed her up the four flights of stairs to her apartment, panting and struggling to keep up. "Shame on you," she said, as I plopped down on the nearest chair, breathing hard. "I do those stairs four or five times a day and I'm almost sixty years older than you."

Kagan's reminiscences about her experience as a feminist legislator presaged my own. She'd been elected as a feminist, and though there were a few other feminists in the First Knesset, none had been elected because of their pro-woman beliefs. Kagan told me how it felt to be a woman and the only committed feminist in the Knesset. How her knees knocked and her legs trembled each time she walked from her seat to the podium. How easily intimidated she felt by the loud, angry, belittling voices of the hecklers. How the women Members always overprepared for every speech and every committee hearing, afraid to be found wanting. And finally, how hard it was to remain true to her constituency. They criticized her endlessly for every vote she cast that wasn't on a women's issue. The members of WIZO and the UER did not agree among themselves on many of the political issues of the day. By the end of her term, Kagan's party decided not to run for a second term.

Kagan also told of the dubious cooperation she got from other feminists in the Knesset, whose party loyalty always took precedence over their feminism. One of these women, a Labor Member, once took her aside to give her some advice. Kagan's lips smiled, but her eyes were angry as she spoke. " 'Stop talking about women all the time,' she told me. 'You're becoming a joke.' 'Fine,' I said. 'I'll stop if you'll start.' "

Although Rachel Kagan never did stop talking about women, she could claim only one victory for her four years in office, a victory that she herself discounted. She sponsored a bill called the

Equal Rights for Women Act that granted married women equality before the law in civil matters—the right to sign contracts, own property, and bring suit. Kagan's version included a section providing for civil marriage and divorce as well. Under the Mandate, jurisdiction over "personal affairs," marriage and divorce, had been given to the religious courts of Palestine—Jewish, Christian, and Moslem. With the declaration of the state, Kagan proposed that jurisdiction over marriage and divorce be returned to civil authorities under laws ensuring the equal rights of both spouses.

On the day of the final vote on her bill, Rachel Kagan received a handwritten note from David Ben Gurion, then Prime Minister. The note apologized for not supporting her. Maintaining religious control over marriage and divorce was one of the conditions for the support of the National Religious Party. Ben Gurion, a socialist, knew that he had sold out women for a coalition with the religious minority. Kagan's angry eyes filled with tears as she told me that she'd been forced to vote against her own bill to protest what had been omitted.

I thought of Rachel Kagan often between 1973 and 1977. She was a singular point of reference to which my self-esteem and sanity desperately clung. I thought of her one last time on the morning of the final vote on abortion and my last speech before the Knesset. I sat alone drinking coffee in the Members Dining Room, picturing Kagan, then ninety. I caught my reflection in the large window that framed a view of the Jerusalem hills. A small, delicate, quickly turning white-haired woman with a sad but belligerent expression. I, too, would vote against the legislation I had invested years in getting passed.

That afternoon, following one another to the podium in ritual procession, the women of the Knesset, feminist and nonfeminist, rose to proclaim a great victory for women. In a way it was. Our issue had dominated the Eighth Knesset. The bill about to be enacted acknowledged the existence of abortion. The silence had been broken. Nothing had changed, but this was a promising beginning for a struggle yet to be won.

Once again I stood alone, a feminist opposed to abortion reform. Once again, and for the last time, I spoke to the Knesset about women's right to choose. Four years of speeches made me confident this last time. I was at home on the podium. The faces that filled the chamber were familiar. The hecklers no longer intimidated. And I no longer had any illusions.

◄●►

Israelis acquiesce to governmental secrecy as well as censorship not only from a lack of sensitivity to democratic process, but also because of deeply rooted insecurity. For most Israelis, freedom of expression is a luxury that Israel cannot afford. There is no equivalent to First Amendment rights in the Israeli legal system, and though for the most part there is minor actual governmental interference with freedom of expression, it's occurrence is possible. At such times, there is usually little or no protest. When, for example, in 1988, the military virtually sealed off the West Bank and Gaza to the press, opposition within Israel was minimal. When alternative news services were closed down, there was no protest. Until recently, plays were banned or heavily censored because of their political content, and only a few were concerned.

In 1976, a well-known author and critic, Dan Ben Amotz, was barred from expressing his belief in selective conscientious objection on television. The whole affair took only a few days and aroused no outcry. Geula Cohen learned of his taped interview two days before it was to be broadcast. She presented an urgent motion to the agenda to censor Ben Amotz. The Knesset voted her motion to the Education Committee. The Committee met the following day. Without hesitation, the Minister of Education and Culture concurred. Both Labor and the Likud supported Cohen. Only Meir Pa'il and I opposed. It all happened very quickly, and the press gave it a paragraph on an inside page.

That same day I walked down the dark underground corridor from the Education Committee meeting room to the auditorium where a high school civics class waited to hear a Member of Knesset talk about the parliamentary process. It was my turn to deliver the lecture. I was shocked to the core by the Ben Amotz affair and brought it up with the students. I wasn't prepared for their responses.

—"Ben Amotz is subversive. It's right to censor him."

—"What if people listened to him? Maybe we wouldn't have an army at all."

—"It's a security issue."

—"You can't allow everyone to say anything they want whenever they want to say it. It's dangerous."

—"Security is more important than freedom of speech in this country. We're fighting for our survival here. This isn't America."

This last from one of the teachers.

◄●►

We are a people whose survival has been challenged so often and so regularly that we have come to believe we need to prove to the world that we deserve to exist, as individuals and as a nation. Being "just like everyone else" has become the ideal, being better than everyone else the necessity born of anti-Semitism. Insecurity, personal and national, blurs the distinction between that which we do not wish to admit because we are ashamed of it and that which we do not admit for reasons of state. In such an atmosphere, every secret is a state secret.

Whether it was the covert sale of arms to South Africa, abortion, or violence against women, the issues I talked about to the Eighth Knesset had one thing in common: each was surrounded by a conspiracy of silence. The walls of denial are especially thick around family concerns. Women's issues always seem to reveal shameful secrets about family life, secrets that the Jewish state has a vested interest in protecting. It took me two years just to bring wife-beating to the Knesset floor. Even the feminist leader of my own party opposed bringing it up. Her office had a standard reply to letters from battered women: "We do not interfere in matters between him and her." Nobody, really nobody, wanted to know anything about wife-beating.

I learned about domestic violence first from these letters and others addressed to me. These were the first and for a long time the only hard data on wife-beating in Israel and, to my knowledge, among Jews in the world.

"Arabs beat their wives, not Jews," I was told by the Chief of Haifa's police. "They say that even if they don't know what she's done wrong, she'll know," he finished, smiling at me across his desk, inviting me to share the joke. No, I was told, the police keep no statistics on complaints of domestic violence. They're lumped together with the rest of the battery complaints.

"Do you ever investigate such complaints?" I asked.

"Only when there's blood or broken bones," he said. "Then it's a matter for the police. Otherwise, we consider it to be a private family affair. We can't get involved in every argument between a husband and a wife."

The police kept no statistics, nor did the Welfare Ministry or the hospitals. Wherever I turned looking for information on wifebeating, I was told that what happened between husbands and wives was protected by the right of privacy. Besides, it didn't happen.

So complete was the conspiracy of silence that the search for information would have turned up nothing at all if it were not for the Israeli chapter of WIZO, the Women's International Zionist Organization, which operates a network of legal bureaus in which volunteer paraprofessionals practice family law. The bureaus are an important remnant of the period before the establishment of the state, when Israeli WIZO had been a militant feminist organization. In 1975, I met with Tanya Levinfish, who directed the operation of the bureaus. In her sixties, she was one of the younger feminists in WIZO. "We know all about wife-beating," she said, and for a second she looked profoundly depressed. "We tried to get a law passed fifteen years ago and didn't even get it past the first reading. I wish you luck." There was no conviction in that wish.

Tanya didn't mean to be discouraging. She was only telling her story. Fifteen years earlier, wife-beating had been on the Knesset agenda. There must have been some media coverage. Fifteen years later, not a single government agency acknowledged its existence. But they had to know. If WIZO knew, then the police, the courts, the health and welfare establishment had to know what was going on.

Armed with data from WIZO's bureaus, I asked the Knesset to put wife-beating on its agenda. After months of procrastination, it finally came to the floor. The Chair announced the subject. The chamber filled with a loud buzz and a few bursts of laughter. I heard them as I walked to the podium. I began with the standard "C'vod hayoshev rosh, Knesset nichbedah...," Honorable Speaker, honored Knesset, and got no further when the first heckler interrupted.

It was Akiva Nof, he who had first welcomed me so warmly. "Why this discrimination? Why aren't you talking about women who beat their husbands?"

"Maybe there are some husbands who deserve to be beaten." That with a laugh from Meir Pa'il.

Esther Herlitz, a feminist, complained in polite tones of my sexist attitude. Why was I not talking about "spousal" abuse.

The heckling never stopped. I spoke above it, in spite of it. As I did, I looked out over the horseshoes of power below. Which of these men beat their wives? A few years later, there was an answer. The wife, a well-respected journalist, accused him in open court. It was Akiva Nof.

I doubted that I could be heard in the Chamber, but it came out loud and clear on the evening news. I told the millions who saw it on television what I'd heard and seen. Women with broken noses, blinded, bodies covered with scars from knife wounds and cigarette burns. Pregnant women who had been punched in the stomach, pushed down stairs, beaten and tortured with household weapons, a chair leg, lamps, even hot irons.

Speaking for the government, Shlomo Hillel, then Minister of Police, expressed doubt that there were any but occasional instances of wife-beating in Israel. Though there was undoubtedly some violence in Israeli society, there was no reason to believe that there was a specific problem of family violence. And even if there were, he continued, it was not and should not be a matter for the police, no more than pushing and shoving to get on the bus is a matter for the police. Wife-beating, if it existed at all, is a private affair. Hillel asked that my motion for a full debate in the plenary be stricken from the agenda.

Normally, the Knesset does the Minister's bidding. When Hillel asked to strike the motion from the agenda, that should have been that, but it wasn't. The Chair called for the vote of those in favor of my motion for a full investigation. Slowly and defiantly, hands went up on both sides of the aisle. All the women in the Knesset voted with me and enough of the men. It was a self-declared individual vote of conscience. Not one of those who voted with me expected to be in the majority. Hands raised, we looked at one another and our numbers in surprise.

The next day, I was approached by one of the hecklers, Yoram Aridor. He is a tall man whose body parts behave like beads on a string. His head, especially, seems to wobble loosely on his neck, perhaps an illusion created by a large Adam's apple. Aridor was then only a midrank Member of the Likud. In the eighties he won dubious notoriety as the Finance Minister who nearly bankrupted the state with a preelection giveaway, reducing taxes and increasing entitlements for the poor. "The woman who cleans our house saw you on television last night," he explained. "This morning she told me she was one of the women you're talking about."

Aridor chaired the committee to which wife-beating was referred. Thanks to his housekeeper, he appointed a special subcommittee to investigate the problem. Thinking of a comparable British subcommittee and the impact it had had on public opinion, I became hopeful, a hope that didn't last beyond the subcommittee's first meeting. Why was no stenographer present? There was no one available. A tape recorder? None available. Was this legal? Yes, it was. By relegating wife-beating to a subcommittee, Aridor assured that the information revealed during the hearings would never escape the confines of the hearing room. Wittingly or not, the man so moved by his cleaning woman's confession outmaneuvered me on a parliamentary technicality, a procedure I was unaware of until it was too late. There is no record of the meetings of this committee, and no report was ever issued. All that remains is a yellowed draft of a preliminary report I submitted to the chair.

The government fell in February of 1977, three months earlier than its scheduled demise. Because four American F-15 Phantoms were delivered on a *Shabbat*, the NRP broke with Labor, and Israeli politics were never the same again. The subcommittee's work was disrupted, no doubt to everyone's relief.

Even the press conspired to keep the secret of wife-beating. Once the jokes disappeared from the headlines, not a single reporter took it upon him- or herself to investigate. One columnist outdid herself with an outraged tirade against women who abused their husbands and against me for coming to their aid. The television coverage which claimed a few minutes of the attention of the nation wasn't enough. Tanya was right after all. Wife abuse, the shameful vice of at least one hundred thousand Israeli men, remained one of Israel's best-kept secrets.

◄●►

I was known in Israel as a radical extremist not because of the positions I took, but because my subject matter was unseemly. I raised issues that were either believed not to exist or not to be issues. Like the New Jersey official who accepted my father's invitation and opened the peephole, I was smeared with that which was hidden within. I do not hear my father's laughter at this tale. For he, too, was a survivor of European anti-Semitism. He, like many Israelis and many Jews, accepted his fellowship in the conspiracy of silence and denial that surrounds Israel's shortcomings. Jews, as I had been taught, hold the moral high ground. We do not acknowledge wrongdoing because we believe it will be used against us by our enemies.

But if we cannot acknowledge our errors, we cannot correct them. It is a habit of human nature that the abuse of power unchecked does not diminish but escalates. Israel's crimes increase in seriousness and frequency from one decade to the next, while the growing minority of those like me who have peeped inside the fortress of denial are blamed for having looked in the first place and, worse, for reporting on what we've seen.

Chapter Five
The Natives
◄●►

*Among us. . . since the Six-Day War, live one-and-a-half mil-
lion people—men, women and children, whom I call "the natives."
I have no other name, and I don't wish to use other names for the
million-and-a-half Palestinian Arabs who live under Israeli rule. . . .
Why do I choose to call them this?*

*Between the Six-Day War and the Yom Kippur War, the authori-
ties refused to call these more than a million people by any meaningful
name. They did not wish to call them "Palestinian Arabs" and used
all sorts of substitutes: "the population," "the population of the territories," "the Arabs of Gaza," "the Arabs of the West Bank." It
is so much more comfortable, so much easier on our consciences,
to use these amorphous terms. . . . One could, of course, call these
Palestinian Arabs. . ."the population under Israeli military government" or "the population under occupation." These terms are much
closer to reality and perhaps a little easier to swallow. Nonetheless
I choose to call them "the natives" in this sense: the native inhabitants of a territory ruled over by others under coercion.*

Ariye (Lova) Eliav, Israel's Ladder: The Shattered Dream

When the United Nations granted observer status to the Palestinian Liberation Organization in 1975, most Israelis were confounded. In their eyes, the nations of the world were celebrating the triumph of terrorism.

At that time, many were still under the illusion that the occupation was temporary, though prolonged, and that those under occupation suffered it, if not gladly, at least patiently. These same people considered Lova Eliav's choice of terminology to be merely inflammatory.

Israelis thought this way because they were encouraged to by their leaders who, typically, referred to the Palestinian people as refugees and to the PLO as a gang of murderers. Each new act of Palestinian terrorism was seen as a senseless crime against innocent people committed by those who were filled with hatred toward Jews.

Both major parties in the Knesset, Labor and Likud, as well as the Citizens Rights Movement and all the religious parties, formed a wall-to-wall coalition that denounced the UN decision and refused to recognize the PLO as the legitimate representative of the Palestinian people. Only the Communists and Moked, the most left of the Zionist parties, opposed the majority resolution.

I was at odds with my own party. Though today the CRM is an outspoken advocate for Palestinian self-determination, the Citizens Rights Movement in the 1970s was cautious. An ad hoc coalition of civil rights advocates, environmentalists, and feminists who had come together to elect Shulamit Aloni, we were still searching for a common identity. In the meantime, Aloni was the party's only identity. Privately, she agreed with the two-state solution and the ultimate necessity of dealing with the PLO. But on the day of the vote on the UN resolution she announced that she would vote with the majority, meaning, of course, that we all would.

Carrying out the threat I'd made during the drive to Jerusalem for the swearing-in ceremony, I refused. It was the first but not the last time I voted against my party, and it was always on the Palestinian issue. Standing in the corridor that ran alongside the Knesset chamber, smoking one cigarette after another, Shulamit and I argued. Aloni was a Labor Party maverick, independent now not because of ideological differences but because of her feud with Golda Meir. Her vote was crucial to the left because she provided the legitimacy of the Labor mainstream.

"Without you," I said, "the rest of us look subversive."

"I'm not going to align myself with anti-Zionists. The press won't make fine distinctions between minority positions," she replied, stabbing her cigarette out in one of the sand-filled metal tubes that lined the corridor.

Though Moked and the Communists submitted different minority resolutions, the major vote of the day was the vote for or against the majority resolution. I raised my hand against it together with Meir Pa'il and the Communists. Shulamit and Boaz glared at me. It was a declaration of independence, the first noticeable step in a process that eventually split the Citizens Rights Movement. The next day, as Shulamit foresaw, the media reported that Moked, the Communists, and Marcia Freedman had been the only opposing votes.

I was already infamous as a militant feminist in a country where the liberation of women was seen as a threat to national security. I was an upstart immigrant who went too far too fast. By coming out, in 1975, in favor of a two-state solution, I became more notorious and more isolated, even within the feminist community.

◄●►

Official government policy called for maintenance of the status quo in the occupied territories. That policy meant that Israel would continue to hold on to the territories until a comprehensive peace settlement could be reached. By the mid-1970s, however, status quo was a serious, even misleading misnomer. The situation, particularly on the West Bank, was anything but static.

Beginning in 1967, the Israeli government secretly acquired title to more and more land in the West Bank, controlling about a third of it by 1975. During the early 1970s, in the name of security, the government sanctioned civilian Jewish settlements in the Golan Heights, the northern Sinai, and the West Bank. As the years went on, Israel became economically dependent on the Palestinians of the West Bank and Gaza who provided a large pool of cheap labor as well as a significant expansion of Israel's domestic market. The residents of the occupied territories added a million-and-a-half people to the consumers of Israeli goods and a new source of tax revenue. Slowly, the country became used to the idea that its western border was the Jordan River.

In March of 1976, the pattern that in 1987 became known as the *intifada*, the Palestinian uprising, emerged. Three Palestinians were killed on the West Bank by soldiers breaking up a demonstration. That week I spoke in the Knesset as harshly as I ever had. I spoke of reports in the foreign press that Israeli security forces tortured political prisoners in order to secure confessions. Hecklers responded that these were lies published by the enemies of Israel. I spoke of the settlers' vigilante groups and their unchecked violence against the occupied population. I spoke of the covert purchase of Palestinian land. I pointed out that the Israeli press reported so little of all of this that the average Israeli did not know what was really going on in the occupied territories. "Our most recent actions against the residents of the occupied territories," I said, "provide ammunition for those who claim that Zionism can be realized only be dispossessing the Palestinian people." When I descended from the podium and walked back to my seat, Menachem Begin whispered loudly, "*Maideleh*, you sound like an enemy of the state."

The predictable but long-in-coming revolt of the Palestinians on the West Bank and in the Gaza Strip is now a reality. The Israeli government still refuses to negotiate with the Palestinian Liberation Organization and seeks negotiations only with Palestinians who do not support the PLO, though those who do not are either collaborators working for the Israeli government or supporters of Hamas, a militant organization of Moslem fundamentalists much more dangerous to Israel in the long run. The handful of stone-throwing children have become armies of stone-throwing children. The few hundred Palestinians in Israeli jails have grown to six thousand. The hundreds of illegal settlers on the West Bank have now mushroomed to seventy thousand, legally settled in sprawling West

Bank suburbs of Tel Aviv and Jerusalem. A handful of vigilante extremists among the settlers have now become thousands, organized into permitted but unsanctioned civilian armies and armed individuals. Jerusalem, a united city in 1976 where Jews and Palestinians mingled, is now divided once again. Most Jews dare not go into Palestinian East Jerusalem, and most Palestinians will not go into Jewish West Jerusalem.

There are today, as there have always been, a few voices in the Knesset who speak out repeatedly against the growing violence in the occupied territories. In 1975, Lova Eliav, Meir Pa'il, and I openly advocated the right of the Palestinians to self-determination and the necessity of a solution to the Middle East conflict that would ultimately have to include a Palestinian state alongside Israel. We found ourselves beyond the pale of the national debate on the future of the occupied territories.

Anyone who was looking hard enough could see the writing on the wall. But few Israelis and supporters of Israel were looking. Perhaps if I had not been in the Knesset, I would have remained as oblivious as most others to what was happening on the Palestinian front. But being so close to the sources of information and power, I could not avoid the conclusions expressed in the 1976 speech. I anticipated the unchecked rise of the right, growing Palestinian resistance leading to a full-scale rebellion, the increasing brutality that would be needed to control a population in revolt, and continuing unwillingness to seek a negotiated settlement. I was not the only public figure who prophecied doom, but I was one of a few, and the only female, the only American-born, and the only feminist. Therefore, I was an extremist, my name was linked to Arafat, I was called a liar and a self-hating Jew for speaking out. The Shin Bet, the secret police, I was told by a colleague who knows such things, had a growing file on me. I was considered a security risk. Despite my protestations to the contrary, many in Israel believed I was anti-Zionist.

◄●►

Members of the National Religious Party, the most moderate

of the religious parties, are indistiguishable in their dress from other Members of Knesset except for the black *yarmulkes* they wear. There were two, however, Zvulon Hammer and Yehuda Ben-Meir—another American immigrant—whose *yarmulkes* were small, colorful knitted circles held onto their heads by a hair clip. I didn't know at first that these knitted *yarmulkes*, the *kipah srugah*, was an emblem of adherence to a group of nationalist religious fanatics who would determine the future of Israeli politics—Gush Emunim, the Bloc of the Faithful.

More than anything else the emergence of Gush Emunim irrevocably altered the status quo in the occupied territories. The ideological and moral vacuum left by the sons and daughters of the labor Zionist pioneers was filled by the sons and daughters of the religious Zionist pioneers who made up Gush Emunim's membership. They were graduates of the moderate Orthodox Bnai Akiva youth movement. The men were recognizable by the *kipa srugah*, the women by the kerchiefs they wore on unshaven though Orthodox heads. Their politics were inspired by Rabbi Avraham Yitzhak Hacohen Kook, the first Ashkenazi chief rabbi of Palestine. Rav Kook believed that Zionism was a prelude to the coming of the Messiah. His disciples believed that the conquest and settlement of Judea and Samaria, the West Bank, was a necessary step on the road to redemption.

At a peace conference of Palestinian and Jewish women held in Jerusalem in 1988, Leah Shakdiel, a religious feminist and now a supporter of the religious peace movement Oz V'Shalom, described how she became enamored of Gush Emunim during her early twenties. She was attracted by the pioneering spirit of the movement. It reminded her of the Zionism of her parents. "But the older I got, the more confused I got," she said. "The Jewish values I'd been taught at home, the values that underlie my religious belief contradict the elitism of those Zionists who deny the humanity of others, almost as if they don't exist."

In spite of its eventual acceptance in Israel, the ideology of Gush Emunim was too esoteric for immediate public consumption, and in the mid-1970s the members of Gush Emunim were few in number. Many Israelis did not take them seriously. Had their message remained merely verbal, they would have had, at most, an important minority voice within the Greater Land of Israel movement which, in turn, was an important minority voice within the national consensus.

But the Gush was not merely verbal. The passion and tenacity with which Gush Emunim began to dot the West Bank with tiny Jewish enclaves was heroic. Small numbers of young men and women, some with children, set up campsites on chosen pieces of land and gave them names—Kadum, Ofra, Givat Ephraim—sites that had been claimed by the State of Israel as military zones, or that had been purchased by the Israel Land Authority. In establishing their campsites and vowing not to leave, the illegal settlers trespassed on Israeli government property. They could have been removed and prosecuted, but the settlers threatened to resist eviction. The military, without clear orders from the politicians, refused to act.

The spectacle of young religious zealots angrily squaring off against the Jewish army sent chills through the heart of Israel. It was Cain and Abel, brother at war with brother. To a nation of survivors, nothing was more unthinkable. The government was afraid to order the settlers' removal, and so they stayed.

Once they were allowed to remain, the campsites took on the air of permanence. Housing, roads, electricity, and water had to be supplied. Though it came slowly and grudgingly from the Labor government during the 1970s, a primitive infrastructure was built. With the vanguard of settlers successfully ensconced, there was no way of stopping the others who followed. Living conditions were difficult, and the number of settlers willing to pioneer on the West Bank was limited. By 1975, there were only five thousand.

It could have been different. Polls taken in Israel during the mid-1970s showed a majority of Israelis still in favor of exchanging land for peace. Had peace been made then, the illegal settlers could have been removed without great public outcry. The occupation would have ended with the blessing of most Israelis.

Reflecting the government's intransigence, most Israelis were apathetic in the face of Gush Emunim's tenacity. The policy of the status quo was successfully internalized. Public apathy and political immobility meant that the field was clear for Gush Emunim. The tiny peace movement that actively opposed it was fragmented and severely outmatched. Gush Emunim was militant, it was Ashkenazi, and it was driven by a religious fervor that was not unlike the Zealots of old. Most important, during a period of extreme malaise in Israel, Gush Emunim offered new content to the pioneering vision of the founders. In the absence of anything standing in its way, these sons and daughters of Bnai Akiva, a small minority of religious Zionists, determined the history of their country for decades to come.

Encouraged by Gush Emunim, the Begin bloc in the Knesset called for annexation of the Golan Heights and the West Bank. Begin's rhetoric was not messianic but political. The Jews, he claimed, had an historic right to sovereignty over *Eretz Ysrael Hagdolah*, the Greater Land of Israel, which stretched from the West Bank of the Jordan River to the Mediterranean Sea. The Labor coalition had a strong faction of hawks led by Moshe Dayan, who espoused the permanent occupation of the West Bank—not for reasons of God or State, but for reasons of Security. Slowly, what had been inconceivable in 1967 became the policy that dominates Israel today, a policy that decreed Israeli dominion over the most populous of the territories conquered during the Six-Day War.

◄●►

In Israel critical events follow one another with frightening rapidity. During the same week that the first three demonstrators were killed on the West Bank, Meir Kahane, still a new and largely unknown voice in Israel, but precursor of the overt racism that would come to be acceptable public speech in the 1980s, made an attempt to pray on the Temple Mount. During that week, too, on March 31, the events that came to be known as Land Day took place. It was a day whose anniversary has since been marked by Israeli Arabs every year since.

Israel's Arabs, 18 percent of the population, most born since 1948, i.e., *sabra*, are as much Israeli as Palestinian. Throughout the 1970s, their discontent was not nationalistic. They did not demand, for instance, that the Galilee, which is overwhelmingly Palestinian, become a separate state. They did not speak out against the Israeli occupation of the West Bank or for Palestinian self-determination. Their identification with Israel was so strong that when, in 1967, the border between Israel and the West Bank ceased to exist, the two Palestinian populations found that their estrangement from one another was no longer just a matter of a closed border.

The demand of Israeli Arabs was, and for the most part still is, for equal rights and equal opportunities, the end to second-class citizenship within Israeli society. Their struggle has not been particularly successful. Until 1966, those Palestinians who did not flee or were not expelled in 1948 lived under military rule. Most of the land they farmed was confiscated and given to neighboring Jewish agricultural settlements. The 1948 war left them leaderless and traumatized. For the next twenty years, they were a docile subject population. In 1966, they were rewarded with citizenship in the state of Israel, nominally enjoying all the rights and all the obligations of Jewish Israelis but one. They do not serve in the army. By 1975, a generation of Israeli Arabs born into Israeli citizenship had come to maturity.

Israeli Arabs see themselves as loyal citizens of the state of Israel, and so they are. For whatever happens, they share the fate of the Jews in Israel. I remember Nomi's boyfriend, Ramzi, during the Yom Kippur War, saying that if the Syrians were to break through to Haifa, they would rape me but shoot him. I remember watching the news together with Aida, the first Arab feminist to join the movement. Palestinians tried to hijack a plane bound for Tel Aviv with Aida's father on board. Together we cheered the Israeli security guards on the plane who overcame the hijackers. No doubt, so did her father.

For many reasons, not the least of which was covert action by the Shin Bet, there was little independent political organizing in what is called the Arab sector. Most of the voting population supported the Labor Party. A minority voted for the Communists, a mixed Arab-Jewish party. The first all-Arab party to run in Israeli elections did so in 1988, electing a Labor Party dissident. Outside the electoral system, there has been very little political activity and hardly any protest activity.

Land Day, therefore, came as a surprise to everyone, a spontaneous expression of outrage at a policy that went too far. Land Day was the culmination of a policy of land expropriation in the Galilee, all of it owned by Israeli Arabs and earmarked for "Judaization." In fact, the expropriations were excessive, almost punitive. In some cases all the land beyond the existing perimeters of the villages affected were claimed by the state, making it impossible for the villages to expand beyond their present size. In other cases, all or almost all remaining farm land was expropriated, driving the last of the villagers into Jewish-owned factories as day laborers. On March 24, the day the expropriated land was to be fenced off, the Arabs of the Galilee sat down on the roads leading to their villages, blocking access. Aida led the protest in her village. The government responded, not with the police but with the army. It seemed like 1948 all over again, and what started as a nonviolent protest became a riot.

The media underreported the confrontation for several days. In press coverage, the army claimed it had met with violent resistance, shots had been fired into rioting crowds, and when it was all over, three Arabs were dead. Later a few journalists, only a few, traveled to the Galilee to hear the Arab side. They claimed that the army used tear gas to disperse the sit-ins and that soldiers fired into fleeing crowds. One of those killed, a woman, was shot in the back on the doorstep of her home.

The occupation, the close proximity of "the natives," the constant reminders that they, too, are "natives," had made Israeli Arabs more conscious of their Palestinian identity, more divided in their loyalty, and more resistant to discrimination. Land Day was far from a revolt, even far from an organized movement, but this writing, too, remains on the wall.

◄●►

In August 1976, the daily newspapers carried a small story. Christian Falangists in Lebanon had carried out a pogrom in the Palestinian refugee camp of Tel-al-Zataar. Hundreds of civilians were massacred. I am a survivor among survivors, raised on horror stories of the pogroms of Russia and Poland. Surely, I thought, there is no Jew in the world who doesn't hear the echo of genocide. Surely the government of Israel would condemn the Falange, even though the victims were Palestinians and the massacre was the work of our allies. Surely someone would say something.

I waited, but no one did. Finally, unable to contain my horror not only of the atrocities of Tel-al-Zataar but also at the silence of the Jews, I wrote an article that appeared in *Davar*, the Labor Party's daily newspaper. "The massacre at Tel-al-Zataar is an act that calls up the specter of genocide and crimes against humanity," I wrote. "It is regrettable that not a single official Israeli voice thought it proper to unequivocally denounce the barbaric crimes of the Christian Falangists."

In all of Israel there was only one response to the article. A right-wing columnist, Zvi Shiloach, called me "an admirer of one of the greatest murderers of all times," Yasir Arafat, and concluded that I must be taking orders from Moscow.

Arab lover is a term reserved for those Jews in Israel who concede humanity to the Palestinians and who dare to speak out for their rights and against their victimization. It is hissed visciously whenever spoken, the worst thing an Israeli Jew can say about another Jew.

By that time, my alienation was extreme. I had become an enemy of the state that I had chosen as my home and I was beginning to question the choice. I came to Israel because I was a Jew. I spoke out in Israel against its wrongs because I was a Jew and because I believed in the justice of a Jewish state. Vilified for espousing values that seemed to me preeminently Jewish shook my faith in the humanity of the Zionist enterprise and in Judaism. It was no longer clear what my commitment to Zionism entailed.

What did it mean to be a Zionist? Was I a better Jew for living in Israel? What did it mean to be asking these questions?

The Palestinian issue, as no other, set me apart from the country I loved. That the country was sexist, that it was not as egalitarian or democratic as it presented itself, were difficult though not impossible issues to integrate. Is there a country in the world that is not sexist? Every nation-state practices censorship, has a secret police. If anything, the growing list of injustices deepened my commitment to political activism within Israel.

But that a people so recently victimized by messianic nationalism and racism was becoming what it ought to despise cracked the bedrock of my belonging. That Jews separated by only a generation from the Holocaust could deny the humanity, even the existence, of another people whom it defined as enemy seemed inconceivable. I didn't understand then that the need for an enemy, the potential for brutality, the adoption of the oppressor's role are themselves part of the legacy of the Holocaust, as much a part as the lessons of resistance and empathy with the persecuted that I'd been taught at home.

◄●►

After my father's suicide in 1970, the heroic image I'd carried with me all my life shattered. What had happened to his strength, his fierce sense of self, the life force that I'd known? I understood little then, though I have learned a great deal since, about the devastating contradictions—grandiosity and self-destruction— characteristic of narcissistic personalities. But twenty years ago I could make no sense of the self-destructiveness that lurks in charismatics.

I could make no sense of the occupation either, and for remarkably similar reasons. No doubt I displaced much of the grief and shock, the anger and the bitterness I felt toward the father who abandoned me onto the state of Israel. It was, no doubt, easier to castigate the state than it was my dead father. But it would be foolish to overemphasize the personal and lose sight of the political. It is the parallel here that is important, not the projection.

Sometimes, in my moments of worst despair, it seems to me that Israel as a nation is arcanely self-destructive, intent on a second Masada. High on a mountaintop in the Negev Desert, the last survivors of the revolt against Rome drew lots for who would go first in a ritual of mass suicide that is celebrated in our history as the ultimate act of heroism. Until a few years ago, every new group of Israeli army recruits graduated boot camp with a ceremony held on Masada. Looking for the explanation of why Israel should so obstinately and obsessively refuse to give an inch to the Palestinians when doing so could lead to peace, I understood that this is a country that fears to live *without* an enemy at its doorstep.

Today, the anger, the bitterness, and the pain of rejection of those years have abated. Having returned to what in Hebrew is the *galut*, exile, I can be a Jew again, a Zionist again. I can comprehend both my father and Israel. Charismatics crave martyrdom, and so do survivors. Only time, the passage of generations, can alter the deep-seated need to be an aggressor.

Meanwhile, the distrust, the insensitivity to oppression, the willingness to colonize, and even to consider "transfer" as a viable option, continue to mark Israel as a nation dominated by the Jewish history of survival. We are still under what Robert Lifton calls the "death imprint," the legacy that marks survivors individually and collectively. *Tov lamut b'ad artzenu*, it is good to die for one's country, is taught in the schools as if it were a universal truth, a self-evident axiom of national life. Is it ever good to die, even for one's country? Necessary, perhaps, but good? It is a strange concept and one that only makes sense for a people more dominated by the solace of death than by the possibilities of life.

Having an identifiable enemy, a "gang of murderers" who wish to drive us into the sea, is a psychological necessity, not a political one. But in Israel, a nation of Jews, the personal has become political. The politics of the Middle East are incomprehensible if we do not factor for the role of the irrational—the unconscious need for an enemy. In the meantime, the deeply disturbed search for meaning, the "survivor mission," holds sway. In the meantime, Never Again, the great cry of resistance of the Jewish people, has become, Don't Give an Inch. Not an inch of territory, not an inch of leniency, not an inch of compromise. The Palestinians have become our Nazis, and we theirs.

Chapter Six
Marcia, Hamarshah
◄●►

In Hebrew there is a usage that renders *bedroom* as *chadrei chadarim*, inner chambers. Syntactically, the usage echoes *Kadesh K'dushim*, the Holy of Holies, that place of mysteries in the Temple that only the priests were allowed to enter. *Chadrei chadarim* connotes privacy, but it also rings of the holy, the mystical, the ceremonial. What one does there, it is said, is one's own business. There is a powerful silence around what goes on in *chadrei chadarim*.

"Marcia, *hamarshah*" was coined by an Israeli journalist and stuck. It means permissive or free. I didn't mind. In fact, I liked its anarchist overtones. But of course that's not what it meant for the Israelis who used it. It meant what goes on in *chadrei chadarim*.

From the very beginning, Israeli feminists were vilified with sexual epithets. At first we were castrators and man-haters. With time and because we talked about sex so much, we began to be seen as sexual Amazons. We could hardly help talking about sex. In Hebrew, the word *min* means both sex and gender, as in male and female, masculine and feminine. It also means, as it does in

English, what goes on in *chadrei chadarim.* When we spoke of our issues, we could only do so by talking about sex—sex discrimination, sex stereotyping, sexism. *Min*—a subject that most Israelis do not talk about at all (except, perhaps, in *chadrei chadarim*) was the subject of most of our conversations and public appearances. The semantics were bad enough, but grammar—because it demands masculine and feminine endings for modifiers—compounded the problem. Sex discrimination, for example, is *haflayah minit. Minit* also describes a sexy woman.

As the years went by I began to understand that this talk about sex was no mere coincidence of semantics or grammar, but that sex—how we do it, what we do, when we do it, why we do it, and with whom we're allowed to do it—is at the heart of women's oppression. And so I found myself talking less and less about gender and sex-based discrimination and more and more about sex itself.

In 1972, I spoke to an all-female audience about female orgasm, or rather, the lack of it. By that time I was used to talking about my own and others' sexuality in our consciousness-raising groups. So I felt comfortable telling this public gathering of women what most knew, but did not wish to acknowledge, that they probably weren't enjoying sex much. I said it quickly, in passing, wanting the audience to barely hear it but to remember it in the night in *chadrei chadarim.* A little spasm of fear passed through me as I noticed a woman in the front row writing it down. She sat opposite me, taking notes. I could see the paper on which she wrote. Her tight, jagged scrawl slanted erratically across the page. She and her inaccurate notes haunted my political career. Because of her, what I had hoped would be remembered only in the night became, two years later, a page-one story.

The woman in the first row was a journalist. She wrote in 1974 that the newly elected Member of Knesset, Marcia Freedman, intended to press for legislation guaranteeing women the right to orgasm. I could have sued but thought it would be the better part of wisdom to let the story die. It never did. A few months later an article about me appeared in *Bul,* a Hebrew-language porn magazine. It revealed nothing new, but my picture and name on the

front page of *Bul* was enough. Years later, I was still referred to as
the Member of Knesset who wanted to legislate orgasm reform.

◄●►

Eleven months and twelve days after the election, on the thirteenth anniversary of our wedding, Bill and I separated. We had
been the ideal couple and had created a model marriage. We were
both twenty-three when we married, two sweet, small people who
liked in one another what each had attained at high cost—self-
control and an even temper. Our relationship, except toward the
end, was never stormy. We rarely fought, and our anger, when we
allowed it to surface, was expressed only by protracted silences. Bill
was a graduate student, good-looking, witty, wrote poetry, and, in
those prefitness days, he lifted weights. I, too, was a graduate student, with a B.A. from a prestigious Eastern women's school. I was
ambitious for a career, for achievement and recognition, but also
needed, more than anything else, to be loved and to be "settled."

When I married, my own ambitions took second place to Bill's.
My degree unfinished, I moved to Chicago where he was going
to school and took up my ministry to him. I worked to support
us both, typed his dissertation in the evenings, shopped, cleaned,
cooked, and did the laundry on the weekends. But most of all I
tried to keep him happy and content. Bill, like so many of us, needed
mothering. And Bill, like most men, got it.

Everything changed in the 1970s. Feminism, my father's suicide, and my sudden leap into activism opened us up to ourselves
and to the unequal nature of the compact between us. We struggled for years to make it an honest and equal one, and by the time
the election took place, we succeeded in once again creating a seem-
ingly model relationship. Except that slowly, gradually, we stopped
being sexual. We lay in bed, night after night, side by side, not
touching.

"What's wrong?" I said finally, fearing to hear the answer.

Bill hesitated, not looking at me. "Since I've learned to respect
and admire you as a person," he said, "I can't relate to you as a
woman."

I had feared correctly. The pain of rejection, a physical pain, flowed from the tight place in my chest where it had been stored and usually locked away through my whole body. But there was anger, too. Of course a *person* cannot be sexy. *Person* is neuter.

Ours was a relatively amicable parting. We had a hard time letting go of each other and our model marriage, but we both wanted out. We separated civilly, equitably, with shared property, shared custody, and no legal formalities. I feared the publicity of a divorce. Even more, I feared what Bill could do to me if our separation became contentious.

In Israel, marriage and divorce are under the jurisdiction of the rabbinical courts, presided over by the ultra-Orthodox. The law governing divorce is Halachic, Jewish religious law, last amended in the eleventh century. Accordingly, only husbands can initiate divorce, only men can bear witness, and all the judges are fundamentalists. Though a wife can refuse to consent to divorce, it isn't too difficult to force that consent. According to Halacha, disobedient wives can be declared *moredet*, rebellious, divorced against their will and deprived of all rights, including property and custody. A woman is rebellious if she leaves her husband's home, if she has sexual relations with another man, if she refuses conjugal rights, or if she fails to provide domestic services.

I didn't believe that Bill would ever divorce me in this way, but I always knew he could. When we separated, realizing that I would be able to hide nothing, I lived and I loved openly. I was a famous feminist. Surely the rabbinical judges in their long black kaftans and *pe'ot*, sidelocks, had heard of "Marcia, *hamarshah*."

◄●►

"Do you know what they say about you?" said my kibbutznik lover. "That you've had seven men at one time."

"Well, not seven," I said, "but I have had several lovers at the same time."

"All on the same night?" he asked incredulously.

This mythic sexual reputation did not stand me in good stead politically, though personally, of course, it was a major asset. I was in my mid-thirties during most of the Knesset years, and as attractive to men as ever I'd been or would be. That, together with the intensity of political life, combined to create an insatiable sexual appetite that I hadn't known since adolescence.

Jerusalem's social life revolved around a bar called the Little Gallery, where artists, writers, and the press gathered nightly to drink, cruise, exchange information, and make connections. For the younger Members of Knesset, it was a nighttime Members Dining Room. Most of the well-known figures at the Little Gallery were men; the women were there as wives and girlfriends, with a few writers, artists, and socialites among them. I was the only female politician to frequent the Little Gallery. With title to one of the highest offices in the country, I had right of entry and instant popularity.

The intense pace and endless tension of political life heightens the need for uncomplicated intimacy and release. Since the late hours of the night are about the only private time politicians have, the only time left over for companionship and relaxation, it is inevitable that orgasm is the politician's drug of choice. The drug is in abundant supply. The sex appeal that attaches itself to men as soon as they are elected surrounded me as well, perhaps especially well. I was not so much a sex object as a sexual achievement, courted by both men and women. Obeying the laws of a market that had once seemed inaccessible, desire increased to meet the supply.

With two streaks of grey beginning to stripe my long brown hair, I was the Marcia of all my adolescent fantasies. For how many years had I put myself to sleep with a nightly serial in which the most handsome of men fell instantly in love with me. At eight, it was Roy Rogers. At fifteen, a football hero. At thirty, a handsome student. In spite of my feminist politics, I was more than willing to be a sex object. I felt beautiful and loved it.

There were many lovers—artists, writers, intellectuals—for one-night stands and brief affairs. Some, I am ashamed to say, were other women's husbands. Again, feminist consciousness gave way to desire, rationalized as free love. I was scrupulous about only one thing. Politicians and even would-be politicians were strictly off limits. Everyone else was fair game.

One of these men was a more constant companion, an affair with a journalist that lasted through the four years of my term. We met in the Knesset Dining Room. The first time I saw him, he was at the other end of the room. I couldn't take my eyes off him. What an ugly man. Why did I keep staring at him? Our eyes met in a long, charged look. I got up and went over to him, knowing that I wouldn't have to introduce myself, knowing that it would be easy, that the advantage was mine. We arranged to have a drink that evening, after the session. It was midnight before I could get away. He waited, though years later he still complained about it. We went to a cafe in Ein Kerem, once a lovely Arab village, now a bohemian Jewish suburb of Jerusalem, the home of artists and intellectuals. Sitting on cushions lining the walls of the cafe that, before 1948, had been the home of a well-to-do Palestinian, we could not keep from touching one another, but we had nowhere to go. I was still new to Jerusalem and hadn't yet found a place of my own. Avi was married. After a few months of being thrown out of cafes and checking into motels, we rented a one-room apartment in Jerusalem together. It was mine half the week, his the other.

I loved that room, filled with fragile collectibles that had no place in the busy Haifa household. A worn Persian carpet, an antique *hookah*, water pipe, the mattress on the floor covered by an old Moroccan rug, a Victorian crazy quilt on one wall, a Russian tapestry on the other. Over my desk was a stick-figure drawing done by my daughter, labeled in childish print, "Woman Plowing a Field." There was a photograph of Tallulah Bankhead looking mean and derelict, and another of my father when he was my age, at the height of his career in the labor movement.

In that room, my lover and I came together in an uncomplicated way—with one another and with others, demanding little. He was a survivor. During the war, in Hungary, at age twelve, he had returned home one day to find his parents gone, taken away in one of the roundups that terrorized the Jewish population of Europe. He never saw them again. Like many others, he lived the remaining war years in the streets, begging and stealing food, finding shelter where he could. After the war, he was taken to Israel by Youth Aliyah, the Israeli organization founded by Henrietta Szold that rounded up refugee children and raised them collectively in youth villages. Even in his late-forties, Avi had an emaciated, hungry look. He never talked about the war, except to tell me these bare bones one night. But his nervous energy, blackened teeth that gnashed as he slept, the way he ate, as though there might not be another meal after this one, and how much he drank, betrayed the fact that he still lived with the terror of sudden loss. His frenetic life was dedicated to the art of keeping anxiety at bay.

In Haifa, the men in my life were mostly students, though not mine. George, an Arab from Nazareth who played the guitar and did not talk much, was only a few years younger than I. As I got older, they got younger. The last, when I was thirty-eight, was twenty-one. What was it about these young men that was so pleasurable? They were nonthreatening, the lesser power in the relationship. They were flattering. They were admiring, fascinated, adoring. They knew their place. They were beautiful. My lovers had long brown hair, a red afro, a black mane, blond curls. Each was high on something—drugs, the edge of madness, revolution, even religion. Their adolescent grandiosity matched mine.

◄●►

Nomi moved in the day that Bill moved out. The rumors were wild and contradictory. That Nomi and I were lovers. That Bill and Nomi were lovers. That we had divorced because he had another woman. Because I had another woman. When Nomi became pregnant, Haifa gossiped. Is Marcia the father of the baby? In one newspaper, almost in passing, I was referred to as the lesbian Member of Knesset. Lesbian women and gay men, strangers, called to invite me to parties. Bill's friends began to flirt with me, my friends with him. For a while he was drawn only to feminists. His lovers were my sisters.

I wrote home to my mother about how I was living. What she read was bizarre, even worse. After a few months, she could contain herself no longer and announced she would be paying a visit. She was nervous when she arrived, but for the first few days she said nothing, carefully watching everything going on around her. Finally, her first question. "Are you and Nomi...uh...lesbians?" she asked, choking on the word. We were in the kitchen. I washed and she dried. It was one of the few places in the house we could be alone. "No, Mom, we're not, but I wish we were," I answered. I've always told the truth to my mother. No matter how much of a trial I have been, and no matter that she didn't always understand, she had eventually come round and been supportive.

That evening, Arnon came for a visit. My mother stared at the black-bearded blue-eyed young man who walked in. I introduced him to my mother, and he went to play with Jenny.

"Who's that!" my mother almost shouted. "One of Nomi's boyfriends?"

"No, Mom, he's one of mine."

"How am I going to tell my friends about any of this," she complained. "They'll think you're crazy. What kind of life is this for Jenny?" she said. "She sees too much. Wherever she goes, someone is sleeping with somebody, and not always the same body."

It was true. Jenny had knowledge of things that are still a mystery to my mother, that would have been a mystery to me five years earlier, an ability to be at home with complicated human emotions and relationships. My mother, like many in Haifa, made dire predictions about the effect of my "experiment" on my daughter. How could she possibly grow up normally in such an abnormal household?

What they feared, I hoped for. Jenny's life was full of people. She was mothered by Bill, Nomi, and Cholit, Bill's lover and later mine. Bill was a patient and loving father. Jenny adored him and he her. She lived with him half the week, the half I was in Jerusalem. Jenny went with me to meetings, lectures, sometimes to the Knesset, and almost always to demonstrations. At abortion demonstrations she wore a sign hung on her chest, I Am a Wanted Child.

"You're Moses and I'm Joshua," she told me one day. She called herself a feminist and was one at the age of nine. When her gym teacher told the children, "Do it like a man," my daughter said, "Some of us will do it like women." When I complained about how uncomfortable my bra was, Jenny said, "Stop wearing them." When I muttered to myself about cosmetics ruining my skin, she said, "Don't use them."

I wanted to believe that it was all simple, secure, and uncomplicated for her, but it wasn't easy to be Marcia Freedman's daughter. She sometimes introduced me as Marcia Freedman to her friends. "Well, that's who you are," she said. "You're famous." By definition, so was she. I imagined there were parts of it that she gloried in, her mother on television giving speeches in the Knesset, her mother on stage addressing an audience, herself often the center of attention among adults. But I also knew that people said things to Jenny about me, or allowed her to overhear them, that were never said to my face. Once, when Jenny and Nomi were eating ice cream in the Mercaz, an acquaintance of Nomi's asked, "Who does the little girl belong to?"

"She's Marcia Freedman's daughter," Nomi said.

"Oh, *that one*," the woman replied, not bothering that Jenny was there to hear.

How did it feel to be *that one's* daughter? Throughout puberty and adolescence Jenny toughed it out, defending her mother's reputation and trying to protect me from knowledge of it. I didn't know what to do about it.

◄●►

Nomi and I were never lovers. Though I was in love with her, I could barely acknowledge the thought, let alone act on it. During the last few years of my marriage, Nomi's apartment was my refuge. Just as I had run to my grandmother's as a child to escape my parents' fights, now I ran to Nomi's home to escape from the silent tension of my own. I ran there for shelter, for privacy, and to be with Nomi. But we were rarely alone. I wasn't the only one who sought refuge at Nomi's. There was usually a small crowd.

Nomi is a big and beautiful woman. She wears her thick chestnut hair long and pinned up. The weight of the hair is too much for the pins trying to restrain it. It breaks loose and spills down over her chest and back, a lush radiance. *Schmates*, my mother said of her clothes. "She wears rags and looks beautiful." Oversized T-shirts, cotton wraparounds from the Old City, worn leather sandals that flopped off her feet as she walked. It was the jewelry that changed rags to riches. Large pendants of stone or wood, antique Bedouin earrings, a row of bracelets on her arm, huge silver rings on her fingers. Nomi's smile is a blessing, the full wide mouth opening to reveal large, perfectly even white teeth, dimples creasing her cheeks, eyes shining and impossible to resist. Everyone falls in love with Nomi. She behaves as though unconscious of her beauty, of the longing around her for a smile. But I have seen her examining her face closely for flaws, creaming her lips, brushing her hair and pinning it up this way and that until it is just right, arranging the *schmates*, selecting the jewelry.

The home that Nomi and I made together remains a golden age of personal history. A time of comfort, warmth, support, informal domesticity. The crowd that always gathered around Nomi followed her to the home we shared. The women in our lives, mostly movement women, visited freely and frequently. We formalized the fact that we'd become the local women's center by holding monthly open houses. Many who came were strangers, wanting to see for themselves the growing legend of the women's community in Haifa.

We became a ritual community, too, celebrating many holidays together. We made up our own rites, naming ceremonies for baby girls, and weddings for lovers. Nomi and I devised our own Shabbat. On Friday morning, instead of shopping at the crowded supermarket, we took our straw baskets down to the lower city, Wadi Nisnas, and shopped in the Arab *shuk*. The fruits and vegetables were cheaper and fresher there, the pita bread came hot from the oven, and fishermen spread their catch on streetcorners. Nomi made *chulent*, a traditional Sabbath stew of beans and potatoes that got better the longer it simmered on a low flame. For Orthodox housewives, *chulent* was the perfect answer to the prohibition against turning gas jets on and off during the Sabbath. We cleaned the house and then laid down to rest, separately and chastely. At four we rose, dressed for dinner, pulled the phonejack out, and sat together in the living room reading the weekend papers. In the evening, with or without lovers, with or without friends visiting, Nomi and I remained at home, together, in candlelight.

At *Pesach*, Passover, forty women gathered to celebrate an alternative *seder*, the ritual meal. For the occasion, Nomi and I moved all the furniture out of the living room and covered the floor with cushions and mattresses. We placed dozens of candles all around the room. The women brought traditional Middle Eastern food—*hummus, t'china, tabouleh, koobeh,* pita bread. We reclined on the mattresses, leaned on pillows, were bathed in soft candlelight, and read together from the *Haggadah,* the Passover story, that Nomi and Esther Broner had just finished writing. Nomi led us, wearing her dead father's cantorial robes. We spoke of the few women mentioned in the Talmud—Bruriah, Ima Shalom, Rachel, the wife of Akiva, and lastly, the unnamed daughter of Rabbi Gamliel. We spoke of Miriam the prophetess, and we spoke of ourselves, the oppression of the Jews in exile flowing naturally into the oppression of women in Israel. We talked through the night and into the morning, dozing off now and then on the floor. The *seder* lasted until noon the next day.

Young men, alienated and searching for meaning, came to our home like moths to a flame. The Yom Kippur War, still referred to as "the debacle," produced a generation of agitated, searching young men. They had faced death and survived. Once again, the endless rite of Jewish sacrifice and guilt was played out through these young men. Some turned to dope, some to religion, a few escaped into insanity. Our home felt safe to them, and hopeful. "Only women have energy now," Arnon said.

Our home became a gathering place for Palestinian students as well. They were only one or two generations removed from the land and accepted Israeli nationality as a fact of life. They'd been Israelis from birth, spoke Hebrew as a native language, and valued the expanded degree of civil and personal liberty they enjoyed within Israeli society. These young men complained cautiously of discrimination in jobs and housing and inadequate funding for

education in the Arab sector. They did not refer to themselves as
Palestinians. The very word was considered subversive, and these
men, though politically aware and active, were not subversives. All
they wanted was a fair share of what the West had to offer.

I thought about this home both romantically and politically
and, of course, I assumed it was forever. We were, I believed, creating change from within. We were demonstrating what a feminist
environment could be. We were offering an alternative model of
domesticity, of family. Nomi and I often talked about the politics
of our family life. We found our inspiration in the *chalutzot*, the
women who pioneered the Jewish state.

Among the early Zionists, there was a radical minority, men
as well as women, for whom Zionism was a utopian vision. They
called not for the establishment of a state, but of a new social order in which sons no longer obeyed their fathers or wives their
husbands, equality between sisters and brothers, free love. Instead
of family, community. The children parented by all, marriage an
anachronism. Jews would relearn how to live as whole human beings by returning to the land and laboring to rebuild it. There would
be a cultural renaissance with the revival of Hebrew leading the
way. There was no need for a state to make this happen, some
thought. Others, that a state would only interfere with the process. The women understood their role as crucial to the process.
"We create the homes that will create the homeland," they said.

When Nomi became pregnant, as far as I was concerned, the
fantasy was on. For the first time, I let myself think that we would
be a permanent family. She would have a daughter. We were both
convinced of that. We would mother our children together. By the
time Nomi's water broke, my fantasy was already in ruins, though
I was unaware of it.

Her water broke in the afternoon, and Nomi ran to the store
to buy toilet paper to mop up. That was the way the rest of the
birth went, too. We cleaned closets and drawers to pass the time
between contractions. We dressed as though for a party and waited.
Hagai, Nomi's lover and the baby's father, was on his way from
the kibbutz. Nomi's mother, who lived only a few blocks away,

came to the house for the first time. "Isn't it exciting?" I burst out. She looked at me angrily. "I can think of better circumstances for a baby to be born into," she said icily. She, the cantor's wife, saw Nomi as an unwed mother, me as the cause of her corruption. I was the unfortunate circumstance of the baby's birth.

I took Nomi to the hospital and signed her in. The woman at the admitting desk was confused. "Where's the husband?" she kept asking. "Who are you?" she wanted to know. Suddenly her eyes flashed with recognition. "You're Marcia Freedman, aren't you?" she asked, as if that explained everything.

Hagai arrived finally, and we both went up to the delivery room together. Nomi was just starting active labor. I had never seen a woman give birth before and hadn't been conscious when I gave birth myself. I was awed by the effort, the power, and the pain. With each push, Nomi's face puffed out and foreshortened forehead to chin, all her energy concentrated in her pelvis, struggling to free itself of an obstruction. It went on for hours, until I, a bystander, was desperate for it to end. "Push! Push!" the midwife shouted. And suddenly it was over. A bloody mass that they called the baby's head, then a slimy bundle emerged still attached to Nomi by a long purplish weave of tissue. And then the placenta, the umbilical cord cut and knotted near the baby's stomach, the washing and presentation of the baby girl we knew it would be, now laying warm on Nomi's suddenly flabby stomach.

It was three in the morning when Hagai and I left the hospital and went home. I couldn't sleep. A real baby had been born, and so had a new mother. It was one thing to share Nomi's pregnancy and dream dreams of alternative family. But would Nomi and I have the courage, the wisdom, to mother communally? How would Hagai fit in?

We did not, and he did. What I thought was a beginning was, for Nomi, the end. Hagai came every weekend. The house filled with the baby's grandparents, Hagai's and Nomi's siblings, cousins, aunts, and uncles. Nomi didn't seem to want either Jenny or me to get close to the baby. Jenny felt rejected. Nomi had been a mother to her and now exclusively mothered another. We became two unrelated families uncomfortably sharing space.

When Nomi's mother died only weeks after the birth, and Nomi inherited her childhood home, she began to think about moving. I knew this, though the idea was never articulated until the decision had been made. Nomi and I were in the kitchen, preparing our separate meals. She put some raw vegetables on her plate. I picked at a chicken carcass left over from Shabbat. Her vegetables seemed ascetic. In comparison, the carcass looked disgusting. We can't even eat together any more, I thought. The silence grew uncomfortable.

"I have something to tell you," she said. There was only one thing it could be. Living together was too difficult. She needed her own space; she wanted to raise her child in her own home. She planned to move. And there it was, settled at last. I had nothing to say, no words to try and persuade her to change her mind. It was no longer important to say anything. The fiction shattered, and I felt suddenly freer, lighter. I love this woman passionately, but she does not love me. It would be a relief to part.

◄●►

Malka-Marcia and I were friends despite the thirteen years between us. When the troubles at home with Nomi began, Malka was there to share them. We met at the cafe because there seemed to be no privacy at home. We drank *cafe hafuch*, cafe-au-lait that for some reason was called upside-down coffee. The Mercaz was filled with shoppers and strollers. The coffee drinkers sat around small tables shaded by umbrellas. The cafe was full, and the sounds around us were, as usual, shrill. Conversations sounded like arguments, laughter exploded aggressively.

Malka spent a lot of time, as I did, in bed. She loved only one of her partners, Mustafa, a Palestinian poet, but complained that he was distant, emotionally unavailable. "I feel so close to you," she said, "and to other women, too. I never feel that way with men. They all seem to be holding something back, keeping their distance, maybe even from themselves."

"I know," I said. "I used to think it was just Bill. Now I wonder. It's different with women. The connections go so deep. I wonder why so few are lesbians. You'd think sex would be a normal part of our relationship."

The sun shone through Malka's light-brown afro. She looked at me sharply, her golden-brown eyes fixed on mine, frankly sexual. I could feel myself reddening. The heat spread from my face to my genitals. The passersby, the laughter and arguments around us didn't exist. There was no cafe, no noise. All was foreground. Malka with the sun in her hair seated on the other side of a table filled with empty coffee cups and an overflowing ashtray.

"You're very beautiful," I whispered, but couldn't go on. I looked away. The sights and sounds returned. The moment was over.

"I have to go," she said, looking at her watch. "Mustafa is waiting."

We stood to leave, facing one another, suddenly awkward. Usually we hugged and kissed lightly on the lips, exchanged a few words of affection and said good-bye. Neither of us moved. We just stood there.

"What are you doing Saturday night?" Malka asked. "Do you want to go to the movies?"

"Sure, I'll pick you up," I said, as casually as I could.

"Well, so long," she said. "See you Saturday."

The Cinemateque is next to a small park, a dark, safe haven for lovers. At intermission, Malka and I went for a walk along one of its paths. We sat in the dark under a tree. Was there a full moon, or do I just remember it that way? "I want to be your lover," Malka said.

We were both very frightened. Neither had ever touched a woman's body before, and we struggled with our inhibitions. Women's bodies were foreign country. It was my first experience lying breast to breast with another woman. I was overcome by the softness and warmth of it. No wonder men want us so badly, I thought. Who wouldn't want this? But we were unable to make love. We couldn't find passion, couldn't overcome inhibition and guilt. Malka and I fumbled through our relationship trying very hard not to hurt one another with our hesitancy and fear. Somehow, through it all, we remained friends.

And I, in my journal, wrote a repeatedly anxious entry: "Does this mean that I'm a lesbian?" The word terrified me.

◄●►

A day with Esther Broner stands in memory as a marker of the disintegration of Marcia, *hamarshah*, though there is no direct connection. It has always been so between Esther and me. Though most of the time we live on different continents, or on different sides of the same continent, our lives come together on occasion, always marked by symbolic moments. Things happen that we do not know the meaning of until later, when they become material for books. Early in our friendship, we took a walk through the deserted streets of the German Colony in Jerusalem late one night. She talked of needing to write not only a great novel but one that would be acclaimed. I spoke of feeling trapped and diminished by marriage. We walked the narrow streets and alleys bordered by old stone houses, immersed in our conversation. The first time we came to the Dead End sign, we paid little attention. The second time, we looked at one another questioningly, but neither she nor I had the answer. The third time, we knew it was telling us something.

"We're lost," said Esther.

"We need to concentrate on where we're going," I said.

Toward the end of Nomi's pregnancy, Esther came for a visit, and we decided to go off to Jerusalem together for a few days. The day that presaged the future began happily. We were both dressed in *jalabiot*, long cotton dresses from the Old City, mine maroon and gold, hers blue and silver. We packed lunch, took a bottle of wine, and set out for Jerusalem. Esther's book had been published and acclaimed. I was no longer married and was now a Member of Knesset. We had different things to talk about.

We drove down the old road toward Tel Aviv and stopped for our picnic on the beach at Caesaria. It was littered with broken pillars and shards of the Roman seaport and fortress built in Herod's time. The beach was deserted, the sky was bright blue, and the sun was hot. The calm sea rippled gently onto the shore. Esther and I talked about our work.

She: The frantic competition in New York for reviews, advances, publicity. Angry friends and family who had become material for her fiction and didn't like the experience. Teaching women and becoming involved intimately in the lives of her students. The responsibility she felt for growing numbers of protégées.

I: A dream about a crumbling old mansion inherited from my father and my anxiety in the dream that I couldn't possibly maintain it. Being "that one." The young woman doing security at the airport who, when she saw the name in my passport, told me I was her hero. Without intending to, she made me feel guilty for not serving her well enough. The loneliness of public life and the terror that my incompetence would be exposed. "Do you think you're being compelled by your father?" Esther asked gently. I shrugged, not yet ready for the question.

We left Caesaria and drove to a nearby kibbutz. I wanted Esther to meet one of the string of lovers that lined the road from Haifa to Jerusalem. Joe wasn't there when we arrived. Instead, Shlomit answered our knock. I knew Joe had a lover on the kibbutz, but it hadn't occurred to me that she might be in his room. Shaken, I tried to maintain my composure. I believed in free love, didn't I? She looked at me, at Esther, at our long dresses, at our slightly inebriated gaiety.

"Oh," I said, "you must be Shlomit. Joe's mentioned you." I introduced Esther, "Is Joe around?"

He would soon return, she said, but first she wanted to talk to me. Wouldn't I please come in. Esther tactfully went for a walk. Shlomit made coffee. She served cake. She spoke. She was divorced, she told me. Did I know what it's like to be a divorced woman on a kibbutz? Exclusion, isolation, a failed woman, a dangerous woman. She had three children and she wanted to get married to Joe. "Don't you see that you're hurting people with this freedom of yours?" she chastised. I felt shame. Promising I wouldn't see him again, Esther and I left the kibbutz, the glow already off the day.

Back on the road, I stopped for gas. "You've got an oil leak, lady," the attendant said, showing me the puddle beginning to form under the car. Reaching for my wallet, I discovered it gone. So was Esther's. Stolen from the car, probably, as we sat on the beach. We had to turn around and go back home. Our pretentious dresses mocked us now, and we sat in silence. A bird flew into the windshield, dying on impact and leaving a spatter of blood and feathers. A porcupine crossed the road in front of the car and died under the wheels. Our journey of celebration was turned into a day of loss, the beginning of loneliness.

Soon afterward, Esther left, Nomi told me she was moving out, and Malka announced she was going back to America. Malka's last night in Israel was Nomi's last night in our home. For the occasion, Malka chose to bring her lovers together, Mustafa and I. The three of us went to a nightclub in the lower city frequented by sailors, prostitutes, and pimps. It was a huge place, mostly empty. We sat isolated at our table while a noisy group of men and women drank and danced. The women looked at us from time to time with a look that said, "Get out of here. You don't belong." We were two white ladies from the Carmel, slumming. Were it not for the protection of our Arab escort, we would have been in trouble. The women knew that. Late that night we took Malka to the airport, and Mustafa and I consoled ourselves together in his bed. When I got home in the morning, Nomi was gone.

◄●►

There is a shoemaker in Haifa, a *sandlar,* who occupies a small cubbyhole under the stairs in a courtyard that once was the center of a group of houses and is now lined with stores. I brought my shoes to him. I had only one pair, and they were beginning to look scruffy. I waited, barefoot, while he worked. We sat across from one another in the tiny space.

"I bet you're an artist," he said.

"Why do you think that?" I asked, stalling, dreading having to tell him who I was. It felt so good that here was a person in Haifa who didn't know me.

"You look like an artist," said the *sandlar.* "You have a good eye for color." He held up the creamy orange sandals.

"No, I'm not an artist," I said.

"So what do you do?" he persisted.

"I'm a Member of Knesset," I said.

"A Member of Knesset? In shoes like this," he shouted at me, holding up the scruffy shoe again, no longer admiring its color. "You should be ashamed of yourself. Be a *mensch*," he said. "Buy yourself a new pair of shoes."

I walked home on my new soles and heels. Be a *mensch*. It was what my grandmother always said. Am I not a *mensch*? The houses at the top of Derech Hayam are older and larger than those below. Some of them were still private villas then. They are made of roughly cut stone, in the Middle Eastern style, or rubbed smooth as the British colonialists preferred it. Those who built the villas were rich, mostly German Jews who emigrated before the war. These houses once commanded unobstructed views of the city and the bay below. At the top of the road, many of the shops that had served their needs for imported coffee and chocolates, travel and fancy notions, were still there. They had an old, dusty look. Feathers Cleaned and Washed, it said in one storefront. In the showcase were pillows and featherbeds there since the day the store opened, in need of cleaning and washing. There was never anyone inside. No one had featherbeds anymore.

The Sea Road is lined with palm trees, the houses set back from the road and fronted with retaining walls. Flowering vines spill over the walls down to the sidewalk. I passed the synagogue, one of the largest in the city, with a separate entrance for women leading directly to a flight of stairs and a curtained balcony. I remembered climbing those stairs to say *kaddish*, the prayer for the dead, for my father, and leaving because I could not stand being curtained off as though contaminated. My grandmother wouldn't understand not saying *kaddish* for such a silly reason. Be a *mensch*, she would have said.

I passed the Pension Wohlman. Now there's a *mensch*, I thought. Even my grandmother, who used the word sparingly, would agree. Geveret Wohlman, the woman who owned the pension, inspired respect. She was in her seventies, a short, round woman who didn't often smile. She ran the pension with great dignity, though it had obviously once been her home. My mother had stayed there. Geveret Wohlman, according to my mother, thought the world of me. She is a feminist, my mother said. Visiting, we shared our dim view of Israeli society, of the ill-treatment of Palestinians, the justified anger of the mostly Oriental poor. Geveret Wohlman had never expected the state to turn out the way it did, but she had never been and would never be an activist. She rarely stepped outside the dark rooms of the pension. Would she, I wondered, still be a *mensch* in my grandmother's eyes if she left the overstuffed furniture behind and fought publicly for her causes? Does a woman have to stay indoors to be a *mensch*? *C'vod bat melech pnima*, the tradition says. The king's daughter is honored for staying indoors. No, Grandma, there is no way that Marcia, *hamarshah*, can be a *mensch*.

Chapter 7
Politics

◄●►

When Shulamit Aloni called on the women's movement for support and offered me, as a feminist leader, third place on her list, I hoped I would be at home in the new party and that Aloni would be a mentor. I joined the ticket to help her get elected. The possibility of being elected myself was remote, and neither Aloni nor I anticipated it. Even as she made the offer and I accepted it, neither of us thought it important enough to first come to a meeting of minds. Our association, we thought, would be brief; only two months remained until the election.

Shulamit Aloni is in many ways a great woman. Starting with almost nothing save the force of her own personality, she created an enduring political party that she continues to lead more than fifteen years later, a party that has become an important progressive force in Israel. I genuinely wanted to see her elected in 1973. But from the start, we disliked and distrusted one another.

The dislike and avoidance became enmity as soon as the election results were in. Although she had refused my offer to resign before the election, she wanted me to do so afterward, but it was already too late. It would have been a betrayal of the movement and of myself to turn my back on the possibility of the political power that was now mine. When I refused to resign, she shut me out of the party's decision-making process, denied me access to staff, cut me off from money, and never missed an opportunity to badmouth me even though, for half of the four-year term, we were ostensibly colleagues and allies.

Aloni had wanted me on the ticket because she needed the women's movement to provide some organizational support until she could develop her own organization. She took on the mantle of women's liberation for anyone who might approve, but she didn't want to call attention to it for those who might feel threatened. The first platform of the Citizens Rights Movement reflected her assessment that women's issues should play no part in the campaign. Her actions on women's issues made good electoral sense but did little to advance feminism politically. Aloni, I felt, betrayed me, and in doing so, she betrayed feminism as well.

My name and the women's movement were inextricably linked by the media. Marcia Freedman and Women's Liberation were synonyms for the average Israeli, who knew little about either. Whenever Aloni sullied my name, which she did often, she reinforced the negative stereotypes about the women's movement. Later, once I was out of the country and therefore out of the picture, she reembraced feminism. But throughout my Knesset years, she seemed to many in the movement more enemy than friend.

◄●►

I was elected to the Knesset on the list of the Citizens Rights Movement and left under the banner of the Women's Party. In between, I represented Ya'ad and the Independent Socialists—four parties in as many years. This was an odyssey facilitated by the peculiarities of Israel's electoral and parliamentary system. Though Members of Knesset are elected by their place on a list of candidates for a particular party, once elected, each owns her or his seat, making it possible to switch parties at will.

During the entire period of my Knesset career, there was only a brief moment of respectability. As the partner and colleague of Ariye (Lova) Eliav—who tried repeatedly to clean up my act—I was as much of a *mensch* as ever I was going to be.

Eliav rose to political power as a protégé of Levi Eshkol during the 1960s. He was twice a Deputy Minister and in 1970 was elected Secretary General of the Labor Party, its highest office.

Following the Six-Day War, Golda Meir replaced Levi Eshkol as Prime Minister. Meir, following Dayan's lead, believed that the occupation could continue indefinitely, that each year of occupation optimized Israel's chances of dictating peace on its own terms. Together, Dayan and Meir developed the policy of maintaining the status quo. Do nothing, hold the Palestinians hostage to a comprehensive settlement in the Middle East, redraw the future borders of Israel by strategic settlement of Jews in the conquered Arab lands. Lova opposed the policy, vociferously and openly. Golda wished to be rid of him.

Meir removed Eliav from his post as Secretary General of the Labor Party, stripping him of power and function. By 1975 when Eliav came into my life, he was a tragic figure of Israeli politics, his rise and fall a trajectory later repeated by the Labor Party itself. Cast out of the inner circle of leadership, he found himself, like me, on the outside looking in. We discovered one another on the margins.

In 1975, Eliav began to look for a new political home. There was a rumor that he might join Moked, Meir Pa'il's party. I knew Pa'il, whom everyone called Meirkeh, very well by then, but Eliav hardly at all. Then in his fifties, he was known as a writer, a thinker, an activist, and an idealist. His sad eyes and the deep furrows that lined his wide brow and drew long frown lines around his mouth suggested a worried man. In repose, Eliav frowned. In sorrow or anger he frowned more deeply.

My difficulties, personal and political, with Aloni and the CRM had only gotten worse. From the very beginning, the CRM feared I would bolt and join Moked. Pa'il and I consistently voted the same way, the two of us often casting pro-Zionist antigovernment votes on peace issues. The possibility that Eliav might join Moked suggested that the time was right for me to do the same. With three representatives in the Knesset united under one banner, the peace movement would have a more solid base in Israeli politics.

While I thought about these possibilities, Aloni acted. It was a mark of my alienation from Aloni and the CRM that I was unaware that she had negotiated a merger with Eliav until the deal was done. So I do not know how it happened, or even why it happened. Only that it was a disaster for them both, but a move toward salvation for me.

Eliav, I suspect, believed he was taking a first step toward unifying the peace camp, bringing Aloni—who until then avoided the left—into its fold at the outset and building from there. Aloni, probably, believed that the merger with Eliav and his followers who had left the Labor Party with him added stature to the amateurish group she'd hastily put together in 1973. Perhaps she also realized that if Eliav went with Moked, I was sure to follow.

Eliav and Aloni clashed on grounds of politics as well as temperament. Aloni was a capitalist and Eliav a socialist. Eliav was an idealist, Aloni pragmatic. Aloni believed she had much to gain by fudging her position on the Palestinian issue; Eliav had already lost as much as he was ever going to by not fudging. Aloni's style was aggressive. In the pursuit of power or headlines, she could be unscrupulous. Eliav was quietly contemplative. He valued his personal honor more than political power.

Eliav refused to join the CRM. Instead he insisted that a new party be formed. It was called Ya'ad, mission. He brought with him a small cadre of Labor Party intellectuals, mostly university people and writers, who had been his policy advisors. It was part of the deal that they were disproportionately represented in the new party's governing bodies.

While it lasted, Ya'ad revived the hopes of the peace camp, or "the left," as it is known in Israel, that its several movements and parties could be unified under a single banner to run in the 1977 elections. The peace camp was never able to attract more than 2 or 3 percent of the vote. But it was badly splintered into competing groups—Moked, the Black Panthers, a group of university professors who called themselves the Movement for Peace and Security, writers and editors of the English-language Israeli journal *New Outlook,* Eliav's followers within the Labor Party, a scattering of people from the rank and file of the CRM, and the remnants of Uri Avneri's party, Ha'olam Hazeh. As much as anything else, the fragmentation of support assured the impotence of the peace movement throughout the 1970s. That became immediately obvious in 1973, even to the competing principals. Moked ran against Ha'olam Hazeh, and only Meir Pa'il was elected. Three potential seats were reduced to one because the movement competed with itself.

During the term of the Eighth Knesset, representatives of all these groups had often met on a Tel Aviv roof, sitting on hard chairs in a small circle. I was there not to represent the CRM, but in spite of it. Over coffee and cake, the men fantasized together. Shulamit will come around, they had said. Then they could win six to eight seats in the Knesset. Mapam, the left-most faction of the Labor coalition, might join them. Some of the Labor Party doves would cross over the line. The peace movement united could have fifteen to twenty seats, be an effective block of votes, a strong counterweight to the right. With the merger between Eliav and Aloni, many of this group believed that the opening move of the grand design had been made.

Shortly after its founding, Ya'ad held a get-acquainted weekend retreat at a hotel in the Negev. Perhaps to mark my newly gained status in a party in which I no longer stood ideologically alone, I was scheduled to chair the opening session. Two hundred people, mostly men, filled the room. A few were seasoned politicians; many were well-known intellectuals and writers. A few, including most of the women, were committed amateurs like me.

I hated making formal political speeches in showcase forums in which the politicians and the hopefuls display their rhetorical abilities to one another and reveal subtle nuances of style. As chair, mine was the first speech, and I was nervous about it. In the best of cases I have no rhetorical ability in Hebrew, far too many nuances, and a barely understood feminist agenda.

That speech, meant to be a settling into a new political home and a display of recently acquired political power, revealed all too clearly that I was still a long way from home. The morning of the speech, fifteen kilos of dynamite exploded inside an abandoned refrigerator in one of the busiest sections of Jerusalem, Zion Square, not far from my lover Avi's office. Fourteen people were dead, another sixty-five injured. The PLO immediately claimed responsibility.

Coming from my room to the session I was to chair, the day's events weighed heavily. The names of the dead and injured hadn't yet been released. I worried about Avi. And I worried about the hate in the voice of a chambermaid I overheard shouting to a young Arab cleaning the floor of the hallway. "Murderers," she screamed, "you should all be killed!" But most of all I worried about the blouse I wore, the only one I'd brought with me. It was made from a *kafiyeh*, the checkered scarfs that Arabs wear as head coverings, that Yasir Arafat made his trademark. I had chosen it carelessly that morning, not meaning to make a statement now so glaringly inappropriate.

Someone else would have opened with a reference to what had happened, expressed outrage, extended condolences to the bereaved, wished speedy recovery to the injured, and gone on from there to something else. Out of step once again, I spoke of the significance of the Zion Square incident for Ya'ad. What could be more appropriate for a meeting that was to inaugurate a new era for Israel's peace movement? But how could I? Especially in that blouse.

Acts of terrorism bring Israelis together in a defensive posture. It is impolitic at such moments to talk about concessions and compromise, impossible to talk about recognizing the legitimacy of Palestinian national aspirations. Yet, as I understood Eliav, and as I myself believed, this above all was our mission. The fact of our founding on that particular day highlighted the urgency of that goal and the greatest obstacle to be overcome, the fear and distrust that informed Israel's foreign policy. The timing could not have been worse. Nor could it have been more instructive. It won't make us popular, I said, but we have an obligation to say the unpopular. These are not the acts of anti-Semitic brutes. They are the acts of a disenfranchised, displaced people seeking political self-determination. They will end only when a political solution is available. Did not our own national liberation movement have its terrorists? As horrendous as it was, the explosion in Zion Square was a political act by a political movement using tactics whose effectiveness, unfortunately, has been borne out by history. It won't make us popular, I said, but it is a statement incumbent on this gathering to make. We must urge support for a Palestinian homeland to be established beside the state of Israel. We must urge negotiation with the PLO toward this end. In these times, and for this group, votes are less important than vision.

The speech, like the *kafiyah* blouse, was unseemly, perhaps even in bad taste. And in bad Hebrew. Out of kindness, perhaps, no one said a word to me about it, but from the silence I knew that, once again, I had not resonated with those I addressed. Even here, surrounded by many who on any other day would agree with me, I was the foreigner, alien and alienated.

It was a hot August day in 1975 when the troubles in Ya'ad first began to surface. I was in the Northern Galilee with Avi, for the first vacation we'd taken together and the only vacation I'd had in years. Stretched out in a deck chair on the lawn of a kibbutz guest house, I read the newspapers, glancing only quickly at the paid political ad calling on the government to accept the two-state solution. My name appeared in the ad, along with many others, but more prominently listed. I was the only non-Communist MK who had agreed to sign on. The lead story was more worrisome. Rabin had flown unexpectedly that morning to Stockholm. No one knew why. Ford and Kissinger were in Helsinki. The talks with Egypt over an interim agreement seemed to be at the breaking point again. The Arab states were organizing to demand that Israel be expelled from the UN. Did Rabin fly to Stockholm to warn the Americans of a preventive strike?

I laid the paper aside and closed my eyes, letting the sun do its work. The white light glared through my closed eyelids. Thoughts flitted harmlessly through my mind, none staying long enough for serious consideration. I felt only the heat of the sun on my parts.

"Marcia Freedman, telephone." The public address system pierced through my sun-induced trance.

It was Boaz Moav. "You have to come to Tel Aviv this afternoon," he said, "for an emergency meeting."

"What happened? Rabin in Stockholm?"

"No," he said. "It's the talks Lova's been having with Moked and the Panthers. And the Communist petition you signed. Shulamit is furious."

It was not the first time that the Communists had asked for my support, but it was the first time I'd consented. Within the CRM I'd been censured for associating with Moked, with the peace movement, with the Panthers. They had all been beyond the pale of the liberal consensus of the CRM. Now Ya'ad, or at least Lova, was talking with Moked and the Panthers about merger, and it was time, I thought, to break down the barriers between moderate Palestinians and leftist Jews.

"We can't afford the stigma of anti-Zionism," Boaz said as the meeting began.

"A year ago you said we couldn't afford the stigma of the left," I said. "Now you're sitting among some of them. Rakach is the only party with grassroots Arab support. But Rakach is not the point. The point is whether there's only one voice in this party. Do I and each of us have freedom of association or not?" I demanded a vote and, with Lova's support, won it narrowly.

Lova Eliav's merger talks with Moked and the Panthers, the second item on Shulamit's agenda, was more difficult. She was determined to stop him; he, I knew, was determined to continue. I had only been a dress rehearsal, but the vote made it clear that Ya'ad was split evenly down the middle on the peace issue. We were only two months into our history as a party. A split this early was unthinkable, yet it seemed unavoidable.

The debate went on for hours, no one wanting to concede and no one wanting to bring closure. Except for Shulamit, everyone around the table spoke once, then twice. Shulamit remained silent. Finally, after midnight, when everyone else was talked out, all eyes turned to her. She was brief. "Never," she said, "I don't want to be a Panther. If you want to be Panthers, go ahead. But if so, I leave."

The Black Panthers were a group of militant Moroccan Jews that originated in the early 1970s in one of Israel's poorest neighborhoods, the Musrara section of Jerusalem. They were, in fact, a street gang turned political force by the intervention of a left-wing American-born sociologist, Naomi Kiess. The Panthers were dark-skinned, spoke with the uneducated accents of the Sephardic working class, and, unlike most of those they represented, opposed the Palestinian occupation. When the Panthers first took to the streets to demonstrate against conditions in Musrara, the police broke up their demonstrations with force. Most Israelis were shocked and frightened by visions of class and ethnic warfare among Jews. Golda Meir summed it up when, after a particularly violent confrontation between the Panthers and the police, she said they were not "nice boys." Shulamit's pronouncement, which singled out the Panthers as those with whom she wished not to be associated, rang uncomfortably of racism.

It was a hard drive home. The night was dark, and the Tel Aviv-Haifa road was unlit and nearly deserted. The headlights of my old VW cast a dim beam. Wanting more than anything to be home in bed, I drove fast thinking about how it would all end. Surely Ya'ad couldn't survive long. The first ultimatum had already been delivered, papered over by Lova's agreement to postpone further talks until our own party platform was completed. That would only take a few months. How would it end? What would happen to me in the process?

A split down the middle would divide the party's coffers and its weight in the Knesset in half. The legal precedents were clear. Without me, Lova would be a lone figure in the Knesset, recognized for nothing but the right to vote, a faction of one, but unrecognized as a party because he had not run independently. With me, we would constitute an independent party. Without me, Shulamit's power in the Knesset and the CRM's financing would be reduced by a third. My position in the jockeying for advantage that was soon to come was central. The time for cunning was at hand. Like everyone else, my political future could be assured or broken by the events of the next few months.

The issue on which Ya'ad ultimately split was, ironically, foreshadowed not by the dissension over Lova's merger talks, but by the issue I'd raised in signing the Rakach petition. Freedom of association, not with Rakach, but with the peace movement. The same people who had met on a Tel Aviv rooftop and called themselves the Third Force came together once again to establish the Israeli Council for Israeli-Palestinian Peace (ICIPP). Lova joined, and so did many of his followers. I joined for the same reasons I'd gone to the rooftop meetings, but also because of the new organization's name. However impotent the group might prove to be, it recognized Palestinian nationality in its title. In 1975, these were radical semantics.

For Aloni, it was the final straw. She did not wish to be associated with the peace movement. She did not wish to be associated with the left. She did not wish to be associated with anything that had the word *Palestinian* in its title. And, finally, she no longer wished to be associated with Lova Eliav. She hoped to outmaneuver me once again and keep me within the CRM, but she could not. She lost not only me, but much of her political standing in the process.

Soon after the media announcement of the ICIPP, Aloni issued a statement to the press. In the name of the Citizens Rights Movement she denounced Lova Eliav for acting unilaterally and overstepping the party's mandate. She did not denounce me. She did not even mention me. But in speaking for the CRM and in not mentioning my transgression as well, she tacitly claimed me for her own.

The next move had to be mine. Silence would mean acquiescence, and it was time to part company. The temptation I'd felt earlier to get out from under her had sharpened to determination during the past six months. For two years Aloni rode roughshod over me with an ease of which I am not proud. With Lova beside me, I found my voice.

According to Knesset precedent, Members cannot single-handedly found new parties at midterm, but if an existing party splits in half, both new parties can be recognized and assigned their share of the original party's assets. Eliav was as determined as I to break with Aloni. The relations between them had deteriorated to mutual avoidance. We needed one another. Though I knew that the split would be a crushing blow to Aloni, and that it would be difficult for her to recoup politically, I felt no guilt when I issued a statement to the press dissociating myself from this move of the CRM's. It was tantamount to an announcement of intention to split the party, and so it did.

Moments of truth being what they are, they tend to drag on. The next month was a nightmare of endless meetings, ostensibly to patch things up, but in reality they were confrontations between Aloni's supporters and Eliav's, between Eliav and Aloni, and Aloni and me.

Aloni's and my final confrontation was witnessed by two hundred people. It was as though we exchanged mirror images. For the first time, I saw her looking shaken, uncertain, and groping slowly for words. And I, for the first time in her presence, was self-assured and articulate, even in Hebrew. I entered a room filled with hostility. These were the activists of Shulamit's campaign, those who said, one moment, that they had elected me and I was responsible to them and, the next, that they certainly hadn't meant to elect me. The room was crowded. I could not find an inconspicuous place off to the side. There were no sides left. Though it was December it was hot, and the smell of sweat was strong.

One after another, Aloni's supporters spoke. The words *left* and *leftist* punctuated their speeches. I was accused of selling them out to the devil, of betraying my mandate. One retired army officer said, "What does she know about politics anyway? She's never even served in the army." There were no defenders.

It took hours for them all to finish, and then it was my turn. I accused Aloni of betraying her own positions on the Palestinian issue and of participating in an Israeli variant of McCarthyism, stigmatizing those farther to the left in order to appear moderate. There was a second part to the speech, left unspoken. I wanted to tell Shulamit Aloni and her followers the other reason for my defection, that I'd been personally oppressed by her and that, if she were me, she would have done exactly as I was doing. Had Shulamit been a friend, a mentor, a sister, I would have been hard-pressed to betray her because of a political disagreement, even one as serious as the occupation. As it was, to remain in the CRM would be political and emotional suicide.

Aloni spoke last, slowly, haltingly. There was no easy rhetoric on her tongue that night. She looked tired and depressed. She wore no make-up and made no attempt to smooth out the blonde curls that, uncombed, looked disheveled. She'd had the spoils of victory stolen from her, she said. She accused Eliav of stealing her "dowry" and me of taking part in an ugly conspiracy. Though unsettled and downhearted, Aloni was still angry. I was not sorry I didn't try to reach out to her. All that she said was true. Despite the wreckage, I was not sorry. I was sorry only that Aloni and I could not tell one another of the pain we both endured and the scars we bore.

On New Year's Eve 1975, the end of Ya'ad was formalized. Lova and I called a meeting of supporters and announced the establishment of a new party in the Knesset, the Independent Socialists.

I celebrated the New Year alone in my car on the road from Tel Aviv to Haifa. I drove up the Sea Road, stopping at Nomi's to pick up Jenny, who was already asleep. So was Nomi. The light on in the front room was for Esther Broner, bent over the dining room table writing. She and Nomi were working on a women's Passover *Haggadah*. Esther, in Israel for a limited stay, was determined to finish before she left. I took both Esther and Jenny home, and when Jenny had been put to bed, I lay down on the couch and cried.

"What's wrong?" Esther asked, sitting opposite me to offer comfort at two in the morning.

"My stomach hurts. It's been hurting for weeks."

"Poor baby," she said. "You don't have the stomach for politics."

◄●►

Lova and I were outcasts thrown together by the peculiar fates of Israeli politics. Strange as it was for both of us to find ourselves political allies—he a father of Israel and I a daughter of Eve—we had an easy personal and political rapport. During the two years of our partnership, we discovered we had much in common. We championed equally unpopular causes and both preferred writing and teaching to the nitty-gritty of politics. Following the downfall of Ya'ad, we were equally discouraged and undecided about whether to run again. We were both socialists and agreed that changing consciousness, not winning votes, was the goal of our political activism.

As an Independent Socialist I was part of a group of a dozen men and a few women who stood at the forefront of progressive causes. For the most part, they knew nothing of feminism, but they understood that their liberalism required assent. One, Naomi Keiss, who helped to found the Panthers and was one of the Jerusalem feminists, was a friend. There was never opposition to including women's issues in the party's agenda.

I was able, during those two final years of my political career, to raise the issues I wanted as I wanted to raise them. I was published in progressive publications and had a monthly column in a mass-circulation women's magazine. For the first time in my political career, I had real control of my party's resources. I was able, with the party's money, to fund feminist activities. Because of the role I'd played in Ya'ad's split and Lova's support, I was taken seriously by the press for the first time. How ironic that the one thing I'd done in politics motivated solely by my own personal advantage had made a *mensch* of me.

Only days after our announcement of the Independent Socialists, Lova and I met at a cafe in Tel Aviv to do what Aloni and I never did—discuss the terms of our partnership. I asked for and got his agreement to use half the party's monthly income to establish the Women's Aid Fund to support feminist projects. By 1977, when the term ended, the Fund had accumulated half a million pounds. Lova made a pledge to me that he never broke, even under the most intense pressure from his colleagues: my mandate, my right to run for reelection if I chose, and control of the government money to fund a campaign belonged to me to use as I wished.

◄●►

On December 21, 1976, the Rabin government fell. The official reason was that four Phantom jets delivered by the United States landed on Shabbat. The National Religious Party resigned from the government and the coalition was now a minority. New elections were scheduled for May 17, 1977, my thirty-ninth birthday. The serious business of putting together a list that would unite the left began in earnest. All around me, politicians and hopefuls scrambled to secure their places. The peace camp had three incumbents—Eliav, Pa'il, and myself. There were, we knew, no more than three seats to be won. Ordinarily, the incumbents would be the candidates. But there was nothing automatic about my candidacy and no priority for the issues I represented. The peace camp wanted to bring in the Panthers, more Arabs, and Uri Avneri's Ha'olam Hazeh. There would be fierce competition for third place on the list. If I wanted it, I'd have to work for it.

You better know what you want, my father told me many times, repeating a maxim of Trotsky's, because you may get it. Was he thinking about the end of his own career in the labor movement? In the late 1940s when the unions were mainstreaming, idealists, leftists, and mavericks like my father were no longer welcome in the leadership. My father threatened to pull his locals out of the State, County, and Municipal Workers of America to form an independent movement, but he lost the power struggle, and that was the end of his public life.

Now it was my turn for an equally fateful decision. Did I want to run for office? This time, it would be a conscious choice. I retreated to my one-room apartment in Jerusalem to think. Three days of seclusion in a room that for years had been a sanctuary. All the ghosts were there. Some of them old and familiar, but some relatively new. My father had built the table in the kitchen. The Persian rug and Victorian crazy quilt had been stored in a warehouse my father once leased. When Mary Watson Cole had died, her effects were left in lieu of rent. I am the keeper of your ghost, Mary Watson Cole, Daughter of the American Revolution. A print by Bob Broner on the wall and Esther's new book on the table. A mosaic table I made while a student at Bennington. Pictures of Jenny and her drawing of "A Woman Plowing a Field." The Bukharan tapestry that Malka-Marcia gave me when she left. A picture of a younger me giving a talk at the women's center, my hair long then, and seeming so sure of myself. And a more recent picture, hair cut short, my mouth gaping in wonder and doubt. An unsigned Cruikshank that Bill had bought in New York—Tom Paine taking the measure of George V's britches. Power measured in penises. Tom Paine had been a hero of my childhood, along with Spartacus and Emma Goldman.

I sat at my desk staring at Jenny's drawing or lay on the mattress on the floor staring at nothing, worrying my thoughts to the surface. Smoking too much and eating little. Trying to get in touch with myself. Knowing what it was I wanted didn't come easy. Politics had put me out of the habit of feeling my feelings too deeply. There was always the need to perform, to achieve, to compete, to stay in touch with the world as created by journalists and insiders. A thousand antennae spread for all that might require a response. My body was chronically tense. I lived with a crowded schedule that never eased off, swinging widely between highs and lows, elation and depression. Experiences tumbled in on me, too fast and complex, with never enough time to make sense of them. Alone in my room, I remembered and took stock of what my life had become—increasingly isolated, aloof, and self-protective. Personal needs mostly unmet. Is this what I want?

Had my father chosen wisely? The answer to his threat had been an offer to move him up to a highly paid but uninfluential post in the union. Knowing, perhaps, that it was all over, he accepted on condition that he could address the upcoming national convention during prime time. He used the time to expose the offer, denounce the union, and resign. Should he have stayed in, actualized his threat? Would he be alive today? Would there be a militant independent union of public employees?

If I should fight and win somehow, it would be an important victory for women, a personal victory for me. It meant a good income, a secure pension. How would I make a living if I left the Knesset? I'd been warned many times that no one would hire me. Reelection meant continued status and access, publicity, fame. Would I be able to readjust to living without them? Winning would be legitimation as a politician in my own right. After four years, I finally had begun to learn the ropes. I would know how to do things, how to get along. I'd be a *mensch*.

By the third day the only thing left to eat was oatmeal, called *kvacker* in Hebrew because the only brand available was Quaker Oats. The round tube, the smiling face of William Penn on the box, were familiar from childhood. I could never look at that box and talk about *kvacker* without being reminded that somewhere else used to be home and that there were ways that I would always be a stranger in Israel. Reelection would mean spending another four years of my life mostly in the company of politicians, men whose bombastics are in inverse proportion to their power. Theirs was a false version of reality, to my eyes a perversion. I was sick of the deception.

If I were to run for reelection, it would be voluntary this time, with intention. If I lost, it would be an upset. I would be upset. I ate oatmeal and wondered. Perhaps, Marcia, you're just scared?

I remembered all the things that used to inspire me. Love, pleasure, sensuality. Freedom, justice, *tikkun olam*, repairing the world. During this past year I had begun to lose them. I no longer belonged to myself. There was no time for love and intimate connection. I wasn't changing the world; I wasn't living in my body. My facial muscles ached with the effort of smiling. I hardly ever cried anymore, and I suspected everyone of being out to get me. I was becoming like the rest of them, the politicians, and surely it would only get worse. But, perhaps, Marcia, you are just scared?

Pacing now, round and round the small room plus kitchen. Suppose you do want a second term? How do you get it? What do you need? A support group first of all, women I would bring into politics for the express purpose of supporting me, women I could trust. Making our demands together and preparing to run independently if they weren't met. The mandate, Lova promised, is mine. He would, I knew, keep his promise, but if he didn't, I could split the Independent Socialists and it would still be mine. There were women in Haifa, Tel Aviv, and Jerusalem who could be called upon. I had always known that, although I had never asked them for political support before. I had always tried to keep the movement separate from politics, and it had been a mistake.

The oatmeal was badly cooked, slimy and hard. I thought about food. The body's need for food. The skin's need for touch. The brain's need for rest. The imagination's need for play. The spirit's need for solitude. Must I really try for a second term though I did not like the work, did not even believe in it? Slowly the idea made its way through my questioning. Someone else, one of this group of women who could be called upon, could be the candidate. It doesn't have to be me. Same organization, same strategy, same demands, but a different candidate. I could be liberated from this burden if I chose. And realizing that, I knew I didn't want another term in office.

◄●►

There was little sense in early 1977 that the Likud might really win the election, though everyone expected they would remain a very significant opposition potentially posing a challenge to Labor. The Likud came into being in 1973, an alignment of centrist and rightist opposition groups. In 1973, Labor lost votes to the left and to the right. A two-party system was in process of coming into being. In 1977, Alec Bassin believed that the Likud was a serious threat, but he, too, did not expect them to win. No one expected the Likud to win. Even when Ygal Yadin, a world-famous archeologist and former Chief of Staff, one of the few who had never pursued a political career, announced the formation of a new centrist party, the Democratic Movement for Change, the threat posed to Labor was not fully appreciated. Labor was too entrenched. A government in Israel without Labor at its helm was inconceivable. The ascendency of Menachem Begin and Israel's right wing could not yet be imagined.

Against this background, the splintered left tried to form an alignment of its own. Everyone agreed that two seats were secure and a third possible, but only if there was a united front. The grass-roots demanded it. The peace parties would lose support if they ran against one another once again.

Lova's supporters, the Independent Socialists, took the initiative. Lova himself refused to run, though he changed his mind toward the end. He turned his mandate over to his followers, to negotiate in his name, even if he were not the candidate. But, he told them for the first time and to their complete consternation, he could not speak for me. They would have to negotiate with me separately.

A delegation of ten men asked to meet with me. They arrived late, stalled in traffic, and angry that I'd insisted they come all the way from Tel Aviv. Their spokesman took the offensive. "We haven't come to bargain with you. We know you have veto power, so either you agree or you don't." Agree to what? To let him become the decision-maker for the Independent Socialists. To let him decide my fate. Why, I wondered, did they bother to come? Did anyone really expect me to give up so quickly and so easily? They made speeches, one after the other, saying nothing and offering nothing. I waited silently. Finally, hours later, they conceded.

"We'll give third place on the list to a woman."

"To a woman and a feminist," I added.

They hesitated, looked at one another, finally nodded their heads and agreed.

"I'll think about it," I said.

I called Judy Hill in Haifa and Shoshana Eilings in Jerusalem. Within a few days, the women's caucus was formed. Two weeks later we were ready with our demands. We asked for a meeting with the Independent Socialists. As we walked up the stairs to the party offices, the fuses blew. We entered to find five or six men and one woman, Naomi Keiss, sitting in the dark. Unable to find the fuse box, we held the meeting by candlelight. Not the usual political ambience. The women's shadows loomed large on the walls as we filled the small room. There were fifteen of us. Only Naomi knew some of the women. The men had never seen any of them before, knew only that these were feminist militants, like myself. For the first time, they found themselves in a political meeting where the majority were women. The darkness, the candlelight, the women unnerved them.

"I've decided not to run," I began. The sigh of relief was audible. "But my mandate belongs to these women. I will negotiate for them, but I won't be their candidate. We'll operate as a caucus in the new peace party, but only if the budget we bring to the party is used to promote feminist issues, and only if a candidate of our choosing has third place on the list. We are prepared to run independently if we don't reach agreement."

"My hat's off to you, Marcia," said one of the leaders. "You've won round two."

Though the Independent Socialists were willing to accept our demands—they had no choice—the rest of the peace camp was not. Until then, these men had only to deal with a handful of women in politics, divided among themselves and safely competing with one another. Now there were many women, in solidarity with one another and speaking with one voice. It was obvious that we frightened them. "You think that we all beat our wives," Charlie Biton, a Black Panther, exploded one evening. We hadn't been talking about wife abuse. We hadn't even been talking about women.

"I bet he does," I said to Shoshana as we left the meeting.

"So I've heard," she said, "but what he really means is that we're beating him."

Negotiations with the peace camp went on for months, but from the start it was clear that they were only stalling, hoping to keep us hanging and drop us at the last minute. They could hardly agree on how a united front would be formed and who among the many political hopefuls would represent them in the Knesset. Though the Panthers, Avneri's group, Moked, and the Independent Socialists more or less trusted one another, the newly constituted women's caucus was a total unknown. Whoever supported whom for what, no one supported the choice of a feminist for third place on the list. The left was willing to pay the price, a third of their campaign budget, to rid themselves of this disturbance of their peace.

I made the rounds of the women's movement, holding meetings in Haifa, Tel Aviv, and Jerusalem, to see what they thought about running an independent feminist party in the election and to state clearly that I would not be the candidate. Haifa was unanimously in favor. Jerusalem and Tel Aviv were split, the majority opposed. In Jerusalem, the women of the left saw a new party, even or especially a women's party, as a threat to the men they were in the habit of supporting politically, in some cases the men to whom they were married. In Tel Aviv, the women were thrown into confusion by my offer. Many refused to believe that it wasn't all a ruse to get myself reelected, that I wasn't trying to win them over from Shulamit Aloni.

In the final analysis, there were enough women in Tel Aviv and Jerusalem who favored an independent women's party. On January 29, 1977, thirty-five women responded to a call to discuss a feminist run for the Knesset. The room was crowded and buzzed with excitement. After several hours of discussion, not about whether, but rather about how to proceed, the vote to run an independent women's party in the elections for the Ninth Knesset was unanimous. It would be called, simply, *Mifleget Hanashim*, the Women's Party.

◄●►

With the formation of the Women's Party, I felt safe in politics for the first time. Women in groups connect and bond. We keep in touch with one another's personal lives. We do not make unnecessary speeches to impress one another. We express our feelings. And in the beginning, at least, we did not compete for power.

Following what had become traditional feminist patterns, we organized collectively. We established committees with specific responsibilities, but no chairs, no fixed membership. All meetings were open to anyone who wished to attend; decisions were made by consensus. We paid some salaries on a sliding scale, beginning with zero for most of us and supplementing as needed the income of others. In these ways, we avoided, we thought, the sticky issues of power with which we could not deal. The women's movement believed in empowerment, but within our organizations no one was supposed to have more power than another.

Most of us did not believe in the possibility of winning. Our goal was to use the election campaign—newspaper ads, TV and radio spots, house meetings, and rallies—to expose, as widely as possible, hard data on the status of women in Israel. We wanted to define the issues and to suggest ways they could be redressed. Our priority was to raise consciousness, not to win votes.

The budget of the Women's Party was 350,000 pounds, the amount per seat allotted by the government to each party for its reelection campaign. Since I was not a candidate and the Women's Party was a new political entity, our funding could not come directly from the government. It would have to be given to us by the Independent Socialists, and they were under no legal obligation to do so. To secure the money, Lova's pledge was crucial. I met with him one last, painful time. I did not like what I had to do, to tell him that unless I was sure I could count on him to honor his pledge, I would have to split our party formally in order to be recognized by the Knesset as the leader of the Women's Party. "No, no, no more splits," he said. "I never break a promise."

He didn't. I met, the first in a series of strange meetings, with the lawyers representing Shelli—the new peace coalition that included the Independent Socialists, Ha'olam Hazeh, the Panthers, and Moked—to arrange for the transfer of funds. They faced me triumphantly. "You can't have the money," one said. "It's illegal."

By law, one party cannot fund the election campaign of another. I knew that. This lawyer, one of the best civil rights lawyers in Israel, was sure he had me, and that I could be divorced from the Independent Socialists Israeli-style, as a *moredet*, a rebellious wife, without property rights. But I had become an expert on the body of law and precedent relating to party funding when Ya'ad split. "There's nothing illegal about a party contributing to a non-profit organization," I said, "nor for such an organization to contribute to an election campaign representing its mission. The Women's Aid Fund can accept Shelli's donation."

Once again, the men of the left were bested and angry. They refused to make the "donation." Lova, however, demanded they honor his pledge. Because of his stubborn insistence, 350,000 pounds were contributed to the Women's Aid Fund, in cash. I met one last time with the lawyer to receive a briefcase full of 350 hundred-pound notes that I carefully counted before leaving.

◄●►

Hoping to reach out to Arab women, Ruth Resnik and I made a trip to Kfar Yasif, a village in the Galilee, to talk to Violet Khouri. We had first met in 1972, as copanelists on a radio talk show about the status of women. Violet Khouri was the only Arab woman in Israel to hold political office. She was then mayor of Kfar Yasif.

Like all Arab villages, Kfar Yasif nestles unobtrusively into the side of a hill. The road leading to the village from the main highway was unpaved, muddy and rutted. We passed small cultivated fields, groves of olive trees, and wide expanses of rocky hillside barren but for the goats who grazed on the sparse greenery.

The houses had been built with respect for privacy. They did not face one another or stand closely side by side. These homes were gracious, built around courtyards full of flowers. The streets wound around them in whatever random pattern emerged.

We were greeted at Violet's with ritualized hospitality. A tray of fruit and chocolates was brought out together with four bottles of whiskey, two imported and two local. It was still morning. No one touched the whiskey while we made small talk and ate. Violet excused herself, bearing the trays of fruit back to the kitchen and returning with platters of Middle Eastern delicacies. We were expected to eat it all, leaving just a mouthful to show we'd had enough. We complimented Violet on her cooking. She is known as the best cook in Kfar Yasif, she told us. She had to be, she said with sudden bitterness, in order to be elected. Her feminine credentials were automatically called into question when she entered politics, and they needed to be proven over and over. "The women in the village don't really like me much," she confided. And she, for her part, was bored in their company.

Violet was elected through family connections, but she decided to run only because she dared. In all of Israel there were only a few women mayors, and only one Arab woman—Violet Khouri. It began when her husband had been mayor and council meetings were held at her home. In and out of the room, serving the council members as she had us, she overheard their discussions. "Listening to them, I realized that the issues they discussed were the practical concerns of daily life in the village. I understood the needs of the village as well as they did, perhaps even better." Khouri was a social worker, an educated daughter of a prominent Christian family, one of the few in her generation encouraged to have a career. When election time came, her husband had served the maximum number of allowable terms. She asked his permission to run. "He had to agree, of course, or I couldn't do it. But once he did, the whole family gave its support. We are a large family." She smiled. The Khouris are an enormous Palestinian clan, and it is traditional among Arabs that clan members vote for one of their own. She was elected to the council, and because everyone thought she would be the weakest among them, she was chosen to head it. Ruth and I looked at one another. When Golda Meir was chosen by the Labor coalition to serve as Prime Minister, it was for the same reason.

We talked about the Women's Party. "We have money, and we're going to run." Violet's face suddenly turned shrewd. Now we're talking politics, it seemed to say. Her eyes narrowed and the lines around her mouth hardened. This must be how she looks when she's dealing with the men, I thought. "We can't promise you anything," Ruth said quickly, seeing what I saw. "We're not here for that. But we'd like you to join us. We'll hold internal elections to establish the slate. You'll have to take your chances, like everyone else." Violet's face softened. She liked the idea of a women's party, and if she was on the list, she felt sure she could bring in enough votes from Arabs, women and men, to insure a seat. But she couldn't yet consent.

"I have to wait for my brother-in-law," she explained. "He's trying to get a place on Mapam's list. If so, the family and I are obliged to support him." She would join us only if Mapam turned down her brother-in-law. Will the Khouris support her if she runs with us? "Of course," she said. "That's our tradition."

Mapam took its time letting Violet's brother-in-law know that he wouldn't be given a secure place on the list. With only three months until the election, we couldn't wait for Mapam's decision to select our own slate, too early for Violet to be available as a candidate. Slate selection turned out to be stormy and divisive. It meant, after all, ranking ourselves in order of leadership, and this was something that feminist groups didn't do. Though the list included everyone who wanted to be on it, we still had to determine an order of preference and, most particularly, who would head the list. The possibility of winning a seat was remote, but it was at least conceivable. We were, we knew, selecting the woman who might become our Member of Knesset. Two women campaigned actively, if secretly. Ruth Resnik for herself, and I for Shoshana Eilings. Shoshana, a seventh-generation *sabra*, articulate and knowledgeable, had always been the one I thought should lead the movement, but she had refused. Now she had stepped forward to accept the mantle that, to my mind, was rightly hers. But to Ruth Resnik, the memory of 1973 had to be haunting. Had it not been for ill-health, she would have been the Member of Knesset, not I. Ruth wanted very much to win the Women's Party nomination, but lost to Shoshana.

With the strict feminist norms of collectivism and egalitarian process we held for ourselves, there was no room in the Women's Party for politics as usual. But the fact of having to select our candidate for the Knesset, and the fact that success could lead to real power in the real world, meant politics very much as usual. There were several, it turned out, who wanted to be number one. We hadn't foreseen the feelings of disappointment and distrust that slate selection entailed. The anger of some of those who lost insinuated itself into the collective. Everyone who had ever felt frustrated about anything was infected.

Inevitably, Shoshana and I were trashed. Though I wasn't a candidate, I was the acknowledged leader of the party, the only one with political experience and, as chair of the Women's Aid Fund and campaign manager, I controlled the funds. We were accused of elitism, of controlling the collective, of not sharing power. Shoshana sat stiffly and silently as the angry voices of women detailed a list of complaints. I felt like a bird with a broken wing, flying so high on the success of my political maneuvering to bring about the Women's Party and suddenly grounded, not by the men I struggled against, but by the women who were my sisters. Hadn't I, after all, given up power willingly and handed it to them on a platter? I'd never felt so betrayed. Years of accumulated fatigue made it impossible for me to fight back. All I could do was cry, long and bitterly. Why can't these women let me exit gracefully? Why do they have to fight me for the power that I have already relinquished?

The party splintered into cliques that poisoned the joy and pride with which we'd begun. The wonderful joining together with one voice and one purpose turned to acrimony and factionalism. The disappointment and distrust caused by slate selection were still fresh when Violet Khouri called a month later to say she was ready to join us, but only if she could have second place on the list. In return, she pledged to deliver 10,000 votes to the Women's Party.

There was no reason to doubt her. In fact, it might even have been an underestimate. For the first time, I thought seriously about the possibility of winning, not with apprehension but with excitement. Violet's presence on the list could elect Shoshana. It would bring Arab women into the party on an equal footing. We would become a bicultural and bilingual women's organization. We might succeed in doing what only the Communists had done so far. The Women's Party would also become a binational peace party.

The collective met to discuss Violet's offer. It was a marathon meeting, lasting eight hours. That day, and for several more, it seemed that we were going to self-destruct. Ruth Resnik, who had been elected to second place, refused to relinquish it. Since she'd once before given up the possibility of being a Member of Knesset, I could hardly blame her. Everyone understood Ruth's feelings, but we didn't address them. Instead we argued about violating our own internal democracy. Shoshana suggested that the elections be held a second time. Ruth would have another chance at first place. If Violet didn't win, she could withdraw. It seemed workable. But when we took a vote, Shoshana's proposal lost, and Violet's offer was rejected. "I don't want to belong to a party with Arabs," one of the women said, and a few others nodded agreement. It was our most shameful moment. It was the end of my last illusion about Israeli society. The women's movement, too, was permeated by racism. I wanted to believe that feminists were better, but I no longer could. For the first time, I began to dread the unlikely possibility that we might win, comforted only by the knowledge that without Violet, we had no chance.

◄●►

The election campaign of 1977 was a three-way struggle between Labor, the Likud, and Yadin's new party. The election atmosphere was tense with the potential threat to Labor's dominance. No one paid much attention to the peace camp. The Women's Party was, at first, a humorous diversion. As such, we attracted a lot of media attention. As the campaign went on, we climbed to the rank of dark horse. Of the twenty-two parties that ran in the 1977 elections, only ten were covered regularly by the media, among them the Women's Party.

Publicly we maintained that we had the potential for 51 percent of the vote. Privately we hoped we would get enough votes so as not to make fools of ourselves. Because of our presence, women's issues were addressed for the first time by all the major parties. Though they didn't really fear losing votes to us, they could take no chances. Both Labor and the Likud pledged themselves to advancing the status of women. By the simple fact of running in the election, we forced our issues onto the national agenda.

There were never more than fifty activists for the Women's Party, and toward the end, there were only about fifteen. The only political experience we had was mine. Our list of thirteen candidates, the number chosen to honor the witches, was made up entirely of women of whom no one had heard.

Our twenty-five page platform, printed in purple, began with a brief statement recognizing the rights of the Palestinians to self-determination and economic justice for the poor. The rest of the platform detailed every aspect of the discrimination, exploitation, oppression, and victimization of women. It outlined a blueprint for redress that constituted a revolutionary revision of society. Most of what we talked about had never been discussed before in the mass media, and certainly not as part of an election campaign. Shuli Eshel's two-minute videos were subtle but outrageous. One, filmed in the Jerusalem market Machene Yehuda, followed a woman shopping for the week's provisions, carrying heavy bundles home on the bus and up three flights of stairs to the kitchen. The camera filmed her unpacking her baskets and bags, putting the food away, preparing the Sabbath meal. As she gutted and scaled fish, never once looking at the camera, Shuli asked from the background, "What do you do?" Still without looking at the camera, her hands deep inside the fish, she replied. "Me? I don't do anything. I'm just a housewife."

The 1977 elections have their place in history as the year of the *mahapach*, the upheaval, the year Menachem Begin came to power. In the light of that event, how unimportant the Women's Party campaign seems. An electoral footnote, a curiosity. But our campaign made a difference. We set our goal in terms of raising consciousness and we succeeded. Attitudes toward the women's movement changed subtly. The media invariably used the daily press releases we issued. Women told us by the hundreds that they clipped our paid political advertisements and hung them on the walls of their kitchens. Soon the word *feministit* entered the language, though by the back door. "I'm not a feminist but...."

◄●►

The campaign results were directly proportional to the funds we had to spend. Yadin's party spent spent a million pounds for each of the seventeen seats it won. The Women's Party, with a third the amount of money, won a third of the votes necessary for a mandate. These six thousand votes were spread with uncanny evenness throughout the country. In every polling place, without exception, we got between one and five votes—among the Bedouins, in Arab villages, kibbutzim and rural communities, big cities and small development towns.

The most significant, long-lasting result was the impact of the Women's Party campaign on the Prime Minister's Commission on the Status of Women. The Commission had been established, grudgingly, by Yitzhak Rabin just as International Women's Year (1975) came to a close. Its deliberations ended with the start of the campaign and resumed immediately after the 1977 elections. The recommendations adopted were presented to the new Prime Minister, Menachem Begin. Throughout the year-and-a-half that the Commission and its task forces met, the few feminists on it had fought what seemed like a losing battle against the mostly conservative representatives appointed by the Prime Minister. But, after the election, when the final recommendations were voted on, there was majority support for feminist positions on most issues. The report issued by the Commission on the Status of Women reads like a gloss on the Women's Party platform.

◄●►

May 17, 1977 was election day and my thirty-ninth birthday, my last day as a Member of Knesset. I spent it at home, alone. Our members were spread thin by poll watching. My phone was the number to call if anything went wrong. There were few calls and few visitors. Only Judy joined me that night as we followed the returns on television. On the screen were tally columns for Labor, the Likud, Yadin's party, Shelli, the Communists, the religious parties, and the Women's Party. Among the dozen small parties also running, we were the only one to make it to the Broadcasting Authority's chalkboard. Just to be up there on the screen throughout the night, as all of Israel watched, declared the enormous potential of the women's vote. In defeat, victory.

At the night's end, my political career was over and Menachem

Begin, anathema to every Israeli liberal, was to be the new Prime Minister. Shelli won two seats. Shulamit, hurt by the split but also by the Women's Party, won only one. Labor would sit in the opposition for the first time in its history. The Knesset would never be the same.

It was a lonely night, but one of infinite relief. It was the end of an era in Israeli politics. Begin encapsulated the change for the foreign press. "From now on, we will refer to the West Bank by its ancient Biblical name, Judea and Samaria. Get used to it." But I would not, the next morning, have to rise from dreams of political intrigue to face a day of meetings, speeches, frantic travel from Haifa to Jerusalem to Tel Aviv. The spotlight had dimmed, and I sat in the afterglow, exhausted but at peace.

Chapter 8
Feminist Politics
◄●►

Feminist politics, the power relationships within the women's movement, was very different from party politics, not just because of the difference between the internal workings of political parties and social movements, but also because of the difference between how men and women relate to power. My relationship with Shulamit Aloni is a case in point. For though we were brought together within the framework of electoral politics, the dynamic between us can only be understood in feminist terms. It would have been utterly different if one or both of us were men.

From our first encounter, Shulamit Aloni and I brought out the worst in each another. In her presence, I was timid and tongue-tied. In my presence, she was arrogant and contemptuous. Her obvious disdain confirmed my deepest fear that whatever success I achieved was unearned. Perhaps seeing those qualities in me mirrored something of herself, the uncertainty and self-doubt that coexists, as it always does, with an arrogant and supremely confident exterior. Perhaps the hostility had to do with self-hate. Perhaps she thought of me as a potential rival, to be dealt with in the same way Golda Meir had dealt with her. Perhaps the hostility needs to be traced to the deepest archetypal levels of mother-daughter relationships. Golda had disinherited Shulamit, denying her a second term in the Knesset. Shulamit, in a rage, lashed out viciously at Golda, but Golda, the Prime Minister, was beyond her reach. I was not. And I, the rejected daughter, finally rebelled, not caring how much damage I might do.

Whatever the dynamic between us, the outcome—Aloni's dislike of me and mine of her—was immediate and long lasting. The hostility that existed between us only intensified after the election. Since the break, our encounters have been brief, always strained, always grim. We nod coldly and exchange quick hellos.

But once we talked civilly. In 1982, while the invasion of Lebanon was still in progress, Aloni spoke out against the war, virtually alone among politicians. Her stand was courageous and marked an important political shift for the CRM. Israelis do not tolerate opposition to war, especially a war in progress. When she later addressed a feminist gathering in Tel Aviv, I went up to her, determined to let go of my residual resentment. I approached from behind and tapped her on the shoulder. Not knowing it was me, a smile was in place as she turned and remained frozen in place as we spoke. I praised her willingness to stand alone and extended my hand. Surprised, she took it. We said a few more sentences, awkwardly but without rancor, and then it was over, a brief moment of appeasement. It might have been an opportunity to say more, to arrange to meet again for a longer conversation, but we didn't. Not then or ever have we talked about what happened between us.

◄●►

Before, during, and after the Knesset years, the women's movement was home, an ideological, emotional, spiritual, and political home. These were my sisters, and I took sisterhood seriously. It meant bonding, it meant trust, and it meant support. The women's movement was never large enough to be a constituency, nor was it organized enough to be a political base. But it constituted the only public space in which, most of the time, I felt at one with myself.

As true as this was and is, the feminist bedrock of support was never wholly solid. There were cracks that, as my struggle with Shulamit Aloni intensified, widened to fissures and finally, unbridgeable chasms. Even before the difficulties with Aloni erupted, just weeks after being sworn in, fine dividing lines etched themselves between me and all the rest. The title that followed my name set me apart and created expectations not merely of activist commitment, but also of political leadership.

Returning each week from Jerusalem, I was drained by the effort of trying to succeed in a profession for which I had not been prepared. I looked to the women's movement for renewed energy and repair of my badly damaged ego. But even the first movement meeting I attended after only a month as a Member of Knesset was an exercise in objectification that, however innocently intended, taught me not to expect too much of my sisters. I arrived late and walked into a room filled with my closest friends, many of the original consciousness-raising group. We kissed and hugged as usual. We all wore T-shirts and jeans as usual. I warmed to the greeting and the smiles and sat back to enjoy familiarity, to listen and catch up with what was going on. But conversation stopped. Whatever had been under discussion when I arrived was no longer interesting. Everyone looked at me expectantly. "Tell us what it's like."

It was the Knesset, *it* was politics, *it* was life among the powerful and the famous. What's it like? I was accustomed, with these women, to talk about what it was really like, to tell the truth about feelings. I thought they were making space for me to admit to anxiety, to insecurity, to the utter loneliness of *it*.

"I don't know anyone," I said. "When I go into the Members Dining Room, I don't have anyone to sit with. Mostly I hang around with the secretaries. They may be the only ones in the entire Knesset who don't think I'm either crazy or a fool. I'm self-conscious and on guard all the time. It's exhausting."

But that wasn't what my friends wanted to hear. "Did you talk to Golda? What's she like? Did you meet Dayan?" There was awe in the asking, but there was envy, too. I was a celebrity now, their Member of Knesset. They didn't want me to have the familiar responses. They wanted me to be bigger, better than I was. They didn't get it even when I told them that Golda ignored me.

Gradually I and they grew accustomed to my being a Member of Knesset, but the me versus them was never quite erased. I was forever after a public personality in the women's movement, someone to be reckoned with, ascribed power that I did not have and status that I did not want. I was given a role to play. A leader not just by default, not by consensus, but by the title that followed my name. My sisters wanted me to be their mother, omniscient and omnipotent, with no needs of her own.

◄●►

Tel Aviv is built on the sandy wastes that surrounded Jaffa, the small Arab city that was Palestine's port of entry. South Tel Aviv is the oldest section of the city. Its neighborhoods are filled with two- and three-story dwellings built during the Mandate. Many have narrow doorways protected by concrete walls and entryways built to slow down invading armies, grim reminders of the Second World War.

Most of the rest of Tel Aviv is new, hastily and cheaply built to accommodate rapid population growth. It is a flat and uniform expanse of multistory housing and streets too narrow for big-city traffic. Tel Avivians are conscious of their role as Israel's Alexandria. They dress fashionably, support cultural events, and suffer urban discomfort proudly. The main street and city center, Dizengoff, is lined with stores displaying the latest fashions from the West at prices no one can afford but everyone pays. Its broad sidewalks are filled with large outdoor cafes and crowded with strollers. To walk along Dizengoff Street has become a reflexive verb, *l'hizdengoff*. I did not like Tel Aviv and went there only when I had to, mostly for party or movement meetings.

The Tel Aviv branch of the movement, the women with whom I had least contact, changed most after the election. Many of them had been active on behalf of the CRM, some were closely aligned with Shulamit Aloni. The idea for my nomination had come from their ranks. They felt that I was theirs. Our relations during the Knesset years were always testy, sometimes acrimonious.

The Tel Aviv women believed they had elected me and were entitled to share in the spoils of victory. They believed it was my job to carry this message to Aloni and to make good on it. When I tried and failed, they blamed me for the failure. They were frustrated and angry, convinced that I refused to follow through on what they saw as my obligations. From their point of view, I refused to pay my debts. From mine, they obstinately refused to face the fact of my powerlessness in the CRM.

Matters between us only got worse. Our meetings were few and far between. Once, in 1975, I was summoned. In 1976 I went uninvited. The first time I drove from Haifa to Tel Aviv apprehensively. By that time Aloni and I were so estranged that we hardly spoke to one another.

The floor of the large living room in which the meeting was held was covered with bodies wall-to-wall. By the time I arrived, there was no floor space left and only one empty chair. It waited conspicuously for me, alone and set off, facing the crowd. It took a few minutes to wade through arms and legs to take my place on the witness stand. There were no greetings, no smiles. Just a heavy, angry silence.

The recitation of charges began.

—"You don't report regularly. You don't consult before taking positions."

—"According to the press, you support legalized prostitution. The movement opposes legalization. You misrepresent us."

—"Why do you have to talk about prostitution at all? It's too sensational."

—"It's hard enough to be a feminist. You only make it harder."

—"Every time they show you on television wearing a Bedouin dress or jeans, my mother doesn't stop talking about it. I have to defend your clothes to my mother!"

—"We're not extremists. But you make it easy for everyone to think we are."

It was a hot July night, typical Tel Aviv weather, muggy and breezeless. But I didn't sweat. I was cold with anger. Something had changed in me, too. I scolded those who attacked me, meeting accusation with accusation. Am I not to be tolerated because of my clothes? Do you think you can tell me what to wear? Is this sisterhood? Is it even feminism? Since when are we trying to appear moderate? I was misquoted on prostitution, but I shamed them for wanting to avoid the issue. "We're by definition a radical movement, and by definition we're going to be unpopular. Am I the only person in this movement? Raise your voices and you'll be heard. Get out there in front of the media so your mothers can see your clothes too."

"You're an anti-Zionist!"

"No I'm not," I shouted back.

But what, after all, did it matter what I was? Whatever I was, I could not be all that they wanted and needed me to be.

My anger spent, I tried to explain. I can't change who I am, how I dress, what I think just because I've been elected to the Knesset. I don't control the agenda. It wasn't my idea to bring up prostitution. But once issues come up, I have to respond to them, and I can only follow my conscience. I don't want to hurt the movement. I'm always careful to say that I'm not speaking for the movement, that in politics I don't represent the movement. The media has made me your representative in the Knesset. I'm sorry, but there's nothing I can do about it. I'm sorry that I'm so embarrassing to you. I'm doing the best I can. I'm sorry, I'm sorry, I'm sorry.

My apologetic explanations only fed their feelings of resentment. Electing a feminist hadn't legitimized the movement as they hoped it would. They didn't understand why, and so they held me responsible. It was the simplest explanation. The chorus of complaints went on loudly. My hands and feet went cold again, and my head began to pound, the chronic hypertension that lets me know how angry I am. "I need your support, and all I get is a trashing. Maybe I've betrayed you, but you've betrayed me, too." It seemed to strike a nerve. A few of the women noticeably exchanged guilty looks. Are they agents of the Shin Bet? I wondered. Have they been put up to this by Aloni?

Who was, after all, to blame? Had I in fact failed the women's movement? It was true that I took positions without consulting anyone. I was a media sensation. I was the only famous radical feminist in the country. I represented the movement by default. My fault? Theirs for not standing by me, for failing to understand what an impossible position I was in? They are jealous and petty. They want to be liked more than they want to be revolutionaries. I could, then, see only two possibilities. Either I was the cause of the conflict or they were.

A year later, soon after the vote on the Knesset debate on the PLO, I picked up the Tel Aviv feminists' newsletter and read about a meeting scheduled for the following week to discuss "The Movement's Relation to Marcia Freedman, MK." I wasn't invited but went anyway. When I walked through the door, there was already a motion on the floor to publicly disassociate from me. What they saw as my championship of the Palestinian cause had gone too far. Because of me, they said, the movement in Tel Aviv had stopped growing.

I could see the headlines: "Feminists Repudiate Leader." "Freedman Too Extreme, Feminists Say." I became what these women always insisted I was—a politician. I was determined to avoid a split and the bad publicity it would entail. I'd learned a lot about controlling hostile audiences over the years and used it all. I tried to soothe them, to soften their resolve. I distracted them with a discourse on feminist organizing. I lectured on the Arab-Israeli conflict. Smoothly, calmly, I dismissed their disagreement as ignorance. I kept on talking, aiming to wear them down. I spoke softly, trying to persuade, urged them to be reasonable. My voice was so low they had to strain to hear. It kept their attention. The momentum toward a split was broken. The motion never came to the floor. But they still felt frustrated, and I still felt abandoned.

When Indira Ghandi jailed hundreds of her opponents, Avi startled me by saying he admired her. "You'd do the same thing in her place," he said. Would I? Growing up, I had been the neighborhood tomboy. Helene was my only girlfriend. We played mostly indoors—on rainy days or at night when I slept over at her house. Otherwise I was on the street, playing with the boys. My brother's friends, older than I, accepted me into their games as long as I could hold my own in baseball, stickball, and touch football. I was a determinedly good fielder and never ran away from a fight with the Catholic boys at the other end of our block. There was always a place for me among my brother's friends. I was the undisputed leader with the boys more my age and ruled with an iron hand. We played what I wanted to play, and they did what I said. Stanley Karras was the only one who challenged me. I could never beat him in a fight, but even though he won, the gang stood by me. Stanley, the strongest, always waited for me to initiate our games and organize the teams.

Once my breasts began to develop, the older boys wouldn't play with me. They flirted instead, and the younger boys shifted their allegiance to Stanley. Except for playing board games with Helene, I'd never learned much about being a girl. My apprenticeship was long and miserable, but finally I mastered reticence, passivity, and timidity. My grades were too good for some, threatening unpopularity, so I lowered them. I aimed for and made the bottom of the first quarter. I died a blonde streak in my hair and wore the school uniform—tight black pants and big loop earrings. Some of the girls pierced their ears, but I couldn't bring myself to do it. My transformation was so successful that I, who had pulled apart flies and gutted fish, became queasy when I thought about a needle puncturing my ear. I had girlfriends and, occasionally, dates. The closest I came to sports in high school was as a twirler. At least I could wear the brown satin jacket that said Weequahic on the back.

The new me, the girlchild, wasn't created of whole cloth. The transformation succeeded because it expressed a truth that until high school I'd never known about myself. I discovered the other side of grandiosity. Once I had been one of the boys, a leader of boys. Just like my father, a leader of men. And just like him, I harbored a constant fear of having my vulnerability unmasked. It was easy to become a girl. I had all the makings at hand. I was fearful, needy, and profoundly sad. The periodic depressions I experienced, also new to me, were easily explainable as deep sorrow over the loss of a boyfriend or the failure to be noticed by my crush of the moment. I could cry openly, approved feminine conduct. My family did not question why I was crying, why I was depressed. Once I got my period, it was to be expected.

When the women's movement began, it was like recapturing the self I'd known in childhood, a self fondly remembered but long dormant. As I became a leader of women, both grandiosity and self-doubt were there in full measure. In the early years, when leadership meant organizing and facilitating CR groups, the ingredients combined in a successful brew. But once elected and needing to function in the world of men, there was no room for insecurity or doubt, no room for all of me. I had to keep afloat and did so by wearing the mask my father had worn—always confident, always glib, always out front.

◄●►

The women's movement during the mid-1970s was in its prime. The tens of activist feminists became hundreds. Recent immigrants from the Americas and Western Europe joined with those who had grown up in Israel and found a common tongue. We joked that of all the agencies for immigrant absorption, we were the most effective. In Haifa, a new group of young, single women became active. They were experienced agitators, schooled by their work in student politics. The movement reorganized in Jerusalem, this time with recent American immigrants who brought with them the activist style of the sixties. They were soon joined by many women of the left, some from anti-Zionist organizations. These women injected radical experience into the dynamic of the movement. No longer was it unseemly to demonstrate on the streets, to be disruptive, to get arrested.

Two events mobilized the entire women's movement during the mid-seventies. The first was my introduction of the abortion bill in 1974. The second was Shulamit Aloni's introduction of an

Israeli equivalent of the Equal Rights Amendment in 1975. Both caused mayhem in the Knesset. When the equal rights bill came up for its first reading, the Labor government, not wanting to appear antifeminist during International Women's Year, didn't oppose it. There was time to defeat it, they knew, when it came back for the next round of voting. Labor's coalition partner, the National Religious Party, was outraged. The proposed legislation opened the door to civil marriage and the draft of their daughters. It threatened the Jewish family and, therefore, they extrapolated, the Jewish state. That evening, on the nine o'clock news, Yosef Burg, the Minister of Interior, announced that the NRP would leave the Labor-led coalition. He didn't need to add that the move would bring the government down. The following morning, Prime Minister Rabin announced that the Equal Rights Act was dead on arrival, the Labor-led coalition firmly opposed its passage.

The women in Tel Aviv organized a demonstration across the street from Labor Party headquarters. The police refused a permit, but the women demonstrated anyway. Too much force was used dispersing the crowd, and some demonstrators were arrested for resisting. The press, for once, was there. The story made the front page.

Secular Israelis viewed the demonstration, even though illegal, as an expression of their own widespread antagonism to religious coercion. The movement mobilized for a follow-up rally, and this time the Haifa organizers took the lead. To capitalize on public support for an equal rights law, the organizers planned to invite the famous and influential to speak, women who had never before given their names or bodies to a feminist cause—actresses, entertainers, artists, journalists, academics. And politicians.

As a Member of Knesset, I was to be one of the speakers, but the Tel Aviv women refused to allow it. They said that I would get all the publicity, that I was using the movement, that I was too far to the left to be included. They refused to participate if I was listed among the notables. By that time, I wouldn't speak directly to the women in Tel Aviv. Messages were carried back and forth. Tel Aviv suggested a solution—excluding all politicians, except for Aloni. The bile rose in my throat, but I knew enough to take Tel Aviv seriously. They would split the movement if I appeared at the rally.

◄●►

When the CRM split, so did the movement. I was accused in both places of failing to represent my constituency by being too radical. The Jerusalem/Haifa alignment that emerged during my last confrontation with the Tel Aviv women held. Many had come out of left politics. Most, though not all, didn't mind that I'd become vocal on the Palestinian issue or that I called myself an Independent Socialist.

Once again, Rachel Kagan was my teacher. In 1949, she had won a seat in the Knesset as the feminist leader of a feminist party, the Women's Party, which hoped to win several seats and planned for no other possibility. Their representatives would be bound by party discipline only on women's issues. On all else they were to vote their conscience. The list was carefully constructed to accommodate the politics of coalition.

But only Kagan had been elected. As agreed, she consulted the Women's Party on all women's issues but otherwise voted her conscience. By the end of the term, WIZO was so torn with dissension that the party was disbanded and faded out of Zionist history. Kagan, the only woman besides Golda Meir to sign the Israeli Declaration of Independence, did not run for reelection. She returned to WIZO, a marginalized figure.

I knew, from Kagan, that it was an impossible task to represent everyone all the time, especially since the women's movement did not develop positions on anything other than women's issues. That was the real problem underlying the split, but the trigger was pulled on a gun that only partially hit its mark. The specific issue over which the Israeli women's movement split was my participation in the International Tribunal for Crimes Against Women, held in Brussels in March 1976.

I was invited to the Brussels conference because, at the time, I was the only feminist legislator in the world. It never occurred to me to ask anyone's permission to go. I consulted only with the Foreign Ministry. Since the UN's equation of Zionism with racism a year earlier, there had been no international conference that did not reaffirm the charge. It happened even at the UN-sponsored International Women's Conference in Mexico.

The average Israeli's reaction to the international charge of racism was defensive. Whatever else they admit to, Jews view the charge of racism as racist. Though they may or may not be racist, most Jews agree that with reference to Jews—the historical victims of anti-Semitism and survivors of genocide—the question cannot arise.

The official Israeli response did not deny racism but rather affirmed Zionism. Haifa's main boulevard, UN Boulevard, was renamed Zionism Boulevard. My daughter came home from school wearing a large blue-and-white button given to all the children. On Jenny's chest were pinned the words, I Am a Zionist. Political satirists began to popularize buttons and bumperstickers that read, I Am a Guava.

The Mexico resolution sent shockwaves throughout the women's movement. Jewish women "came out" and proclaimed their Judaism, as well as their loyalty and support for the state of Israel. Again no one discussed the merits or demerits of the charge of racism. The Jews of the dispersion agreed with the Israelis that the charge was no more than thinly veiled anti-Semitism. Some American Jewish feminists charged that the women's movement itself was anti-Semitic. "These are men's politics," I wrote to friends. "We mustn't buy into it. Both sides are killers and both sides are racist. That is the nature of nationalism. As feminists we have to oppose it everywhere, even among ourselves."

I was eager to go to Brussels, most of all because I was eager to be with several thousand other radical feminists from around the world. But also because I believed that although Palestinian women were expected to attend, there would be no support for an anti-Zionist resolution. The majority would never allow it.

That's what I told the Foreign Ministry. Though skeptical, they underwrote the trip. Before I left, I went through two briefings.

The first was about how to handle an anti-Zionist resolution if it were introduced; in short, I was to defend the occupation. The second briefing was about security—not to label my luggage, to watch out for suspicious types (e.g., Arabs), to pack my own bags and keep them in sight at the airport.

The Tel Aviv women were furious when they heard I was going to Brussels. Who, they asked, had chosen me to represent the Feminist Movement of Israel? A few weeks later, word reached Haifa that the Tel Aviv women had applied to the Foreign Ministry to send one of their own to Brussels. They selected Joanne Yaron, a Tel Aviv veteran, to officially represent, as they said, the Feminist Movement of Israel. It was Haifa and Jerusalem's turn to be furious. Who chose her to represent us, they asked? Maybe they think you're already represented, I suggested. We didn't choose you and we didn't choose her, they countered, but at least you never claimed to be an official representative. As far as Haifa and Jerusalem were concerned, the action of the Tel Aviv movement was outrageous. They've split without announcing it, some said. If so, then so be it. Tel Aviv was excommunicated.

In the years that followed, the Haifa and Jerusalem movements were united in purpose and trusted one another, while Tel Aviv remained aloof and uncooperative. Their stationery read, "The Feminist Movement of Israel in Tel Aviv," and underneath in small print, "Pro-Zionist, not party-affiliated." The women in Tel Aviv drew closer to Aloni. In Haifa and Jerusalem, they closed around me protectively. For my part, I was tired and felt defeated. I dropped in and out of movement politics.

◄●►

The Tribunal on Crimes Against Women was as radical as I'd promised the Foreign Ministry it would be, but my parochial experience of the women's movement in Israel hadn't prepared me for what that meant. The conference was held at the Palais de Congress, a coldly imposing building faced on the outside with white granite and inside with walls and floors of polished marble. For five days it was occupied by radical feminists from around the world who succeeded in making it their own. I felt, inside that building, like a country bumpkin in the big city, not because of the building—I was used to imposing facades—but because of the women who occupied it.

Hundreds of exhibit tables lined the halls. The walls were covered with political posters, stark and disturbing. The conference poster, printed white on black, depicted a women's symbol crashing through a coffin. The exhibits represented organizations advocating for prostitutes, women in prison, battered women, incest victims, against coercive sterilization and pregnancy, genital mutilation, and pornography. For the most part, these were issues that hadn't yet been raised in Israel.

One corner of the vast foyer that had been turned into an exhibit hall was curtained off. Outside, a long line of women stood waiting patiently to enter. The sign said Self-Help. Help for what? I had no idea. I joined the line. As I drew close to the entryway, I passed a table outside containing nothing but transparent plastic speculums, though I had no idea, looking at them, what they were. Even the sign that said Speculums/$5 was no help. What is a speculum? The booklet that came with it was my only clue, full of diagrams and directions for use. I would, by then, have run away had the curtains not parted. It was my turn to enter.

We were allowed in ten at a time. A young woman standing beside an examining table greeted us. She explained about using the speculum to examine ourselves, how we could recognize the signs of vaginal infection and treat them ourselves with home remedies of yogurt and vinegar. She showed slides of the insides of vaginas with yeast infections and trichomoniasis. Then she called for a volunteer. What now? I froze. A young woman came forth and stripped from the waist down. "I'm going to show you what the inside of a vagina looks like," the self-helper said. "Gather in closely." There wasn't much air in this small space, but it didn't matter. I was hardly breathing. The half-naked volunteer lay down on the examining table, her feet in the stirrups. Our guide inserted the speculum and called for us to come close, one at a time, for a look. "That curved black line you see is the os, the entrance to the cervix," she said. "You see, it's smiling at you."

My trip to Brussels was more, much more, than I'd bargained for. The official proceedings had not even begun when the first of a series of explosive challenges to the conference organizers erupted. Large groups of women gathered in the hall, arguing about the presence of male journalists. The conference organizers, I learned, were meeting in emergency session to decide on whether male journalists should be allowed inside the Palais de Congress. Hours later, a vote was taken. The organizers bowed to the wishes of the majority. Men would not be allowed inside the building. A murmur of satisfaction went through the crowd. I, who lived my life with men in a building very like the Palais de Congress, was amazed and shaken.

The following morning, the same organizers trashed themselves for sitting on the stage, an imposing platform of polished wood that rose high above the heads of the audience. These women, representing several countries, had worked for years to put the conference together but gave themselves no credit. Scrupulously, they shared the opening statements between them. It was a series of apologies.

—"We are sorry to be stuck up here in a God-like position."

—"With a meeting this size and lasting five days, we had to establish an agenda in advance. We realize that others might have done it differently."

—"We're sorry that we have to keep speakers to a time limit. It was the only way to make sure that everyone who wants to can speak."

The organizers had planned the conference with as little control as possible. Sessions were arranged around presentations by country, and each delegation determined its own subject matter. Some of the speakers represented groups organized around particular causes. Most represented themselves, giving testimony to atrocity, victimization, and survival.

But only the first day went in any way according to plan. That night, the lesbian women caucused. The next morning they hung a huge banner over the entrance to the Palais de Congress. Lesbian Nation, it said. No sooner had the conference coordinators taken their places on the dais than the lesbian caucus disrupted. Entering the auditorium en masse, several hundred women poured down the aisles wearing signs on their chests and backs. In front, I'm a Lesbian. In back, Are You?

Am I? As they marched toward the podium, about a quarter of the audience stood in solidarity. At first I stood, then sat down. Then I stood again, and sat down again. When the first of the demonstrators reached the stage, they complained that the conference planners had not made space for lesbian issues and demanded that they be heard. The organizers capitulated. They returned to the dais and announced their decision to abandon it, leaving the conference in a state of anarchy.

Different caucuses met that night and the next. Each day the conference proceedings were interrupted by a noisy demonstration ending in a demand to be heard, and each time the regular proceedings were put aside to meet the new demand. On occasion, one caucus wrested the microphone from the preceding one. Having claimed their time and made their own rules, the groups gave way to one another as gracefully as the organizers had given up control.

It seemed, as it was happening, like sheer chaos. But at the end of the five days, everyone who'd been scheduled to speak spoke, and everyone not scheduled who wished to speak spoke. Everyone was heard, and, it appeared, everyone was satisfied.

I, too, was satisfied and, to the surprise of Israeli Foreign Ministry officials, so were they. I attended only one caucus, that of Third World women. I went shyly—a Third World woman or a colonizer, I wondered. How would I be received? I went to meet Arab women. There were only a few, and like me, they were uncontrolled by their governments. After a hasty meeting, we reached agreement. At the last session of the conference, a joint statement of women from Israel and Arab countries called for the end of hostility between Jews and Arabs and for recognition that as women we are not at war with one another but together waged battle against the patriarchy that oppressed us. The statement, so different from those issued at other international conferences, made headlines in Europe and America, even in Israel.

◄●►

The organizational ideal that radical feminists seek is the leader-less group. We are anarchists not by ideology but by need. We are moved by an underclass appreciation of power—by our certainty that the kind of power that oppresses us can never be ours—to envision a utopia in which there is no governance other than self-governance, a utopia in which the forces of bonding and female habits of caring replace the need for authority. We do this in our literature and expect of ourselves that we will do it in our lives.

In our literature, these utopias are sublime. In our lives and in our organizations, the reflection is often dreary. Our claim on political power is negligible and our claim on personal power is still in its adolescence. We need our leaders but resent them as once we resented our mothers. We empower them consensually but chew them up for exercising the power we give them. We deny, upbraid, perhaps even hate those we need and want to follow. We are jealous of their fame. The leaders, confused by the double mes-sage, appear to renounce power even as we exercise it. We learn to deny, sometimes to hate ourselves. We are, or are expected to be, self-sacrificing and self-deprecating. When we are not, we are overbearing, angry, contentious.

I learned in Brussels that though we may botch the process, the product is nevertheless worthy. Our groups are scrupulously, often inefficiently, egalitarian. They make room for personal growth, for the learned exercise of power, and for the learned exercise of relinquishing power. We are all heard. The center of attention is not fixed. In the end, despite its tumultuous conflict, the Brussels conference gave testimony to the world about atrocities against women as two thousand women wished to present it. In the Is-raeli women's movement, despite the enmity between individuals and groups that was part of its ongoing dynamic, the movement succeeded against terrible odds in breaking through denial and si-lence to place our issues on the national agenda.

The split in the Israeli women's movement that seemed so

damaging in anticipation was, in retrospect, felicitous. It marked an important shift from an early intention to form a single national mass organization to fragmentation into small issue-oriented action groups. Shelters for battered women, rape crisis centers, women's bookstores, magazines, and publishing houses were the result. By the eighties, the women's movement had a dozen centers of power. The Israeli women's movement, like the two thousand women in Brussels, found a mode of organizing that made room for everyone to rise to the top.

Today, when I see the women who trashed me, the women I so disliked, we look at one another oddly. Theirs is a somewhat guilty look mixed with the old righteousness. Mine is still wary, but accepting of the fact that their hair, too, has turned grey. We are wiser now. Some of them have become leaders and have experienced with others what I experienced with them. They know both that they correctly identified their issues with me, but also that others now have the same issues with them. They know, too, that they were instrumental in driving me from the country. They are glad I am gone just as they realize that my going was a loss to the movement.

What we both recognize is that we were helpless victims of a dynamic whose only precedent we experienced in infancy. In patriarchy, the only women we perceive to be powerful are our mothers. We learned to identify with and to reject them, and they us. The residue is the need for unconditional approval and a lasting expectation of betrayal. Feminist politics begin with these unconscious, infantile expectations. As more of us assume and command power in the public sphere, we do not know how to behave with one another, but we are learning—painfully and slowly, we are learning.

PART III:
Yeridah

Chapter 9
Women's Aid

◄●►

"Bubbeleh, are you sure you know what you're doing?" Esther Broner asked when I told her I was leaving politics. I knew I wanted desperately to get out and what I wanted to do next. But I didn't know what I had become used to and what it was going to be like to be exiled from the centers of power. No, Esther, I didn't know what I was doing.

Whatever I was or wasn't as a Member of Knesset, no matter whether I succeeded or failed, the title carried prestige, privilege, and access. It made me important in the eyes of the world. The loss was swift and sudden, marked by stinging events of rejection. Three days after the election, I received a letter of apology from the magazine that carried my column. Since I was no longer in office, they were no longer interested. A week later I was notified, after a prolonged and angry argument within my department, that Haifa University did not wish to rehire me. I wrote to other universities, but no one was interested in letting me teach. I reread the yellowing half-finished dissertation I'd put away four years earlier.

A comparative analysis of Kant and Wittgenstein was as far removed from what I had become as the words on the page from my comprehension. I heard that Yigal Yadin and Israel Katz, liberal Ministers in the new government, planned to establish positions for advisors on women's affairs. I waited vainly for a phone call offering me a job.

I was unprepared to read the day's news without seeing my own name. I was unprepared for the abrupt end of a heavy schedule filled with meetings, interviews, and speeches. The phone did not ring for days on end. I was unprepared for the quiet that shrieked, "You are no one, nothing. We're glad to be rid of you."

I thought about the possibility of leaving Israel to do a degree in women's studies in the States, to start over. But how could I? Impossible, I said. You can't be a former Member of Knesset one year and a *yoredet* the next. *Yored* is Hebrew for emigrant, *yeridah* is emigration. It is the opposite of *aliyah*, ascent. *Yeridah* is a descent from the state of grace. In Israeli eyes it is an act of betrayal, escape from the struggle. It is for many a despicable, unforgivable act.

My self-image shattered into a dozen unrelated fragments. I studied how the grocery store owner handed me my change to discern what he saw when he looked at me. I walked among the familiar faces of Haifa wondering what people said about me. It always seemed to me that they were staring. I put off going to the shoemaker because I feared what he might say this time, he who by my shoes knew me so well. I studied the shoes that needed repair. They looked very tired, perhaps beyond fixing. The leather was stressed, the heels run down. They needed new soles.

The shoes, finally, moved me to action. I had only one pair. I was worried about money for the first time in many years. The pension I received for one term of service to the government would suffice only if I was very careful. New shoes were out of the question. I went to my old friend, the *sandlar*, and found salvation.

I sat in his little *budkeh* and handed over my shoes. The shoemaker, generously, was silent, working for an hour with grave concentration to renew the leather and replace the broken parts. As he hammered the last tiny nail into the new sole, he held them

up to me. "There," he said, with obvious satisfaction. "Like new."
My friend the shoemaker sent me home on feet of serious intent.
Still broken, still tired, but resolved to put a new life together. On
the way home I stopped and bought four gallons of whitewash.

Jenny and I worked for weeks painting the walls, washing and
polishing the furniture, renewing and reclaiming our home together.
I helped her paint over the mural that covered one wall of her bedroom, the mural that she and the Prager children had done years
ago in bright primary colors. I was sorry to see it go, but Jenny,
now twelve, felt it too childish. She wanted a new bed, one that
looked like a sofa during the day. And a larger desk for the more
serious homework of junior high school. We emptied a closet filled
with childhood toys and packed them up to give away. Only a
few of the teddy bears made it through the transition. She waited
for her period impatiently. We hung a full-length mirror on her
door. Each morning, she stood in front of it contemplatively, crit-
ically, brushing her long hair and examining her breasts for new
growth, watching her body take on the shape of womanhood.

Jenny helped me paint and furnish the "extra" room, the room
that had been Nomi's and had served as storage space since she'd
left. Now it would be my studio, my office. I bought file cabinets,
a new typewriter, and made one more trip to Jerusalem to bring
the beautiful things that filled my room there back to Haifa. More
than anything, filling that empty space with the furnishings of a
new life marked its beginning. When it was complete, I began to
write an outline for a book on battered women.

We spent days on the beach, Jenny and I, enjoying a lazy summer together. I let the sea wash over me. Never a swimmer, I could
only float on my back, staring up into the cloudless blue sky, the
sea glittering in the sunlight around me. The sun, as always, did
its magic. The tight places softened. The worry lines on my forehead smoothed out as my skin tanned. The muscles in my jaws
and shoulders began to relax.

That summer, Cholit, my friend and Bill's former lover, became my lover. I knew passion once again, and intimacy. Hiding
our affair even from our daughters, we struggled to understand

that, yes, we are lesbians. We were not yet ready to become part of the lesbian community in Haifa. But each day we traced our growing alienation from the old world of friends and family we still inhabited, wondering whether and how to come out, and discovering in our bodies responses and habits of love we never knew were there.

Taking on lesbian identity was one more irrevocable step toward the fringes of Israeli society and, finally, beyond. I experienced the summer of 1977 as renewal and recommitment to radical feminism. It was the beginning of four years of intense activism and grassroots organizing. Only now, more than a decade later, do I know that each day, each hour, brought me closer to *yeridah*.

◄●►

One morning late in the summer, the usually empty mailbox contained a letter. A woman from Canterbury was on her way to Israel and wished to meet with me. She was one of the founders of a shelter for battered women, she wrote.

It was Judy Hill I had talked to about organizing the first consciousness-raising group. It was Judy I had called to organize women in Haifa for the Women's Party, and it was with Judy I discussed post-election plans. There was money in the Women's Aid Fund, almost half a million pounds. How to spend it?

I called Judy. "I'm feeling strong again," I told her, "and ready to work. Do you want to open a shelter for battered women? There's a woman from Canterbury who can teach us how."

Judy agreed. So did Cholit, and Judy recruited two others, Joyce Livingston and Barbara Swirksi. We were all *Anglo-Saxiot*, three from America, one from South Africa, and one from Scotland, but we'd all been in Israel for a long time. All but Barbara had been active in the women's movement since the early seventies.

We rented a second-floor apartment, five large rooms over a daycare center in a working-class neighborhood in Hadar. We organized a support group from within the Haifa movement. We canvassed Haifa for secondhand chairs, tables, beds, mattresses, dishes, linens. We rented a small truck and drove around the city, collecting musty old furniture from dank basements. *G'dud hanashim,* the Women's Brigade, someone called us as she watched us empty her basement of old iron cots and thin old mattresses that had been her family's beds in the days when these were the only beds available in Palestine. Determined to do it alone, to keep the location of the shelter a secret from all but a few women, we collected the furniture and carried it, including a refrigerator, up the narrow, winding flight of stairs to the apartment-shelter. We cleaned and polished and fumigated. We decorated the walls with militant feminist posters. We found a lawyer, Nomi Gondos, and a doctor, Isa Sarid, who volunteered their services. We located a gynecologist who agreed to do cut-rate abortions. We read and taught one another all we could about battery and rape as we tried to develop skills in counseling. We discussed the differences between what we were doing and social work endlessly, extrapolating from the feminist underpinnings of the project what its purpose was and how the shelter ought to be run. When we thought we were ready, we invited the press to the still-empty shelter and told the world what we proposed to do.

The next day's papers carried the story of a strange new *mo'adon,* a club for women escaping from family violence, called Women for Women, *Nashim l'man Nashim.* The address was secret, the papers reported, but the phone number was published in headlines. The phone rang constantly those first few days. Within a month, the shelter was full.

Among the first was Tzilla, who came to us straight from the hospital, the eye she'd almost lost still bandaged. Tamar who came with four small babies. Sarah, a kibbutznik whose husband had tried to kill her. Carmella, with twenty stitches in her scalp, ominously certain she would never escape her husband's death threats. Shula, mother of five, who pulled up her sweater to show us her chest and back covered with knife wounds and cigarette burns.

All these women came because they were sure that the next beating would be their last. They came because they feared death and because there was no place else to go. This apartment in Haifa, they all said, was their last stop. No, we said, you will move on from here to live again. We were right about most of the women. We were wrong about Carmella.

In the evenings, when the last child was put to bed, the women gathered in the small space we kept as a living room to talk late into the night. Depressed and anxious, each was sure that hers was the most harrowing experience. The transition from depression to anger was negotiated during those evening discussions and their uncanny repetition of details.

Tzilla, blonde and fair-skinned, told a tale of premarital bliss, a fiance who promised to bring her flowers every day of their lives, who treated her like a princess, a fragile, cherished blossom. Tamar nodded. "The night of our wedding, he ripped my dress to shreds, beat me up, and raped me. He said the dress was too beautiful for me. He said I thought too much of myself."

Others joined in.

—"My husband stripped me naked and threw me out of the house. I spent the night hiding under the stairs until he let me back in in the morning."

—"My husband tore off my clothes in front of his whole family. I was wearing a low-cut dress. He said that if I didn't have any modesty, I didn't need to wear anything at all."

—"He put a lock on the telephone so I couldn't call anyone. Then he locked the door so I couldn't leave. Sometimes, he tied me to the bed before he left the house in the morning."

—"He refused to let me see my friends, my mother, my sisters."

—"He said he would cut me off from everyone, that no one could help me."

—"My son and I sat through meals afraid to say anything, afraid to lift our heads, afraid we would annoy him. But it didn't matter. He always found something. The food wasn't hot enough, it wasn't spiced right."

—"Every meal ended with a beating. My children watched it all."

—"He said I was his slave."

—"I tried to run away twice. He found me each time. He threatened to kill me. Even when I tried to kill myself and wound up in the hospital, he came after me. I wanted to die, but I was terrified that he would kill me. He found me in the hospital. He had a knife and attacked me in the bed. He said I would die all right, but only when he said so."

—"The police told me I was crazy. We lived in a small town. They know my husband. They like him."

—"He didn't seem like a violent man. They thought I was crazy at the police station."

—"I went to the hospital with a broken nose. The doctor thought he was joking when he asked if I'd had an argument with my husband."

—"Whenever I was pregnant, he punched and kicked me in the stomach. He wanted to have the babies, would have killed me if I had an abortion. But he seemed to hate me most when I was pregnant."

—"He says that men are masters and women are slaves."

—"He wants me to behave like a well-trained dog, and I'm so afraid of him, I do."

"It's as if we're all married to the same man," Tzilla said.

New women arrived almost every day. Not all stayed. Middle-class women looked at the iron cots, the toilet that could never be kept clean, the mostly Sephardic faces, and left. They took with them the knowledge that their "problem" was a common one, the name of our lawyer, and our suggestion that they empty the joint bank account and load the contents of their home on a truck before walking out.

We developed a routine. One of us sat for hours in the kitchen over coffee or tea with each arrival and listened to her story. The retellings were always new. Always, there was some twist, some deepening of our understanding of woman-hatred. Rage, ours and eventually theirs, filled and fueled the shelter.

Mazal came the first time in the early morning, just after sunrise. She looked old, in her seventies, I thought. She was extremely thin, almost skeletal. Her white hair hung limply, uncombed, down to her shoulders. Most of her teeth were missing. Both her arms and several fingers on one hand were broken. It had happened the night before. She had been beaten every weekend since the day she married, she said. But now her older sons joined in the beatings. Her sons were soldiers. She dreaded when they came home on leave. Last night, the husband and two of the sons had broken her bones. She couldn't stay, she said, because she was worried about the younger children she left behind, ages five and six.

"How old are you?" I asked, unable to make my arithmetic compute.

"Forty-two," she said.

"You're only two years older than me," I almost shouted, knowing that I'd made a terrible mistake as soon as the words were out.

She slumped more deeply into the chair, defeated. "*Kapora!*" she shouted, "Forgive me," the cry of orthodox Jews on Yom Kippur as they swing a chicken over their heads in symbolic sacrifice to God. Mazal believed that her life was God's punishment for some unknown, unforgivable sin.

Mazal came for a few days every few months, usually just before another of her many futile appearances in rabbinical court. Cholit and I went with her. Each time, her husband showed up accompanied by the older sons. Each time, the sons tried to get at their mother, fists raised to strike. Each time, Cholit and I interposed our bodies between the sons and the mother, and the fists pulled back. Hitting us, they knew, was a punishable crime. Mazal never got her divorce and never learned to fight back.

Part of the "routine" was to explain the rules to new women. They were used to this, people telling them what they could and couldn't do. Hearing what the rules were, they stared in amazement. You can stay as long as you want. You can leave at any time and come back whenever you need to. You don't have to see or speak to your husband if you don't want to, and if you do, we will protect you during the visit. You can do whatever you like while you're here, but we advise you to go out in groups of at least three, for protection, or, in the worst case, as witnesses. If you don't take your children with you when you go out, make sure someone has agreed to watch them. That's all. Everything else is up to you.

The women made their own arrangements for communal living, a set of ever-changing rules agreed upon at a weekly house meeting. In cramped quarters, under stress and in recovery, the women had many disagreements. The house meeting was the forum for conflict resolution. Though one of us was always present as facilitator, we imposed ourselves only once, after one of the women beat her child so severely we had to call in Isa Sarid, our doctor. No violence, we said. Anyone who hits her child or another woman will have to leave. The children, liberated from the only discipline most had ever known, ran wild, and for many weeks the house meetings were dominated by discussions of alternative modes of discipline.

We had parties regularly, often to celebrate a divorce. Nomi Gondos, our lawyer, was a patient and crafty advocate in the rabbinical courts. Under Jewish law, husbands are obligated to their wives' support so long as they remained married. "Come to Hillel Street and see the shelter," she invited the black-bearded judges. "No one would stay there if they didn't have to. If you force these women to go home, one of them will be killed eventually. There will be blood on your hands."

The Haifa rabbinical court set a precedent when it accepted Nomi's argument and ordered husbands to mail monthly support checks to the shelter's post office box. For the first time, a wife's right to leave her violent husband was acknowledged, as was her right to take her children with her. It was a form of legal separation that held up even after the women left the shelter. Nomi succeeded in getting divorces for most of the women that wanted them. If the husbands couldn't force their wives to return home by order of the court, if it cost them money to remain married to a woman who could no longer be beaten and raped, they usually gave in and agreed to divorce, on condition that the wife give up her claim to support. "Do it," Nomi urged. "They don't know it, but you can always go back to court next year and reopen the case for child support."

Mostly the husbands responded with rage, but occasionally with genuine puzzlement that anyone thought there was something wrong with their behavior. "But she belongs to me," one said, a sweet-looking young man whom I remember for his yellow shirt. "Just like this shirt. It's mine, and I can do anything I want with it."

Husbands tried to break in. Some succeeded. One night, one of them dragged his wife out with him. When we got the call in the middle of the night, Cholit and I dressed quickly and drove to his home in Tira, a poor development town just outside Haifa. We called the police before we left, but we were first to arrive. "What do we do now?" I asked when we found the house, lights on. "We get inside somehow," Cholit said. She looked fierce, her black eyes shining in the night, her thick, kinky black hair hanging down to her waist, a bushy growth that inspired courage. The husband, surprised to hear his doorbell ring at one in the morning, opened the door immediately. We pushed past him. He first, then we, realized that once inside, it was all over. His private kingdom was now public space. Even before the police arrived, we were helping Smadar fill suitcases with her belongings as her husband, suddenly helpless in the face of three determined women, watched wordlessly.

Not all who came to the shelter were beaten by their husbands or lovers. Some, still teen-agers, were beaten by their fathers. One of them, perhaps seventeen or eighteen, was pregnant. She wanted an abortion, she said, but her father, who threatened to kill her for being pregnant, also threatened to kill her if she had an abortion.

We arranged for the abortion and asked both parents to meet with us at the shelter. The mother's face was a rock, a carving in flesh. Her mouth was grim, her eyes small and hard. Throughout the whole interview, four hours at least, she said not one word. She did not look once at her daughter. The father did all the talking. He threatened to take us to court for operating a brothel. "All these women are zonot, whores," he said, sweeping his hand in an arc to include us all. "Especially her," his daughter. The mother looked stonily at the air. "She can't live without sex, she needs it all the time. You won't be able to keep her here if she can't have sex." The mother's eyes shifted to the floor. The father ranted about his sexual fantasies of his daughter, the pregnant daughter looked at her father with contempt, the silent mother so terrorized that she could neither make eye contact with anyone or utter a word. We didn't understand what we saw and heard. It would be many more years before we knew anything about incest, before we could suspect that the battered, pregnant teen-ager bore her father's child.

Invariably, women came to the shelter depressed, frightened, agonizing over what had happened to them, usually blaming themselves. We taught them anger. We taught them to stand by one another. We taught them self-defense. We taught them to fight back. During that first year, seven out of ten women left the shelter newly independent, healed and ready to begin their lives as single women. Some of them remained close to the shelter, as volunteers or paid staff.

Men were awed by the fact of the shelter, but they also hated the women who ran it, especially me, the famous one. I received anonymous letters weekly, some threatening death. The phone rang in the middle of the night. Male voices delivered dire messages. Mostly, Jenny and I learned to live with it. Whenever Jenny answered, she spoke at length, patiently trying to convince them to change their ways. But sometimes there was something in the voice that was too ominous, and at those times we slept at the Pragers.

For several months, there was a price on my head. One of the women in the shelter, a prostitute, warned me to be careful. Her procurer terrorized me. Every night, at 2:00 a.m., the phone rang. A deep male voice threatened to harm Jenny if he didn't get his wife back. Two men banged on the door one night, shouting my name. They ran away when Leonard Prager came out of the apartment next door. A few days later there was a break-in. I got a dog who learned to snarl at strange men. I got some iron bars and kept them next to my bed and beside the front door. I lived like that for the next six months, until I finally gave up and decided to sell the apartment. My home of ten years, all the time I'd been in Israel, was poisoned by terror, and I began to hate it.

My life was filled with violence and rage. I walked the streets alert to danger, watchful, my hands balled into fists ready to fight. Like the tomboy I'd been, I felt no fear at those moments, only a chip on my shoulder, daring anyone to try. Once, standing with

Judy on the sidewalk in front of my house, I glimpsed a man approaching around the corner. My body tensed with expectation, I felt him bump into me as he passed. Still not looking at him, I threw my elbow into his chest and knocked him down. "Marcia, what are you doing?" Judy screamed. At my feet was a frail old man protecting his face as he looked up at me, puzzled and afraid.

"The octopus," Judy called the shelter. No matter how much we tried to control its demands on us, we were overwhelmed by the needs. A husband trying to break in or stalking the streets; someone's child kidnapped; a new arrival; fights among the women or the children; hundreds of trips to the rabbinical courts, the civil courts, the police; endless phone calls to the welfare agencies and social services, again and again explaining, arguing, confronting, listening, giving our energy to the survivors and being drained in the process.

One precedent at a time, we established a network of police protection, financial support, medical and social services, school for the children, even recognition by the rabbinical courts that the women were not to be sent home against their will. We established second-stage housing where two or three women and their children lived together. The success stories added up. A few women returned home to reformed husbands. Many succeeded in getting divorces. Some, unable to divorce but permitted by the court to live independently, made new lives for themselves though they would never be able to remarry. By the end of the first year, we were accepted in Israel as a vital social service; the policies and precedents we had established became models for others. Ruth Resnik announced plans to open a second shelter in Herzliya, a suburb of Tel Aviv. Later, WIZO opened a shelter in Beersheva, and a group of women unknown to us until then opened a fourth shelter in Jerusalem.

The money in the Women's Aid Fund was almost gone. The shelter needed government support or it would have to close. We lobbied, harassed, and threatened the Welfare Ministry and the Haifa municipality for funding and a permanent home. When they ignored us, we brought the women into the struggle. They agreed to talk to the media. Some wanted their names, faces, and voices disguised. Others, knowing that public awareness of their abuse was the ultimate weapon against the men who terrorized them, insisted on being identified. For months, these women told their stories to the country. They put names, faces, and repetitious detail behind the "problem" of battered women.

The media carried these stories sensationally, week after week. Israel was shocked and ashamed. The Welfare Ministry began to talk about a possible budget of a million pounds a year for the shelter. Enough to replace volunteers with staff, to move to larger quarters, to know securely from day to day and year to year that there was a future.

But there were strings. There are two sides to every story, the officials said. You can't just take the woman's word for things. You're breaking up families. You have to try to save these marriages, make the husbands understand, encourage the women to give them a second chance.

Our conflict with the authorities was unavoidable. For us, the shelter was not social work but political action. We were not interested in protecting the institution of marriage. The government balked. It would give us money if we took the pictures of raised fists off the walls, if we agreed to bring in their social workers to run things. We refused and told the women that we might have to close down. "We'll never leave here, even if you do," Tzilla said. "If we can't pay the rent, we'll camp out on the sidewalk."

We struggled with the officials for months, insisting on having the money on our own terms. Anything short of that, we knew, was failure. Meanwhile, we looked for a new home. The building we found was in Wadi Nisnas, the Arab quarter of the city. There were three empty stories badly in need of rehab. No sign indicated who owned it. Through the Land Registry, we learned that the owner was Na'amat, formerly the Council of Working Women, the women's arm of the Histadrut. We were jubilant. Surely, we thought, Na'amat will let us use their building. Not so.

Na'amat has a checkered history of women's rights. It was founded in 1922 by Ada Maimon, a militant feminist, its mission to agitate for equality within the Labor movement. Ten years later, under the leadership of Golda Meir, it became a ladies auxiliary through which a few chosen women could rise to prominence in Labor politics. Once the story of battered women broke, Na'amat rushed to express sympathy for the shelter and outrage in the name of women, but refused to give us the building. They refused even to allow us to rent it. "The building is for sale," said Nava Arad, then president and soon to be a Member of Knesset. For a million pounds, she added. Carefully groomed, her hair pulled severely back from her face, Arad was all business.

One night we loaded our cars with mattresses, women, and children and broke into the closed building and squatted there. Television cameras filmed the action. Once again the faces of battered women filled the media. The government gave in and agreed to all our terms. It provided a budget and bought the building from Na'amat.

Judy tired first. She wanted to leave the collective in order to finish her dissertation. Cholit was planning to return to the United States. I, too, couldn't last much longer, feeling so angry and becoming depleted. The five of us had worked well together, but once the publicity for the shelter became frequent and intense, friction and power issues began to surface. The media, knowing my name alone among this group of five, gave all the credit for the shelter to me. The government officials we dealt with knew me and tended to ignore the other women when we met together. Cholit, Barbara, and Joyce complained about not being acknowledged and subtly, at first, blamed me. The inevitable trashing was on its way, and I wanted out.

The collective, strained by jealousy and fatigue, came apart. First Judy, then I, then Cholit left. One of the last decisions we made as a group was that Carmella Nakash would have to leave. It was the first time we violated our own cardinal rule—that we did not make decisions for the women, did not presume to know what was good for them, and did not limit their stay at the shelter. Carmella had been at the shelter for almost a year. Her husband would murder her if she left, she said. But during that year, there had been no sign of the husband, not even a phone call. Worried that Carmella had found herself a womb—a noisy, crowded and none-too-clean womb—we agreed that it was right to make her move on.

Carmella left, but only to move to the shelter in Herzliya. There, one evening, her husband showed up, walked through the unsecured gate, and asked to see her. Carmella didn't have to go out, but she did. She walked out to meet the fate that she had predicted all along. Without words between them, her husband took a knife from his pocket and stabbed her to death.

Attending Carmella's funeral was my last act of direct involvement with battered women.

Several years later, fundraising for the shelter in New York, I described the problem and the shelter to a group of potential supporters gathered in a spacious Fifth Avenue apartment. "Shelters are only a bandaid," Betty Friedan insisted. Remembering Carmella, I thought that sometimes they were even less than a bandaid. Was she right? Is the shelter movement a fruitless deviation from revolutionary politics? Thinking about the few hundred Israeli women we'd helped compared to the hundred thousand women estimated to be battered, it was easy enough to agree with Friedan. Except for one important point. The shelters, like rape crisis centers, bear witness. They serve only the few, but they speak for the many. So long as they exist, the raw and brutal facts of violence against women cannot be denied. The Israeli Knesset would never again laugh about wife abuse.

Chapter 10
Lesbian in the Promised Land
◄●►

Cholit and I sat on either side of Sarah in a dimly lit, dirty corridor outside the single courtroom in which the three *dayanim*, the rabbinical judges, heard cases. The corridor was filled with miserable women and men sitting silently apart from one another on opposite sides of the room. Black-coated bearded men wearing small black silk *kipot* walked back and forth between the courtroom and the other rooms. One of them, Nomi Gondos told us, was the scribe, the one who wrote the *get*, the writ of divorcement, in magnificent Hebrew caligraphy. We were a long way from a *get*. This was the first of many times we accompanied Sarah to rabbinical court, trying to convince a nervous, irate husband to give her her freedom and allow her to keep her son. Cholit and I, together with four or five women from the shelter, were there to protect Sarah. Her husband, unlike many others, felt no inhibition about beating her up in public.

Sarah's husband and another man who came with him sat across from us, glaring. Cholit glared back. He wasn't big or particularly muscular, but his lean, wiry body and the glint of malice in his eyes reminded me of a coiled snake ready to spring. "I hear you teach my wife karate," he said to Cholit. "Come on, show me what you can do." The two men stood up and took a step toward us across the narrow corridor, daring us to accept the challenge. My tomboy past resurfaced. Though I had lost every fight to Stanley Karras, I always ached to take him on, perhaps just once to win. Without looking at one another for confirmation, Cholit and I rose and stepped forward. There were only a few feet between us. The two men looked at one another, confused, not knowing what to do next. They had only meant to threaten. They backed off and sat down. We smiled our victory. Frustrated, looking for the most vile thing he could say to us, the husband hissed, "Do you know what you two are? You're *lesbiot!* Do you know what that means?"

We couldn't control the laughter that pierced the somber silence of the rabbinical court. "Yes, in fact we do," Cholit said, as we hugged one another.

There is no Hebrew language for homosexuality. The Old Testament prohibits sodomy in the same breath as bestiality (as did Israeli law until recently). But neither Jewish law nor sacred literature ever mentions love between women. The only Biblical reference to homosexual love is David's words to Jonathan: "*Tzar li aleicha, Yonatan, na'amta li m'od,*" "I am distressed for you, Jonathan; you have given me much pleasure."

Israeli lesbians coined a word for male and female homosexuals, *na'imim* and *na'imot,* based on David's words. It never caught on. Those who give pleasure is not Israel's idea of homosexuals.

◄●►

I was not out during my years in office, not publicly and not to myself. There were rumors, but I was protected by my relationship with Avi. I told myself, during those years, that I didn't identify as a lesbian because I was not yet sure I was one. But it was fear that limited my relationships with women to brief experiments. The lesbian community was very small then, a few dozen women scattered over three cities. It was a scared, often self-hating, and mostly prefeminist community. The straight feminists were frightened by lesbianism. Although I was out of touch with homophobia, and naive about what it could mean to my life, I sensed that I walked a thin line and that coming out would have significant consequences.

During the summer following the 1977 elections, as the life came back into my body, the sexual frigidity that had so unexpectedly become a habit during the last year of my term gave way. And when it did, I discovered that I was no longer interested in men. Only a few months out of office, I found myself hungering for women, and soon after, a particular woman—Cholit.

Her name had been Sandy Klein when she first came to Israel ten years earlier. She Hebraicized it to Cholit Bat Idit. Cholit from the Hebrew word *chol*, sand. *Bat Idit*, daughter of Edith. Cholit was neither a word nor a name in Hebrew before Cholit introduced it. In language and in life, Cholit made her own rules.

When we first fell in love, she was still Bill's lover. They practically lived together, but on those Fridays when Jenny was with Bill and Cholit was on her own, she invited me to dinner to confide her difficulties in the relationship. In this, she was not unlike others of Bill's lovers, often drawn from the ranks of the women's movement. They had a strange need to be my friend and to make me a confidant of their relationship with the father of my child. At first I accepted Cholit's invitations because I was lonely with Jenny away. It was nice to have someone cook a good meal for me. But soon it was more. When her relationship with Bill broke up, I was there.

I was fascinated by Cholit's resistance to the constraints of civilization. She was bawdy, volatile, capable of anger so fierce people were afraid of her. Her thick black hair hung half way down her back. Her body was covered by soft black down. Her breasts were pendulous and large. She wore no bra, and when she walked, they flowed and rippled through the cloth of her shirt.

Cholit made much of her sexual exploits and acrobatics. Along with her temper, they were legendary. Cholit created the legends.

"Oh, Cholit," people would say, as if that were enough to explain her actions. Cholit embodied things elemental and took pride in exaggerating them. She lived alert to possible danger, and, like a siren, she drew it to her. Obscene phone calls, garbage at her doorstep, vandals were commonplaces of her life.

Lusting after Cholit, I understood that it was time to accept myself as a lesbian and stepped over a very fine, almost invisible line to the other side of the sexual tracks. Fear and guilt went with me. As enlightened as I thought I was, as happily in love as I thought I was, the word *pervert* whispered to me.

Separately and together, Cholit and I had many friends in Haifa. Slowly, during the six months our relationship lasted, we began to draw away from them, alienated in the married heterosexual circles where we had always been at home. We could not talk about our relationship with our friends. We were on guard about giving ourselves away. For us, everything was changing, but it was a change we couldn't share with anyone.

Cholit and I gravitated toward the small lesbian community in Haifa. It was the one place we could be together publicly without hiding that we were together. But the closeted community depressed us both. The women were secretive about their lesbianism. At parties, the windows were shuttered to protect against the prying eyes of neighbors. One couple lived behind permanently shuttered windows. Many had families in Haifa. Israel is a small and gossipy country. If you don't come out to your family, you don't come out at all. Within their families, these lesbian daughters —acknowledged as daughters but not as lesbians—are a misfortune. Where women are encouraged to marry young and have three and four children, the lesbian daughters do not marry, they do not have children. They are strange and estranged creatures in a society that knows no generation gap, where the values of family and state are informed by the Holocaust and war.

Cholit and I heard about what seemed impossible fantasies of gay communities in New York and San Francisco, a dynamic culture with its own theater, art, music, poetry. Forty thousand women in the Bay Area alone, Cholit said. She would leave at the end of the year. And I? Again that question. Could a former Member of Knesset be a *yoredet?* Could I descend from this high place that was Israel? It was unthinkable, but unthinkable, too, that I could remain there a closeted lesbian. I was too well-known. My life was a goldfish bowl. The country would eventually find me out and drive me away, I knew that. But until it did, I had to stay. When Cholit left, I wrote in my journal what seemed to be prophecy a year later, but was perhaps only a rationalization of necessity: "The new year will bring a new lover and a new life. Something tells me to stay."

The new lover was Ayala, the new life a committed relationship, building a home together, and building together a larger, more open community of lesbians.

I knew Ayala for several years before we became lovers, and I knew her history, a history like that of many Israeli lesbians. She knew she was a lesbian at the age of twelve. All through high school, she played basketball and pursued women. Gradually, she learned to think of herself as an accident of nature. Her hygiene teacher asked her to leave the classroom during the lesson on menstruation. It is for girls only, she said. Ayala grew up in a small village—a few dozen two-room houses and a *dunam* of land on which to raise chickens. She ate the chickens her mother raised every day of her life.

By the age of nine, Ayala could ride a motorcycle. By sixteen, she could build a house. At twenty, she learned the word for herself, *lesbit,* from a magazine article on sex-change operations. It was the first time she'd heard it. The article confirmed her suspicion that she was born by mistake, a perversion of nature. Later, as a student, she consulted the library. Books on homosexuality were all on the psychology shelves. Ayala learned that she had a disease but that "intelligent lesbians" are the hardest of all to cure. Ayala learned that there are intelligent lesbians.

There was no Greenwich Village to escape to, no gay bars, nowhere to meet others like herself. Nothing at all in the environment offered validation. So she married and tried to cure herself by bearing children, each one marking the end of an unsatisfying affair with a straight woman. She expressed her difference from other Israeli women only by a doctorate in mathematics, thanks to which she landed a postdoctoral fellowship in America in 1974. There she learned about gay rights, lesbian feminism, and the flowering of a culture of open, proud homosexuality.

Ayala was active in the Women's Party, and occasionally she and her lover came to Haifa to visit. When that relationship ended in 1978, she came to visit alone. By then my sexual identity was confirmed. She knew and, more importantly, I knew. I was drawn to this butch woman who wore her jeans low on her hips, whose voice was deep, who was sometimes mistaken for a man, who was a scientist and understood electricity and electronics, things that had always seemed so mysterious. She came to dinner on Friday the thirteenth, along with eight other women, to celebrate a witches sabbath.

We ate in the living room, sitting and then lying on cushions on the floor. We passed sweets from mouth to mouth, drank a lot of wine. It was winter, and we huddled around the kerosene heater. Consciously rejecting the God of our fathers, we were trying to create our own rituals. I lit a candle to welcome the Sabbath Bride. We called her Ashtoret, the Caananite Goddess who, the Bible says, was worshipped by Solomon in the Temple at Jerusalem. I placed my hands over the candle, thumbs and forefingers together. The silhouette on the ceiling was a graceful vulva, flickering in the rhythms of the candle's flame. We all watched the shadow dance on the ceiling. Everyone saw the shadow of Ayala's hand, approaching and then stroking the shadow vulva. She made love to me for the first time there on the ceiling, openly and unashamed, as the others watched in fascination.

It was a wildly passionate falling in love, ecstatic with the spirit of pagan sexuality we'd conjured. Ayala lived fifty miles from Haifa. We spent hours on the road just for the pleasure of as many hours together. I could not imagine ever wanting to make love to a man again.

I was too happy and too certain that I'd found the love of my life to keep it a secret. I wrote to my mother and sister-in-law in

New Jersey. "I've fallen in love with a wonderful woman," I wrote. "I am a lesbian and I couldn't be happier." After a long wait, my sister-in-law answered. My mother, she said, was "extremely upset." She felt guilty, trying to figure out what she'd done wrong. She was nauseated by the thought of women in bed together. She was angry that I'd stigmatized her. Jewish girls are not supposed to do such things. My brother wrote to me. He, too, was angry, he said, because I wrote to his wife but not to him. He believed that I now hated men, including him. It would be many years explaining to my brother that I loved him very much, that there were other men that I cared for. It was many years, too, explaining to my mother that lesbianism is not a perversion, demanding that my relationships be honored by the family, and assuring her that she has nothing to feel guilty about.

Ayala and I decided to live together in Haifa. The only women in the lesbian community over forty, both mothers, both professionals, we believed that our fates had conspired to bring us together at this time and in this place. The home we moved into contributed to the fantasy that we wove around our romance. It was a large house, faced with roughly carved stone and roofed with red tile, an architectural landmark built a hundred years earlier. It had towers, turrets, terraces, and balconies looking out over Haifa Bay. On a clear day we could see as far as Lebanon. Orange and pomegranate trees grew in the wild, untended garden. *Esquadinias*, loquats, grew outside my bedroom window. Late at night I sat on the broad marble windowsill of that bedroom, watching the lights twinkle around the bay, the French windows framing the view that filtered through the *esquadinia* tree. Inside, the house had fifteen-foot ceilings, walls a foot thick, carved wooden doors five-feet across, bay windows, an enclosed sun porch. The rooms were so large that with partitions and lofts, we all had separate bedrooms—Ayala, myself, Jenny, and Ayala's children. It was a house made for gracious living.

In that home for the first year our love was larger than life. We were part of the Middle East—the sights and sounds of modern Israel reduced to the twinkling lights of Haifa Bay at night and

the magnificent view of the city by day. Our view was a favorite
subject of picture postcards bought by tourists. Lying on the terrace, nude under the bright sun, I felt more connected than ever
to this land. At sunset we watched the birds leave the thicket of
trees around us to fly out for their last swing over the bay before
settling in for the night. On that terrace in the evenings we had
our family dinners, and we entertained guests in small groups and
large parties, all women, who came to enjoy the gracious beauty
around them and associate it with what my mother correctly correctly, but for her euphemistically, called my lifestyle.

Our home and our love seemed mythical to others as well as
to ourselves. Women came to visit just to see what it all looked
like, or to take encouragement from this lesbian marriage. Terry
and Nurit, two young kibbutz wives, one a mother, visited often,
drawing support for their decision to divorce, to leave the kibbutz,
and to live together in Jerusalem.

◄●►

It was Ayala's idea that we open a bookstore and women's center in Haifa. She joked about calling it The Closet and hanging
books on hangers in the windows. She thought of the center as
a way of bringing lesbianism out of the closet. I thought about
how reading feminist literature had changed my life. I agreed to
open the store with her.

The first book on feminism in Hebrew appeared in the early
1970s, *Shichrur Ha'isha, Women's Liberation*, by Tchya Bat Oren.
She was well-known among Israeli women. In the 1960s she wrote
books and had a radio program that focused on traditional
homemakers. She told them how to clean blackened pots, how
to keep ants out of the kitchen, how to keep their husbands happy.
In 1971, Bat Oren went through a contested divorce. To win her
freedom, she had to give up her son and all of her property, including the royalties on her books. Impoverished and an outcast,
Tchya discovered the women's movement. Under Shoshana Eilings' tutelage, she wrote an angry but moderate book on feminist
theory. The reviews were scathing, the interviews that blitzed the

women's pages cruel. They said little about the book, much about the author's failure as a wife and mother, all meant to explain how a respectable woman like Tchya Bat Oren had been led astray by feminism. She never wrote again.

The second feminist book to appear in Hebrew was an anthology of translations by American writers published by a fledgling feminist press, The Second Sex. With no capital, two Tel Aviv women did everything themselves—translation, publication, and distribution. They were able to produce a book every year or two, and by 1978, they had three titles. In addition, a commercial publisher put out a Hebrew edition of The Hite Report. That was all there was.

My life had changed because of books a decade earlier. Since then, whenever I made a trip to America or England, I went straight to the women's bookstores to buy the books I wanted to read and then pass on to others. Whatever the subject matter, these books moved quickly from hand to hand. There was tremendous hunger among Israeli feminists for the kind of knowledge and validation that literature from the outside world provided. Even while the shelter was in the planning stages, I had started a small nonprofit mail-order book business, Woman's Voice. As a legitimate bookseller, I was entitled not only to the usual discount, but also had access to the dusty stockrooms of Israel's English-language book distributors. I had traveled to Tel Aviv once a month to comb the shelves in search of feminist literature and to buy up all available copies of the ten or twenty titles I was able to find there. They sold quickly.

Ayala and I traveled to America for a crash course in the book business. With my brother's guarantee of our credit, we ordered ten thousand dollars worth of books to be shipped to Haifa. We returned, found a site, and opened our bookstore two months later.

When we realized we could not afford an actual store in the Mercaz, we decided to rent an apartment, the second floor of an old stone house owned by an older woman who had been active in WIZO. She'd raised her children in this house when there was nothing around her but fields of wildflowers. By the time we came along, the Mercaz had expanded to surround her home and the second floor was for rent as office space. She was glad to have us as tenants.

Not by design, Woman's Voice became a women's center as well as a bookstore. We had only enough books to fill one room. Another became a library and reading room, and a place where women could gather informally, have a cup of coffee and shmooze. A third was furnished as an office where Nomi Gondos, Isa Sarid, and Shoshana Eilings dispensed legal aid, medical advice, and feminist therapy. One room, furnished with pillows and mattresses covered in bright cloth, was given over to meetings and groups. Another became the classroom in which Ayala taught self-defense and electrical maintenance. I facilitated several CR groups a week.

Hundreds of women made their way up the narrow flight of stairs leading to the center on opening night. Rachel Kagan, then ninety, walked the five miles from her home to give it her blessings. The room housing the bookstore was lined with shelves, all neatly labeled in Hebrew and English. Women's Fiction, Women's Poetry, Sociology of Women, Psychology of Women, Women Artists, Women's Science Fiction. There was more women's literature available in this one room than in the entire country. Of all the little signs, there was one that women either rushed by very quickly or lingered near overlong. It said Lesbian Literature. Never before in Israel had the word *lesbian* been writ large and clear. That there was an entire genre of literature so labeled took women, straight and gay, a long time to integrate.

We began a regular Friday evening coffeehouse and held monthly events where women whose work was largely unrecognized in the larger society had, for the first time, a growing audience. Woman's Voice created a women's community in Haifa, a community in which lesbians and straight women felt comfortable, where women's curiosity about feminism could be satisfied, where women could get help when they needed it, and where women could safely explore and proclaim lesbian identity.

Once a month, Ayala and I took all the books from the shelves, packed them in cartons, loaded them into the car, and drove to kibbutzim and campuses where we set up book fairs on the lawn. At the end of the day, we packed the books into their cartons, brought them back to the center, and replaced them on the shelves. It took months to get books from America to replace the ones we sold, so we continued to comb through the musty warehouses of Israeli distributors. Since they did not deliver, we loaded the car with cartons of books, carried them up the stairs, inventoried them, and put them out on the shelves and tables. It was an enormous amount of work, but we knew that books were the key to disseminating the feminist message in Israel. We did it joyfully, counting the receipts at the end of the day, but thinking much more of the numbers of books we'd gotten into women's hands.

A year later, a few women decided to open a women's bookstore in Tel Aviv. We divided our stock and gave them half of what we had. Then Nurit and Terry moved to Jerusalem and opened Woman's Voice there. We divided the stock once more. There were three women's centers in Israel in the late seventies and early eighties, and a growing feminist and lesbian feminist community in each of the three major cities.

The women's centers were magnets for women wanting to find out about or get involved in the women's movement. The bookstore, in particular, provided nonthreatening and noncommittal access. One didn't actually have to be a feminist to browse in a bookstore. Curiosity was enough of a motivation. Buying books allowed women to make contact with the movement while still feeling safe. Once in the door, it was possible to meet other feminists and discover that we were not the monsters the press usually depicted. It was possible to find out about the CR groups, classes, and lectures, and then perhaps to attend one. It was possible to discover what else was going on in the movement and volunteer to help in the rape crisis centers or shelters. The centers, I believe, and particularly the bookstores that fronted them, made feminism possible for the large mass of educated middle-class women who had been taught to be afraid of the women's movement.

They also provided a natural habitat for lesbians. For many who came to the centers because they were women's centers, it was their first encounter with feminism. Woman's Voice encouraged a growing lesbian feminist movement not only by providing the space for lesbians to discover feminism, but also by providing a space for heretofore straight feminists to discover lesbianism. We brought lesbianism out of the closet, and the lesbian community changed remarkably during those years. It became joyful, proud, energetic, and, within the constraints of Israeli homophobia, open. Ayala and I, Terry and Nurit—as yet the only out lesbians—were joined by increasing numbers of lesbian women who did not hide behind a facade and were not afraid to be active publicly.

There was, during that first year at least, great joy in the community. Unlike the society around us, it was life-affirming, radical, creative. I felt once again, as I had when living with Nomi, that we were pioneers of a revolution in lifestyle, this time for lesbian feminists, but also for all women searching for an alternative way of being in the world. Once again, life was a political action.

◄●►

The Jerusalem *hammam*, the public bathhouse, was a remnant of an older, more primitive society, in which a public place to bathe was a necessity. When I was first introduced to the *hammam*, by Cholit of course, it was mostly populated by older Sephardic women for whom gathering at the public bathhouse was a cherished tradition, a moment of privacy, self-indulgence, and rest from housework. We learned from them to scrub ourselves with loofa and cover our skin with a coat of henna. They washed off the henna playfully, throwing buckets of water at one another and giggling. We learned to bring soaps and oils and sit in a steamy bathing room on the stone banquettes that lined the walls. Basins were carved out of the stone at intervals. In the middle of the room were three raised marble slabs—hot, hotter, and hottest. When our bodies were clean, hennaed, and oiled, we lay down on the heated marble, calling now and then for someone to pour a bucket of cold water over our steaming bodies. All this we learned from the older women.

In another room was a hot pool large enough to stand in but

not swim, deep enough for the water to reach the chin. Five or
six women could fit in at one time, breasts floating on the hot
water. Next to it, to cool off, was a swimming pool. A third room,
my favorite, had a vaulted roof and was filled with icy water that
poured in through a large pipe high in one wall. One entered by
descending three steps into a roomful of cold water. In a fourth
room were more banquettes covered with Oriental rugs and soft
cushions. The only light came through a stained glass skylight in
the arched ceiling. There we ate grapes and mangoes while drying
off.

The *hammam* was one of the sexiest places around. Over the
years, it was discovered by the lesbian community who took over
the sunroof, the one place that the older women shunned. The
sunroof was formed from the vaulted ceilings of the *hammam*'s
rooms. In reverse, those ceilings formed the contours of a four-
breasted Aphrodite. The older Sephardic women laughed at our
white-skinned passion for the sun. As though sun-starved for generations, we lay exposed to the sun for hours, needing nothing more
than to warm ourselves, to darken our skin in the heat. We felt
most beautiful, most vital, when our skin turned brown. The lesbians draped their bodies ceremonially on and around those breasts
for hours at a time, oiled and gleaming. They were Jewish women,
mostly dark-haired and dark-skinned. With that much Middle Eastern sun, the bodies were very brown. The sunroof was whitewashed
and gleaming in the intense light of Jerusalem. Lying there, I felt
that we were not perverts, but celebrants.

◄●►

I came out to Jenny when I fell in love with Ayala. "Did you
think I didn't know about Cholit?" she asked. "Do you think I'm
blind?" her voice accused. She offered no blessing for my love of
Ayala, only rage. "It's bad enough you got divorced. It's bad enough
I have the only mother who goes to demonstrations where you're
practically the only one on the street shouting slogans no one un-
derstands. Everyone thinks you're crazy. Now I have to have a lesbian for a mother. I hate you. Why does it have to be you? Why

does it always have to be you? Why can't you just be an ordinary mother!" Overcome by guilt, by fear of losing her, I collapsed into the sofa, silently listening and crying. Is this what I am, what I have been to my daughter? A burden of shame? Am I going to lose my daughter because I'm happy loving a woman?

Her rage spent, she cried for hours. We both cried, huddled together on the sofa, apologizing, both of us pained by the pain we caused one another. I promised that as long as I lived in Israel, no matter what, I would never come out to the media. But I wouldn't give up the relationship. I wouldn't stop being a lesbian. And I wouldn't try to hide it from anyone but reporters. It would be hard for her, harder for her than for me, but I couldn't go back into the closet without poisoning the love I had just discovered. She understood that. "But how am I going to bring my friends home?" she asked, calmer. "They can't possibly understand."

She was right. There was a rumor spread by one of Jenny's teachers that we had orgies at the house and that Jenny participated. She was ostracized by her classmates. Only a few friends remained loyal. Like me, she was branded a pervert.

Though Jenny protected me from most of the abuse she suffered, finally she could live with it no longer. She was jealous of Ayala and angry about the possessive relationship we had with one another. She didn't get along with Ayala's children. She was ashamed to bring her friends home. She thought I didn't love her anymore.

Though our home was a fantasy, living together in it with our four children, aged five through thirteen, was a reality that eventually wore down our passion. The strain of the tense and angry relationships between the children, between the children and us, was ever-present. The children, each differently, remember these years as the worst of their lives. Their mothers, the lesbians that all Haifa was buzzing about, were self-absorbed and not really there for them.

The child who'd had to compete with a country for her mother's time thought she now had to compete with a woman for her mother's love. She believed she had lost it. One morning as I sat with Ayala, Judy, and some other friends at a sidewalk cafe, Jenny marched determinedly by. "I'm going to live with Daddy," she said, and on that day I lost my daughter.

Jenny left with her pain masked in anger, pain so great that I wasn't able to allow myself to acknowledge it for many months. I felt rejected and vaguely guilty, but I responded by rationalizing. It's a normal teen-age rebellion. Lots of kids run away from home. Thank the Goddess she has a safe place to run away to. Only when Jenny and I began meeting regularly once a week for *hummus* in Wadi Nisnas, and sat across the table from one another in tears, did I begin to understand what it was like to be Marcia Freedman's daughter. She'd endured it all, but lesbianism was the last straw.

We were reconciled three years later. It was in Berkeley, however, not Israel, when I was no longer with Ayala and Jenny lived in a place where having a homosexual parent was positively noteworthy, not a liability.

◄●►

In the early 1970s, a few gay men and women organized the Society for the Protection of Personal Rights. Its meetings and dances were, for many years, the only gathering place for gay men and women other than the one bar in Tel Aviv that catered to homosexuals. In 1975, the Society prevailed on Shulamit Aloni to introduce legislation decriminalizing homosexuality. Aloni sponsored the bill but made no effort to get Knesset support for it. During the months preceding the vote that doomed gay rights, I met frequently with SPPR activists, trying to persuade them to lobby the Knesset. Not one agreed. It meant coming out to Members of Knesset, and they were afraid.

I lobbied alone and encountered a stone wall of denial. "We don't need that bill," one Member said. "There are no homosexuals in Israel." I could produce no proof, no living homosexuals, to refute him. Denial fed denial.

Israeli gays do not often lead happy lives. They live in fear of discovery. Their families do not know they are gay. Many, to protect their closet, get married. Even more deny their homosexuality entirely. The men exercised their sexuality in public parks, in the dark of night behind the bushes. During the day, they denied knowing one another. The women formed relationships that lasted a year or years, then changed partners. There are a limited number of possible partners. A lover is the former lover of a former lover. A friend is the former lover of a former lover. Over the years, the relationships became ever more complicated. These women, by default, were family to one another. It began to feel incestuous.

Most homosexuals in Israel try not to call attention to themselves. They close the shutters of their homes. In public they practice the arts of anonymity, particularly difficult in a small country of neighborhoods and families. There is a grayness that hangs over their lives. In such a climate, the lesbian feminist communities that developed in Haifa, Tel Aviv, and Jerusalem were bursts of sunlight.

My mother, unable to say the word *lesbian*, talks about my way of life instead. The euphemism, I discovered, is appropriate. Homosexuality is not, as the more liberal straight Israelis say, what one does in *chadrei chadarim*, the bedroom. It is about friendships, family, community. It is about fashion, taste, and culture. It is about defining one's relationship to others and to the larger society. It is about alienation and connection.

I longed for gay liberation as I longed for women's liberation. In both cases, coming out—being seen and heard—was a necessary first step in the struggle. Forming communities was the next. My life and my political consciousness during the late seventies paralleled what I'd lived ten years earlier. The euphoria of personal liberation first as a feminist and then as a lesbian, the excitement of finding others, the bonding and the energy of activism were the same. The consequences were also the same. Ostracism, being ghettoized, being accepted only by those who all-too tolerantly overlooked sexual preference. While the horizons of possible futures widened and dazzled with utopian visions, the geography of daily life closed in. There was, it seemed, no more room for becoming.

Chapter 11
Taking Leave

◄●►

Life closed in tight in 1980, binding me in bands so tense that my period dried up. The walk between the house on Yafe Nof, the Street of the Beautiful View, and the women's center felt like a daily outing in the courtyard of my prison. There was no air, no space, no solitude other than the short walk between them.

Home was noisy and nervous, filled with small children who clamored for attention they didn't get. To escape their noise, their claims on me that I resented and rejected once Jenny was gone, I retreated to the smallest, most remote room of the house, the room that had been Jenny's. I sat there and wrote—endless beginnings of books and articles that never got anywhere. Though they began in earnest, each was a futile, failed attempt to find a space for myself.

Ayala and I lived side by side in a curious combination of total merger with one another and growing remoteness from the feelings that had brought us together. The endless and unfilled needs of children shut out by a passion they had to destroy in order to reclaim their mothers wore us down. The passion itself, gluing us so tightly to one another that neither even remembered a separate, whole existence, burnt out, leaving us in an increasingly meaningless symbiosis.

There was no space for me in that house, no space for me in that relationship. I felt swallowed up, knew I had to break away, terrified that there would be no self left to reclaim, and guilty for the pain it would bring to the woman I still loved.

The women's center devoured both of us. It needed every bit of energy we could give it just to keep going. Having twice depleted our resources to enable openings of women's centers in Tel Aviv and Jerusalem, we had to work three times as hard just to make enough money to pay the rent. Though American Jewish women had begun to organize funding support for Israeli feminism, the antiviolence facilities received the greatest share. It was more difficult making a case for the subtler contribution of a women's center. It was even harder making a case for the crucial role it played in the lives of lesbian women.

Bringing lesbianism into the open in a feminist environment injected new life into the women's movement but tainted it within the larger society. Woman's Voice in Haifa became known as "the lesbian center." When the women's movement gathered in Jerusalem for our third annual conference, five hundred women attended, perhaps a third of them lesbians. There was an exhibit hall where dozens of feminist groups distributed material on their activities. The women's centers in Haifa, Tel Aviv, and Jerusalem combined to sell books, records, T-shirts, jewelry, and posters. We were proud of the numbers and the feminist activity that been generated in so short a time. The long infancy of feminism in Israel was finally over.

The arts of lesbian concealment were laid aside for the two days of the conference. Women touched, kissed, walked arm in arm. There were workshops on lesbian feminism and lesbian sexuality. The press covered it all. The reporters, some of whom never let on that they were reporters, were horrified by the woman-love they saw. They vilified the conference, reduced feminism to lesbianism, described the women as dirty and oversexed.

On the surface, the Haifa women's center seemed to be thriving. But to keep cash coming in, we had to increase the number of lectures and classes. We had to pack up the books more often to sell them at kibbutzim and campuses. The center could survive, it seemed, only if we fed it with our blood. Ayala and I, both in premature menopause, had no more blood. The center was dying, the frantic activity its last gasp of life. In the fall, we gave in and decided to close.

That same fall, Jenny left Israel with her father for a year's sabbatical in Berkeley. She didn't want to leave, but she didn't want to come back and live with me either. I urged her to go, to experience what the sixties and seventies had wrought in America. I hoped it would help her understand me better, understand the struggle she had had as my daughter. It did. We spoke on the phone once a month. International Women's Day is a school holiday, she told me, amazed because in Israel it was only a day when her mother and a few others once again made fools of themselves. Some of her friends are gay, she reported. More have lesbian mothers, she said. It's very in to have a lesbian mother, she said, incredulous that she was no longer a freak, no longer had to hide her shameful parentage, could, in fact, brag about it. Her high school offered courses in women's studies, she said. Most of her teachers were feminists. "Some of them have heard of you. You're a heroine here." In Berkeley, I was rehabilitated in my daughter's eyes. Once again, America beckoned.

With the center closed, I had time to think about my life. I was forty-three, and my long dark hair had become short and entirely grey. I had no assets other than a small government pension to guarantee my survival. I had no work to do. I'd lost my daughter. My social life shrank to a handful of women, most of them a decade younger than I. Because of my openly lesbian identity, the women's movement, even as it flourished, was forced to battle for its good name yet again. Once more I became a liability to some in the movement. I had no energy and had to fight to keep depression at bay. Looking in the mirror and seeing the grey pallor, the worry lines etched into my forehead, the habitual frown, I knew, too, that I was not healthy. I looked years older than I should.

There is a saying about Israel—*eretz ochelet toshvaiha*, the land that devours its inhabitants, a country that takes the best that anyone has to offer it and returns little, using up its people. My image was only slightly different. Israel sucked me in, chewed me up, and now seemed to be spitting me out. "Save yourself," an inner voice counseled through the fog of fatigue that surrounded me. "Get out of here. This country is draining the blood out of you."

◄●►

The concerns of women, not Israeli politics, formed the core of my existence during the last four of the fourteen years I lived in Israel. But politics, particularly in Israel, is never at a great remove, and because old habits don't change easily, I still read several newspapers a day. I was sanguine when Begin was first elected in 1977. Four years in the opposition might be good for the Labor Party. Yadin and the liberals elected with him displaced the National Religious Party as the balance of power, and Ysrael Katz, an insistent critic of Labor's social policy replaced Yosef Burg as Welfare Minister. Social workers were now allowed to talk to their clients about birth control, and the ministry provided funding for feminist facilities.

Were it not for the occupation, the new Begin regime would have been better than benign during its first term in office. It was, after all, Begin who achieved peace with Egypt. But under Begin, the occupation of the West Bank, Israel's cancer, was not only allowed but encouraged to grow aggressively. By 1980, the first symptoms of threat to Israel's democracy and economy could be found in the two- and three-paragraph items in the papers, only occasionally punctuated by large headlines.

The Begin government quietly authorized the establishment of new settlements on the West Bank and made funds available for the further development of those that had previously been established illegally. "Settlement," Begin said, "is the soul of Zionism." Billions were invested in building for a permanent future on the

West Bank, over the years creating a new map of the Middle East. Private speculators were allowed and encouraged to buy as much land as possible in the occupied territories, assured that permits to construct housing units would be issued. All the "state lands," lands that officially belonged to no one and before 1967 had been claimed by the Jordanian government, were now claimed by the Israeli government. Expropriation of additional land began as the government took the grazing lands and fields of Palestinian farmers and declared them "security zones," closed to the Palestinian population, open for urban development by the Jewish population.

The Likud government concentrated on acquiring land, building residential units, and encouraging Israelis with economic incentives to "pioneer" in these new suburban communities of the the West Bank. Millions were diverted from social services and education to finance the settler movement, to build housing, roads, and schools on the West Bank. The inflation rate rose from 12 percent to 300 percent. The Israeli economy was on the brink of disaster, but to many it felt like prosperity. By 1981, there were sixteen thousand settlers on the West Bank, three times the number in 1977. Begin planned to pack the West Bank so densely with Jews that there would be little left belonging to the Palestinians. The stated aim was to have one hundred thousand Jewish settlers on the West Bank by 1986.

One of my best friends threatened to be among the hundred thousand. I was shocked and bewildered when Nurit first mentioned that she was thinking of moving to Ma'aleh Ephraim, just over the Green Line, only twenty minutes outside of Jerusalem. She had lived most of her adult life on a young, radical kibbutz that aligned itself with the peace movement. She did not, eventually, make the move, but only because of circumstance. In the late 1970s, Nurit studied carpentry and dreamed of opening her own shop. Another woman in the course, the only other woman in the course, proposed a partnership. She had just bought a house in Ma'aleh Ephraim. They could rent two hundred square meters of space for very little, she told Nurit. They would receive generous government loans to buy equipment and get their business going. It was hard to resist. Only the fact of the potential partner's illness with cancer got in the way. Otherwise, someone very close to me, a strong lesbian feminist and peace activist, would today be among the Jewish settlers of the West Bank, and perhaps, like the others, be too entrenched economically, too worried about her daughters' safety, to see that she was an intruder, an obstacle to peace in the Middle East.

As the settlements grew in number and size, and the young and poor of Israel began to see the beginnings of new economic horizons over the Green Line, public opinion in Israel shifted. The growing cancer that was the occupation made a mockery of Camp David, humiliated Sadat, and brought about an increase in Palestinian terrorism. West Bank resistance grew more frequent and more violent, Hussein's more moderate voice was silenced, and the PLO gained in support and stature throughout the Arab world and, for the first time, in the capitols of Europe.

Palestinian protest—stone throwing, general strikes, demonstrations, attacks on Jewish settlers—were infrequent, spontaneous, and sporadic. Nothing like the daily actions of the *intifada*, but surely the beginnings of the full-scale rebellion that erupted in 1987. As the occupation became more and more brutal, young soldiers, eighteen to twenty-one, were exposed to the license of absolute power, unchecked by any but military law. Tales of atrocities committed by these young Israelis began to leak out. Meir Kahana became a celebrity, leading marches through West Bank cities, inciting to violence, and openly espousing racist policies. The settlers began to organize vigilante groups. For every stone thrown at a settler, crowds of settlers rampaged through nearby Palestinian villages breaking windows and destroying property. One morning, car bombs exploded maiming three Palestinian mayors, openly nationalist but duly elected in 1976 under Israeli law. It wasn't yet public knowledge, but a violent Jewish underground was already in place.

Oppression and violence became a way of life for a generation of Israeli men, but the Jews of Israel did not yet wish to recognize it. An exhibition of photographs at the Israel Museum broke through complacent denial, but only briefly and soon forgotten.

Joel Kanter, an American immigrant, photographed the army at work in Gaza in a series of photographs entitled *Routine Check,* the army's term for the military units that patrolled Palestinian streets daily. The gallery was crowded with Israelis who filed slowly around the walls looking at pictures that revealed the terror on the faces of Palestinians as Israeli soldiers held billy clubs to their throats, pinned them to the ground with the heel of a boot on the back of a neck, shoved them against walls, guns in hand. The line of Israelis slowed down at the most violent of these pictures. Occasionally it stopped dead as crowds gathered around.

—"No one should have to see this," a woman shouted. "Why does the museum put these kinds of pictures on the walls?"

—"Everyone should have to see them. He's just showing us what we really look like."

—"It's ammunition for those who hate us."

—"It's the truth about ourselves."

The arguments raged in the normally staid museum gallery, the still-hidden divisions, bitter and deep, exposed by this harsh view of the occupation. Juxtaposed with the photographs of the occupation were those of life on the kibbutz where Joel Kanter lived. The children in the photographs are robust and healthy. The old people, the first generation of pioneers, exude satisfaction. These pictures are full of flowers, alive with light. The contrast with the Israel of the occupation was stark, revealing the contradictions of life in Israel in the 1980s.

Seriously underreported, few Israelis knew what went on in the West Bank and Gaza, and few Israelis wished to know. For me, there was a question growing larger each day, a question I could barely ask. Is this the inevitable turning of a corner in the aftermath of the Holocaust? Are the victims becoming the victimizers? It broke my heart.

◄●►

How do you leave a country when you are a national symbol? How do you leave behind an identity that had become all encompassing? I could physically get on a plane and go, but "Marcia Freedman" would necessarily remain behind. I would not only have to part with my home, but with much of my identity as well. How do you leave when every landscape is filled with memories? The roots I put down in 1967 were so deep, spread so widely, that I could not walk the streets of Haifa without seeing someone, something, that contained a piece of my history. The major stories of my life were stored in this city, this country. How could I leave without cutting myself off from my own history?

"I'm going to visit Jenny," I told Ayala, the first time in the years we'd been together that either of us made plans that didn't include the other. She understood before I did that this was the beginning of our separation.

Jenny told me, soon after my arrival, that she wanted to stay. Berkeley gave her the room she'd never have in Haifa to experiment with who she wanted to be. Feminism was a powerful force in this corner of the world. More was expected of women than just getting married and having babies. Jenny wanted to explore what this "more" might be. And I found the world that visitors to Israel had described to Cholit and me. Not one but three women's bookstores, women's coffeehouses, women's bathhouses, a Women's Building, women's theater, a women's philharmonic, women's health clinics, an active, radical movement, and a powerful, very large lesbian feminist presence. There was no longer a sharp distinction between the gay and straight worlds in Berkeley and San Francisco. Lesbians were everywhere, open and involved.

It was a chance to reconcile with my daughter who, once again, meant more to me than my lover. It was a chance to find the space in which to grow. It was the chance to find some peace and explore who I might become in a supportive environment. It was midlife and the time to make a radical change. "Let me think about it," I told Jenny as I was leaving. Perhaps I'll come in the fall." She had two more years of high school, enough time for her and for me to decide whether we wanted to remain in America or go back together to Israel.

When I returned to Haifa I found out that Ayala had become involved with another woman. The women's center had closed.

My last ties to the country were cut. The prison doors were open, but still I was not ready to walk through them.

There was, as there always is, a final straw, the telling incident that makes the difference. In recent years, the Women's Aid Fund, without any money of its own, had become a handy conduit for funds from America directed toward feminist projects. Different groups did their own fundraising, the money was sent to Women's Aid and then passed on. I kept the books, and Judy and I cosigned checks. The books, however, were a tangle because the money came in in dollars and went out in shekels. During those years, the exchange rate fluctuated almost daily. Reading the books, it was hard to balance what came in with what went out. Angry over things long past, angry with me for my continued prominence in the media, a few women accused me of stealing money from the Fund. It didn't take long to disprove, but the accusation did me in. It was time to leave. My own sisters told me so.

◄●►

I spent my last few months in Israel sitting on the terrace, my back to the country, feeling the sun, storing up visual images of the lower city, the bay, and, on the farthest corner of the horizon, Lebanon. Would I be able to recall smells and sounds? What would it be like to live without them, without the sun that, no matter what state I was in, baked my body into well-being?

I read newspapers hungrily, with an intensity born of the knowledge that I would soon be out of touch. In May 1981, Israel went to the polls and reelected Menachem Begin. Soon after, the Knesset voted to annex the Golan Heights. Arik Sharon removed the legally elected, pro-PLO mayors of the West Bank and imposed an Israeli so-called civil administration that threatened to make the occupation permanent. Begin's government announced its five-year plan to settle one hundred thousand more Jews on the West Bank.

I read about it all sitting on the terrace of my house on the Road of the Beautiful View. I looked across the bay toward Lebanon and down to the headlines in the morning papers.

—"Syrian SAM Missiles Placed in Lebanon."

—"Jets Attack PLO in Southern Lebanon."

—"US Braces for Israeli Raid on SAM Missile Sites."

—"Air Force to Attack Unless Syria Withdraws Missiles, Begin Vows."

—"American Envoy Habib Meets Begin in Bid to Avert War."

—"Last-Ditch Bid to Resolve Crisis."

—"Eitan Says Syrians Are on a War Footing."

—"Time Is Running Out."

—"Israel Losing Patience Over Habib Mission."

—"Arabs Vow Total Aid to Syrians."

—"Israeli Jets Destroy Lybian SAM-9 Sites."

—"Israel Bombs Iraqi Nuclear Reactor; Begin: 'We'll Do It Again If Necessary.' "

—"IAF Raids Terrorist Positions."

—"Israel Downs Syrian MIG Over Lebanon."

—"Terrorists Shell Nahariya and Kiryat Shmona: 3 Killed in Heavy Rocket Attack."

—"Havoc in Terrorist Bases as Air Force Blasts New Targets: Five Bridges Knocked Out."

—"Israel Bombs PLO Headquarters in Beirut: Several Hundred Civilians Killed."

—"Galilee Shelling Continues After Raid on Beirut."

—"Israeli Jets Pound Terrorist Positions in South Lebanon: *Katyushas* Kill One, Wound 23."

—"Habib Makes No Headway on Cease-Fire Bid."

—"IDF Hits Back by Land, Sea and Air"

—"Planes Pound PLO, Shelling Continues."

First they made it impossible for me to stay, I thought angrily, and now they make it impossible for me to leave. If war breaks out between now and July 27, the date set for my departure, I would be stuck for the duration. No Israeli, no matter how disaffected, leaves during a war.

Even as I went through the painful motions of unloading a lifetime's possessions, selling some things and giving others away, even when the shipping company crated the few things I took with me, I wondered whether I'd get out in time. I did not want to be in Israel for another war. I did not want to experience the same sense of impotence and ineffectiveness, the same rage and anger, the same grief and mourning for the brothers, husbands, fathers, and sons who would be its victims.

I was saved by American diplomacy. Philip Habib was sent to the Middle East to negotiate a truce and on July 24, only three days before my departure, the morning paper informed me that he'd succeeded. Sharon still shook his fists in the air, but he withdrew the troops. I was free to leave.

The Victorian antiques I'd brought with me from America were no longer the *alte zachen* in Israeli eyes they'd been fourteen years earlier. Israelis, made affluent by the occupation, were into antiques. To finance my leaving, I sold most of them. The carved rocking chair that I reupholstered myself in black velvet went first. I took the money and saw it go out the door, pained beyond belief. When Jenny was an infant, I sat in that rocker to feed her. Before it was reupholstered, it had been stained with the milky contents of her burps. My life was in that chair. My future was in the cash in my hand. So it was with all the rest. Some things remained with friends, and I was grateful that they bought them. These pieces of my life could be seen again, though not mine, at least available to me. Most went to strangers, lost forever.

After the antiques were gone, I had a moving sale for the pottery dishes I bought when Bill and I married, the imitation Dansk silverware, the pots I'd cooked in for twenty years, the bed linens I received as wedding presents. My life was scattered among strangers, the life I'd assumed was permanent.

I said my good-byes. To Nomi, so engrossed with her four daughters that it hardly seemed to matter to her that I was leaving. To Shoshana, who said ominously that the women's movement could not possibly survive without me. To Barbara Prager, who said truthfully that she would miss me. To Judy, who had been by my side so often.

I returned to 66 Derech Hayam to say good-bye to the neighbors, and especially to Shelly and Alec Bassin. I'd been out of touch with them too long. Alec, my vox populi, was speechless. He giggled, stuck out his tongue, made a gesture indicating that it had been cut out, and threw his hands in the air helplessly. He smiled his big extravagant grin and slumped down into a chair. "He had a stroke," Shelly explained. "His motor function is unaffected, but he's aphasic." Alec couldn't understand much that was said to him and could say nothing comprehensible. Israel's voice, the voice I'd listened to for so many years, was silent. "He can't understand the television news. He can't even read the newspapers. The only thing he seems to understand is *Newsweek*," she said. "Why *Newsweek*?" Maybe he, too, is leaving the country, I thought.

I took my final walk through the Mercaz on the way, for the last time, to the shoemaker. My one pair of shoes once again needed repair, this time for a new life in America. People, as usual, stared at me, their local celebrity. The Cafe Carmel, where the women's movement began, where so many of the crucial moments of my life were set, had been turned into a pub. The Supersol, the supermarket over a bowling alley, had given way to gravity and collapsed, the site a closed area awaiting cleanup and rebuilding. The news vendors—husband, wife, and son—were still on the same corner, selling me the day's allotment of pain and suffering with friendly smiles and the usual small talk. They knew my history in terms of the newspapers I read. The first year, only the English-language *Jerusalem Post*, then the weekly Hebrew paper put out in easy Hebrew for new immigrants, then the five papers a day I read while in politics, and now, post-politics, two papers only, one in Hebrew and one in English. I couldn't tell them I was leaving.

The shoemaker sat in his *budkeh*, waiting for business. He accepted my shoes as always, without judgment, and set to work on them.

"I'm leaving," I told him.

"Leaving Haifa?" he asked.

"Leaving the country," I said.

"Why?"

I took the easy way out. "Because my daughter's in America, and I want to be with her."

"Good," he said. "Children need their parents. Parents need

their children. *Zei gezunt.*" Go with blessings.

Ayala and I sold the house to a young couple who were ecstatic to find a home on Yafe Nof and planned to modernize it.
Two weeks before my plane took off, we watched as the moving
men loaded her belongings onto a truck. We worked silently, the
bond between us still there, but too painful to speak of. The dream
we'd begun three years earlier, carrying this same furniture in the
opposite direction, had ended. What once was ecstatic was now
grim. Only the children were happy to leave Haifa and return to
the suburbs of Tel Aviv, happy in anticipation of my leaving.

I planned to stay with Ayala for the last two weeks, to help
her set up her new home. We followed the moving van in the car,
repeating in reverse the ride that had first brought me to Haifa.
We drove down the Sea Road, virtually unchanged in four years,
past the villas that still lined its beginnings at the Mercaz, past
#66 where I glimpsed the orange and brown of my old kitchen,
unchanged by its new inhabitants, past Stella Maris, the Star of
the Sea, around the curves that revealed ever-changing views of
the city below, and onto the highway between Haifa and Tel Aviv.
We drove past the beaches that I considered my own, where I'd
mindlessly baked for hours on end. Past the kibbutzim where I
had friends, where I'd lectured, where we'd sold books, where I'd
learned of the limits of free love from Shlomit. We passed Caesaria,
where Esther and I spent a day that became mythic in memory.
We passed the fields of corn, bananas, grapes, alfalfa. We followed
the curve of the coastline that marked Israel's outer edge, the
aquamarine sea meeting the sapphire sky, unclouded as always in
the summer. Good-bye, I said. Good-bye. Good-bye.

Two weeks later, on schedule, I left. Ayala drove me to the airport in the early morning. Though dry-eyed, I was sensitive to every nuance of separation—the last look at the Middle East, the
last kiss, the last sentence spoken in Hebrew. The first time I walked
through passport control with a one-way ticket.

◄●►

Habib's truce held for a year, without incident. But with or without provocation, Sharon would have his war. Israeli troops marched into Lebanon in the summer of 1982 to secure *shlom hagalil*, the peace of the Galilee. The name the government gave to that war was not only linguistically contorted, it was also a lie. The Galilee had been peaceful for a year, since the truce between Israel and the PLO negotiated by Philip Habib in 1981. Not a single *Katyusha* had fallen on an Israeli settlement. Begin and Sharon claimed that the assassination attempt on the Israeli ambassador in London was an act of the PLO even though the PLO immediately disclaimed responsibility. The Israeli government agreed to allow Sharon to send his armies into Lebanon, to carry on search and destroy operations against the PLO army in southern Lebanon. The army was not to go beyond the Litani River, twenty-five miles to the north of the Israeli-Lebanese border.

Sharon got his war and ran it his way. He deceived the government and crossed the river. The morning headline, as I sat on the small deck that overlooked other backyards in Berkeley, drinking freshly ground coffee, said that the Israeli army had encircled Beirut and the air force was pounding it with bombs. Sharon, jubilant in victory, vowed to destroy the PLO once and for all. On the table next to me was a roundtrip ticket to Tel Aviv. I planned to spend the summer in Israel, with Ayala, to see if we could salvage our relationship. I thought briefly about postponing the trip, but only briefly. Israelis brag about the fact that *yordim* always fly home when war breaks out. I was in a typically Israeli circumstance, about to fly back to a war that I had fled a year earlier.

I spent the summer demonstrating with the tens and hundreds of thousands who took to the streets to oppose the war. I was awed and excited by the numbers. Perhaps, I thought, I should stay. Something seemed to be stirring that hadn't happened before. My departure date was only a month away, two weeks away. I extended it for another two weeks. The women's movement was, as Shoshana predicted, in disarray and depressed. The lesbian community had become ingrown once again. Many women were angry with me for deserting them. But the peace movement had come into its own. Journalists reported more aggressively. Aloni came out against the war while it was in progress, an act of courage that reminded me of my speech to Ya'ad after the terrorist bomb explosion in Zion Square. The message, too early then, had found its hour.

"Nothing has changed, Marcia," Terry said, when I confessed my thoughts of staying. "It's only gotten worse. Nurit and I plan to leave as soon as we can." Ayala, too, planned to leave. "Even when you're not here, you're still the scapegoat," Terry said. "Imagine what it will be like if you come back."

This time, boarding the plane that would take me "home," I had to say good-bye to hope as well as despair. A year earlier, I had a rush of expectation about a new life in California. Now, the tears streamed down my face. Though life in Berkeley was pleasant, though I was beginning to relax and heal, though I found not only a lesbian but a Jewish community that were welcoming and supportive, California was exile. Permanent exile. Israel would always remain my home.

I return yearly. I am always tempted to stay. The sun, the heat, the landscape, old friends, old intensities of emotion and memory, draw me in just as they did in 1967. The women's movement is thriving once again without me. The peace movement is stronger than ever. But the peace movement and the women's movement are marginal still. And the headlines give no rest. Daily contact with Israel's present is only depressing. The most dire of my predictions are realized in those headlines. Half the country is depressed by the events of the day and the feeling that the course of events cannot be stopped. The other half moves relentlessly toward the extremist right wing of Israeli politics—nationalist, racist, violent, and more xenophobic than ever.

I follow it all from Berkeley, in close touch, but removed. I organize Jewish women's peace activities here, to bridge the gap. But it doesn't. I left, and I will remain cut off from my home forever.

Other titles from Firebrand Books include:

The Big Mama Stories by Shay Youngblood/$8.95

A Burst Of Light, Essays by Audre Lorde/$7.95

Crime Against Nature, Poetry by Minnie Bruce Pratt/$8.95

Diamonds Are A Dyke's Best Friend by Yvonne Zipter/$9.95

Dykes To Watch Out For, Cartoons by Alison Bechdel/$6.95

Eye Of A Hurricane, Stories by Ruthann Robson / $8.95

The Fires Of Bride, A Novel by Ellen Galford/$8.95

A Gathering Of Spirit, A Collection by North American Indian Women edited by Beth Brant *(Degonwadonti)*/$9.95

Getting Home Alive by Aurora Levins Morales and Rosario Morales/$8.95

Good Enough To Eat, A Novel by Lesléa Newman/$8.95

Humid Pitch, Narrative Poetry by Cheryl Clarke/$8.95

Jewish Women's Call For Peace edited by Rita Falbel, Irena Klepfisz, and Donna Nevel/$4.95

Jonestown & Other Madness, Poetry by Pat Parker/$7.95

The Land Of Look Behind, Prose and Poetry by Michelle Cliff/$6.95

A Letter To Harvey Milk, Short Stories by Lesléa Newman /$8.95

Letting In The Night, A Novel by Joan Lindau/$8.95

Living As A Lesbian, Poetry by Cheryl Clarke/$7.95

Making It, A Woman's Guide to Sex in the Age of AIDS by Cindy Patton and Janis Kelly/$3.95

Metamorphosis, Reflections On Recovery, by Judith McDaniel /$7.95

Mohawk Trail by Beth Brant *(Degonwadonti)*/$7.95

Moll Cutpurse, A Novel by Ellen Galford/$7.95

More Dykes To Watch Out For, Cartoons by Alison Bechdel/$7.95

The Monarchs Are Flying, A Novel by Marion Foster/$8.95

Movement In Black, Poetry by Pat Parker/$8.95

My Mama's Dead Squirrel, Lesbian Essays on Southern Culture by Mab Segrest/$8.95

New, Improved! Dykes To Watch Out For, Cartoons by Alison Bechdel/$7.95

The Other Sappho, A Novel by Ellen Frye/$8.95

Politics Of The Heart, A Lesbian Parenting Anthology edited by Sandra Pollack and Jeanne Vaughn/$11.95

Presenting. . .Sister NoBlues by Hattie Gossett/$8.95

A Restricted Country by Joan Nestle/$8.95

Sanctuary, A Journey by Judith McDaniel/$7.95

Sans Souci, And Other Stories by Dionne Brand/$8.95

Shoulders, A Novel by Georgia Cotrell/$8.95

Simple Songs, Stories by Vickie Sears/$8.95

The Sun Is Not Merciful, Short Stories by Anna Lee Walters/$7.95

Tender Warriors, A Novel by Rachel Guido deVries/$7.95

This Is About Incest by Margaret Randall/$7.95

The Threshing Floor, Short Stories by Barbara Burford/$7.95

Trash, Stories by Dorothy Allison/$8.95

The Women Who Hate Me, Poetry by Dorothy Allison/$5.95

Words To The Wise, A Writer's Guide to Feminist and Lesbian Periodicals & Publishers by Andrea Fleck Clardy/$3.95

Yours In Struggle, Three Feminist Perspectives on Anti-Semitism and Racism by Elly Bulkin, Minnie Bruce Pratt, and Barbara Smith/$8.95

You can buy Firebrand titles at your bookstore, or order them directly from the publisher (141 The Commons, Ithaca, New York 14850, 607-272-0000).

Please include $1.75 shipping for the first book and $.50 for each additional book.

A free catalog is available on request.